Global Per Motherhood, Mothering and Masculinities

Edited by Tólá Olú Pearce
and Andréa Moraes

DEMETER

Global Perspectives on Motherhood, Mothering, and Masculinities

Edited by Tólá Olú Pearce and Andréa Moraes

Copyright © 2021 Demeter Press

Individual copyright to their work is retained by the authors. All rights reserved. No part of this book may be reproduced or transmitted in any form by any means without permission in writing from the publisher.

Demeter Press
2546 10th Line
Bradford, Ontario
Canada, L3Z 3L3
Tel: 289-383-0134
Email: info@demeterpress.org
Website: www.demeterpress.org

Demeter Press logo based on the sculpture "Demeter" by Maria-Luise Bodirsky www.keramik-atelier.bodirsky.de

Printed and Bound in Canada

Cover image: Wilma King, Arvarh E. Strickland Professor Emerita, Departments of History and Black Studies. University of Missouri, Columbia.

Cover design and typesetting: Michelle Pirovich

Library and Archives Canada Cataloguing in Publication
Title: Global perspectives on motherhood, mothering, and masculinities / edited by Tólá Olú Pearce and Andréa Moraes.
Names: Pearce, Tólá Olú, 1944- editor. | Moraes, Andréa, 1962- editor.
Description: Includes bibliographical references.
Identifiers: Canadiana 20200375385 | ISBN 9781772582871 (softcover)
Subjects: LCSH: Motherhood—Social aspects. | LCSH: Sex role. | LCSH: Masculinity. | LCSH: Femininity. | LCSH: Motherhood. | LCSH: Mothers and sons. | LCSH: Women—Identity. | LCSH: Men— Identity.
Classification: LCC HQ759 .G56 2021 | DDC 306.874/3—dc23

To the late Olúfémi Kújorè, founder and chair, Department of Nursing at Ilé-Ifè, my mentor and friend, for her lifelong academic and community service to mothers in Nigeria.

And to our daughters Forabo and Clarinha because everything we do is with you in our hearts and souls.

Acknowledgments

The idea for this book developed from the Motherhood Initiative for Research and Community Involvement (MIRCI) conference held in Toronto in October 2016. MIRCI has since become the International Association of Maternal Action and Scholarship (IAMAS). The 2016 conference was titled *Mothers, Mothering, and Motherhood in Today's World,* and it brought together scholars from across the globe to present papers on a variety of topics, including mothers in academia, activism, maternal experiences, mothers and daughters, and healthcare issues. In the session on men and masculinities, papers were presented on different aspects of family life. Following this, the idea for the present volume was fielded, and a global call for papers was sent out in which the editors sought to draw attention to the powerful but often subtle linkages between motherhood/mothering and masculinities. In casting the net across the world, the editors of this volume hoped to contribute to the growing interest in the ways these two phenomena develop and change within specific contexts, which both enable and constrain human agency.

The editors encouraged contributions to explore the following, though contributors were not limited to these themes: Co-constructions of motherhood and masculinities; generational conceptions of motherhood/mothering and masculinities; historical perspectives; Indigenous perspectives; intersectional issues and influences; cross-cultural/trans-national examinations; the feminization of employment and masculinities; mothering and masculinities among sex workers; motherhood/mothering and masculinities: the diasporic experience; autoethnographic examinations; religious discourses; the impact of incarceration on motherhood/mothering and masculinities; mothering, food and masculinities; and maternal activism and constructions of masculinities. We received many responses to the invitation from around the world and selected the twelve that appear in this volume. Our hope is that more interest will be sparked on this important dimension of women's lives and the neglected topic of mothers in the political arena.

The editors would like to thank the participants of the 2016 MIRCI conference, whose public presentations and private conversations brought out many ideas, including developing this volume. Special thanks go to Andrea O'Reilly (founder of MIRCI), Angie Deveau, Tracey Carlyle, and Katie B. Garner for all your encouragement and technical advice. We also extend our thanks to each contributor for the submissions as well as the patience each showed in working through the chapters. Finally, we each would like to thank our colleagues and others who have assisted with suggestions.

Tólá Olú Pearce: I would like to thank Stella Bolá Williams for our many conversations about her continued involvement with working mothers in agriculture in Nigeria and Jay Gubrium, former chair of sociology, University of Missouri, Columbia, who has reviewed several of my publications in this area. Special thanks to Sheila Walker for her analysis of my ideas and for the invitation to present my research on motherhood at Scripps College. Similarly, I am grateful to Ìyábò Fágbúlù for reading my chapter and making suggestions, and to Modúpé Fágbúlù for the many hours of technical advice. My colleague, the historian Wilma King, provided us with the cover design, selected from her great collection of photographs. I thank my brother, Olúwajù Jameson Pearce, for his discussions and insights on motherhood and masculinity among the Yorùbá. Thank you all.

Andréa Moraes: I would also like to thank Cecilia Rocha for the opportunity to contribute to the ECOSUN project in Vietnam, and I express my appreciation for the whole ECOSUN team in Canada and Vietnam. I also want to thank Iara Lessa for the inspiring conversations about my chapter. Finally, the greatest gratitude goes always to my partner, Burkard, and daughter, Clarinha, for their constant love and support in all my undertakings.

Contents

PART III
POSTCOLONIAL DEVELOPMENTS
201

Introduction

Tólá Olú Pearce and Andréa Moraes

The academic study of motherhood and of masculinities took some time to emerge as independent fields of study within feminism (O'Reilly) and men's studies (Hearn). Second-wave feminists in the West, particularly in the United States, initially kept the study of motherhood and mothers at an arm's length, fearing that this aspect of women's lives served to keep women under control in most societies. Feminists yearned for the independence and freedoms that had been denied to their own mothers and saw motherhood as an albatross. Regarding masculinities, men's studies did not initially develop a critical perspective and were often antifeminist. But following second-wave feminism, attention was given to the impact of patriarchy on women, the study of power, as well as the importance of studying masculinities and not just men.

Both topics came into their own during the last two decades of the twentieth century, and the change was also aided by other developments in academia. The "cultural turn" in the study of society—which focused on the way social phenomena are socially constructed rather than rooted in nature or biology—began critiquing many issues that had been ignored. These critiques strengthened the idea that motherhood was a societal construction, a set of expectations that are not fixed for all women for all time. Thus, motherhood as a social construct is now understood to differ with changing historical and sociocultural conditions and to be affected by the impact of intersecting subsystems in society (e.g., class, race, sexuality, age, and geographic location). Moreover, scholarship from Non-western societies, particularly among postcolonial writers, brought new voices and perspectives to the study of motherhood. Scholars from Africa, Latin America, and Asia did not have the same aversion to studying this aspect of women's lives. Many were interested in the way expectations and behaviour link women to a wide variety of relationships within society. Motherhood studies, thus, broadened from a more limited focus on the mother-child dyad to the way motherhood, as a status, links the individual to many other individuals, organisations, and social institutions. From the micro to the macro levels of society and beyond, the impact of, and various issues surrounding this social construct must be further uncovered. What are the positive (e.g., high status) and negative (e.g., workload and conflict) dimensions of motherhood in different societies and why is this so?

Similarly, no one believes today that expectations regarding masculinity are homogenous across the globe or even within the same society. Expectations differ enormously, and as with other social constructions, they change across historical periods. In addition, the resources available to one subset of men (e.g., whites, the rich, and the educated) are often out of reach for other groups. For instance, Kopano Ratele has written about employment or educational opportunities among poor, Black men in South Africa, where the youth now engage in new and negative practices in search of their own manhood, since they observe the behaviour of elite older men enjoying ill-gotten resources. What type of masculinities develop under desperate circumstances, including poverty, racism, the impact of global neoliberalism, and so forth? Where do different categories of men find themselves as their fortunes or status change globally, nationally, or locally? And what do they do about the situation? Thus, the construction of masculinity is no more fixed than that of motherhood. With these ideas in mind, the editors sought to understand some of the ways in which expectations in these two areas (motherhood and masculinities) are brought together and influence each other in different ways in different societies. Motherhood deals with aspects of femininity and, therefore, does have important relational concerns to masculinities. The contributors to this collection were not restricted to any single slice of life in which motherhood and masculinity appear. The chapters introduce readers to topics of interest for each author. In the rest of this introduction, we briefly outline some important issues developing around motherhood and masculinities in the literature, which is followed by an outline of the book's structure and brief remarks on the chapters.

Motherhood and Mothering

Adrienne Rich's distinction between the institution of motherhood and the experience of mothering is widely accepted in feminist discourses and surfaces in several chapters here. As Rich argues and Andrea O'Reilly emphasizes, motherhood under patriarchy has been oppressive for women, given the ideological expectations of so-called good mothering. These expectations not only seek to curtail women's agency but often appropriate the institution for political purposes at both the community and nation levels. Following Rich's distinction, there has been growing interest in understanding the differences in patriarchal systems rather than assuming patriarchy exists in only one form (Kandiyoti). Systems of patriarchy not identical to Western forms are nonetheless still patriarchal, and each affects the construction of motherhood as well as mothering activities. Again, expectations for motherhood under patriarchal systems also differ depending on whether the society is monogamous or polygynous, patrilineal or matrilineal, patrilocal or matrilocal, and even by the degree of matrifocality afforded women. Minority populations in the Global North and women in the postcolonial Global South have consistently pointed to the interacting layers of patriarchal oppression that existed in precolonial Indigenous cultures, that arose out of colonization, and that now emanate from the policies of national governments as well as global financial institutions (Pearce; Santos and Morey).

Although the rules of conduct for mothers differ across cultures, women are critiquing the straightjackets in which they find themselves as mothers. Strict rules and expectations for most women begin with would-be mothers and then continue through pregnancy and into childrearing. Women are expected to accommodate each ideal construct as they move from one status to the next, and the onus is on each woman regardless of her circumstances and situations. Women bear responsibility for early pregnancies, children born out of wedlock, as well as pregnancies that go against cultural ideals of spacing between births. Acts of rape and incest leading to pregnancies reveal the extent to which double standards regarding reproduction still exist. Even in the twenty-first century, women are still being told, "If only you kept your legs together, you wouldn't have become pregnant." This type of statement is being bandied around in the United States today as conservative policymakers seek to challenge Roe V. Wade and limit abortions among women. In a number of countries, including the United States and Canada, women are being advised to dress appropriately in order to avoid sexual harassment, even though in countries where women wear the hijab or the full-length burqa, they have not escaped harassment. Nuns have also reported being sexually bullied by priests.

Regarding childcare, there are also important differences between cultures. In some cultures, mothering is expected to be intensive and exclusive, as among middle-class women in Western countries. In other cultures mothering is extensive but inclusive as it is across much of Africa, where mothers often bear a heavy financial responsibility for their own dependents under polygyny, in addition to the usual emotional responsibilities (Akinware; Clark). At the same time, children belong to the lineage and extended family and any adult in these groups is allowed to discipline the child.

Even though they are socialized into the strictures of motherhood, women develop a world of experience and gain confidence during the actual process of mothering. Some of the contributors to this volume explore the issue of mothering under specific conditions and discuss the way women choose to redefine or expand the role. Furthermore, those who are not biological mothers often take up mothering roles within the family (Collins; Semley). Presently, women are increasingly choosing to speak out as mothers to critique the institution and to expose the complexities involved in mothering and move communities to collective action. In the past, little attention was paid to the problems that mothers encounter, since the role was seen as a natural one, but that is changing. As Sneha Rout points out for Indian mothers: "If an Indian mother were to be asked about how happy she thinks mothers are, she may not give a straight answer. Because even as societal pressure demands that a mother be happy and rejoice in every aspect of motherhood, the social and material realities for women in India are so harsh that the idea of happiness can be an alien concept" (3). Today, women are organizing conferences, giving testimonies, establishing associations, and building movements in an attempt to improve the conditions of mothers everywhere. Movements like Asociación Madres de la Plaza de Mayo in Argentina and the Mães de Maio in Brazil have long fought against state violence and are the forerunners of many feminist activities. While it is true that in many cultures mothers are said to enjoy an elevated status, this perception is being queried: "It is however important to remember that idealisation or sentimentalization of motherhood or mothers is not the same as empowering them or giving them a say in the social scheme of things. Mothers tend to be valued more for their silent endurance" (Vagmita).

In order to address some of the contradictions between veneration and lack of empowerment, O'Reilly has moved the issue of maternal practice to the centre of the discourse on motherhood. The concept she coined, "matricentric feminism," focuses on a wide variety of issues including the need to understand both the oppressive and empowering dimensions of maternity, to take seriously women's experiences as mothers, and to build commitment to social change and justice for all who mother. Mothering, however, is not limited to the home or to women, as discussed in a number of the book chapters.

Masculinities

Although the position of mother has been idealized in many societies, masculinity as a gendered institution is much more privileged than femininity in most cultures. As a construction, masculinity is an expression. It is something to be achieved and is associated with maleness. It is constructed through biological (e.g., penis and large physique), physical (e.g., voice and clothing), and nonphysical (e.g., emotions, marital laws, and politics) dimensions of social life. Values and norms regarding masculinity can also be found in the activities of organizations, occupational groups, classes, religions (Connell), and countries (Leap). Furthermore, there are enormous cultural and global differences in the construction of masculinities, as most of the chapters in this book reveal. Thus, there is no fixed masculinity attached to maleness, only a wide range of masculinities that are context specific. When is male attire perceived as feminine? When men from one cultural group scrutinize the dress code of another cultural group, perhaps. This difference in expectations is revealed by the following exchange. Many years ago, a Nigerian male colleague of mine poked fun at the kilt Scotsmen wear. "How can men be allowed to wear skirts?" he asked. I asked him whether he thought the yards of material that men wrap around their waist into a long garment that reaches the ground, in some Nigerian ethnic groups, counts as female attire. Are those also skirts? "No, that's different," he said. "Those are men's traditional wraps, not skirts!"

In so far as forms of masculinities differ even within the same society, the hierarchies established between various masculinities and their relation to femininities have drawn a lot of attention in research. Raewyn Connell's concept of hegemonic masculinity is defined as the form that rises to the top of the hierarchy in a society or subgroup and legitimates gender relations "between men and women, between masculinity and femininity, and among masculinities" (Messerschmidt 5). Research around the world has pointed to several other masculinities, including complicit, marginalized, dependent, depressed, and subordinated. In reference to females and motherhood, concepts such as "female masculinity" have also been examined and may actually reinforce gender hierarchy, as in the Yorùbá saying: "Obìnrin bi Okùnrin" ("a woman who behaves like a man, tough, decisive, and fearless"). But on the flip side, to say a man is behaving like a woman (i.e., soft, weak, and gentle) is an unequivocal insult. And as the linguist Olóruntoba-Ojú highlights, the Yorùbá also have proverbs that discourage female masculinities: "Àseju ni n mu ewúré hu irûgbòn" ("Excessive and unruly behavior is what make a she-goat sport a beard") (17). Similar sayings exist elsewhere. For instance, in Brazil, female facial hair is associated with masculinity in women and is exemplified by the proverb "Mulher de bigode, nem o diabo pode" ("Not even the devil can deal with a woman who has a mustache")[1]. Such ambivalence to females exhibiting masculine traits, engaging in masculine activities, and occupying prestigious masculine positions is well recognized across the globe; it also encourages not only negative opinions around women in positions of power but also the acceptance of violence to keep women in their place.

On the masculine-feminine continuum, motherhood occupies a feminine role except perhaps when women are expected to defend their babies, and then maternal fierceness, even violence, is allowed. Nonetheless under patriarchy, "father" is above "mother." Even in matrilineal societies, the mother's brother has traditionally had more authority over her children than the biological father. This is important. Jeff Hearn points out that men as a social category generally have power over women as a social category, even though specific women (via class, race, or education) may be more powerful than certain categories of men. But it is understood that men of lower status in a society still enjoy male privileges, even when placed below certain women. Furthermore, being upper class, high caste, or white does not exempt a mother from exhibiting the expected feminine behaviour of her position. A major expectation in patriarchal societies is the birthing of sons. To varying degrees, the expectation is that a woman will produce sons, and in some regions, this has led to aborting female fetuses in the attempt to have a male heir in the family. In other societies, the husband will find another wife or girlfriend who can produce a son. In some cultural groups, one of the daughters is elevated to the position of son. All these practices reveal that the two categories of "man" and "woman" are not equal, since it matters if a mother does not birth a male child. Son preference is a global phenomenon. The world recently witnessed a change in Britain, when the Succession to the Crown Act went into effect in 2015. The act altered a longstanding protocol that allowed the first son to ascend the royal throne, his birth position notwithstanding.

Overview of Book Chapters

Regardless of tradition or former expectations, motherhood/mothering and masculinities are each in flux across the entire world, and therefore relationships between them are changing. The chapters in this volume draw attention to the types of changes women now seek. Twelve chapters have been organized into three sections: Cultural Narratives, Ethnographic Research, and Postcolonial Developments. Although the sections do sometimes overlap in content, the editors believe that these subdivisions will help readers identify specific issues.

Cultural Narratives

In the first four chapters, the significance of social construction, cultural difference, and changing ideals or behaviour is highlighted. The first chapter by Tólá Olú Pearce focuses on historical constructions of motherhood and hegemonic masculinity among the Yorùbá in Southwestern Nigeria. It is part of a larger study on understanding the institution of motherhood within this ethnic group. Her focus, more broadly, is on the relationship between motherhood and masculinity as well as the impact these constructions have on various aspects of family and community life. Many changes have occurred within Yorùbá society from precolonial times to the present day, but there are also many continuities in the culture. Thus, motherhood still elevates a woman's status as in the past. In this group, the mother figure was never constructed as a stay-at-home caretaker. A mother was expected to be the financial backbone of her children and dependents. Mothering was difficult in precolonial times because of the threat of wars, domestic slavery, and the transatlantic slave trade, and is still difficult today due to the exploitative structural adjustment and neoliberal policies of the International Monetary Fund (IMF), which affect mothers in Nigeria. Nonetheless, Pearce argues that the institution of motherhood developed within a patriarchal, patrilineal (mostly), and patrilocal gender system. Pearce also reviews how Yorùbá hegemonic masculinity has developed over time.

The next two chapters focus on the role of the media in perpetuating certain expectations and behaviours regarding mothering and masculinities. Kierra Otis and Miriam Araya analyze memes created by African American youth about Black families. This chapter explores what these memes reveal about Black mothers and expectations regarding masculinities as well as how well the meme compares to academic scholarship in examining these issues. The point is that all groups have their own perspectives, regardless of what others have to say. And as shown here, local perspectives are often quite complex. Memes that focus on the uninvolved father may also help perpetuate negative images of lower-class Black masculinity.

Another dimension of popular culture is movies, as they speak to local, regional, and global publics. Like the Hollywood industry, the films of Bollywood have long crossed national boundaries and play an important role in the messages Indians in the diaspora receive regarding gender roles. Meghna Bhat analyzes the messages Indians in the diaspora receive when they watch Bollywood films. She asks how the institutions of motherhood and masculinities are portrayed in Hindi movies. She argues that mother-hood is depicted through submissive and rigid gender roles, in which women are expected to have little agency. Fathers, as important representations of the notion of masculinity, are portrayed as decision-makers and protectors of the family. The chapter asks whether these constructions promote female oppression and encourage violence against women within the diasporic

Indian population.

Katharine I. Ransom's chapter provides an interdisciplinary and transnational look at matristic and matrilineal societies using historical, religious, and economic perspectives. Ransom argues that these societies have remained egalitarian and continue to function outside of patriarchal norms. The principles found in these societies are said to provide more flexible gender roles compared to other communities, which lead to differences in mothering. This chapter suggests that these societies can provide alternative ways of living and alleviate the problems associated with gender inequality.

Ethnographic Research

The four ethnographic studies in this section deal with different aspects of the motherhood-masculinity relationship. Cheryl Lynch Lawler uses material from her own research and clinical practice as a psychoanalyst in the United States to critique the Western binary gender scheme, in which the male can only assuage the pain of his womb envy by denigrating the mother, who can mysteriously grow life. Lynch Lawler's specific concern is the impact this problem has on sons and their relationship to their mothers as they mature. Her aim is to develop new models for gender relations by looking beyond Western models of community life. Stuti Das looks at mother-child relationships among a group that is not usually discussed in this way—the Hijra in India. They are a religious subgroup composed of individuals assigned the status of male at birth who reassign themselves as women later on. They can be found in several South Asian countries and represent populations around the world who did not follow a strict binary gender system prior to colonization or Western contact. And like others, the Hijra are forced to deal with the impact of Western ideals. Das argues that both the institution of motherhood and mothering practices are used by the Hijra to affirm a feminine gender identity. A complex system of kinship exists, but the Hijra continue to cope with developments in the larger Indian society. An intriguing issue for Das is the fact that although the Hijra as a community subvert binary codes on gender, they simultaneously incorporate normative ideals of Indian femininity. The Hijra also highlight types of mothering not based on biology or birthing.

Victoria Team's chapter explores the meaning of motherhood and mothering for female soldiers. She interacted with female guerrilla fighters soon after the Ethiopian civil war. While probing the complex identity of the guerrilla mother, Team not only assesses these fighters' relationship with their babies, partners, family members, and other female fighters but also examines the impact this interaction had on her, the ethnographer. In addition, Team touches on the meaning of female masculinity discussed earlier and draws her own conclusions.

During times of conflict, but particularly after the fighting has stopped, women often take up additional roles, including political and economic roles, which had formerly been reserved for men, as in the case of Rwanda following the 1994 genocide. In her chapter on Armenian Karabakhi women, Sevan Beukian uncovers how women go about transforming themselves and coping with postconflict situations. After listening to women's own stories, Beukian concludes that Karabakhi women have used the situation of conflict to develop expansive mothering roles, as mothers of the community, of husbands and of sons who were traumatized or exhibit other problems because of the war. She challenges aspects of feminist critiques of the maternal role under patriarchy by noting that while the Armenian environment remains staunchly patriarchal, Karabakhi women argue that the public role of mothers empowers them and counters local forms of masculinity.

Postcolonial Developments

Like other colonized peoples, the Anishinaabeg in Canada seek to protect their past tradition while moving forward in ways that can improve their situation and culture. Renée Mzinegiizhigoo-kwe Bédard, a member of this nation, maintains in her chapter that much can be gleaned from the traditional role of grandmothers as educators of grandchildren, especially grandsons. In the past, grandmothers were viewed as a source of accumulated knowledge, wisdom, and moral teachings. For instance, creation stories relayed by grandmothers drive home important lessons—that humans begin life as members of communities, not as atomistic individuals, and that gender flexibility is part of life, to be accepted. These older women not only teach young males both the knowledge and skills they need for malehood but also introduce them to knowledges about femalehood. Bédard believes that reaching back and reformulating the role of grandmothers is one way to build a more dignified future. Grandmothers should be allowed to participate in the modern school system in order to teach the language and pass on oral literature and civic codes. The wisdom of Indigenous institutions developed in the past can strengthen today's educational institutions.

Zairunisha deals with the problem of colonization from a different angle. Her focus is on postcolonial gender constructs following the denigration of colonized populations. Europeans tended to perceive local constructs of masculinities and femininities among the conquered populations of the Americas, the Middle East, Africa, and Asia as inferior, thus elevating Western ones. Focusing on India, Zairunisha discusses the backlash that ensued when India fought for independence from the British. Among other things, the idea of a pure Hindu nationalism began to take shape in which a specific model of femininity was assigned to motherhood. India became the sacred motherland, and women were to be venerated as sacrificing, chaste mothers. The survival of women and the nation were now in the hands of male protectors, India's sons. Thus, a hegemonic Hindu masculinity started to take form under a heavy-handed model of patriarchy. Foreigners and other religions (e.g., Islam) posed a threat to nation and womanhood. Zairunisha shows how ancient Hindu texts have been used to co-opt motherhood for this political project.

Rasel Madaha's research on the establishment of transformative village community networks (TVCONEs) in independent Tanzania draws attention to an overlooked dimension of women's income generating networks: their impact on gender relations. He argues that TVCONEs not only improve the economic wellbeing of members but appear to play a key role in shaping and redefining relationships between husbands and wives. The new sources of income allow mothers to take better care of their children. Women feel empowered and are less dependent on husbands or partners in fulfilling their responsibilities as mothers. New perspectives on motherhood are developing. Furthermore, villagers often engage in these networks as couples, allowing men to earn income and rebuild masculine identities, which had been shaken by the loss of employment following the imposition of neoliberal policies of the IMF. As women develop their businesses and incorporate husbands into the networks, not only do they gain respect as mothers, but their husbands often participate in household chores, which has had an impact on the local construction of masculinity.

Andréa Moraes explores the close relationship between motherhood and child nutrition. She argues that child malnutrition is often understood and addressed as a problem for which mothers are responsible. Without denying the significance of the work of mothers, Moraes explores gender relations at the household level and the impact of fathers and extended family members on child nutrition. Based on her fieldwork, Moraes discusses the complexities of motherhood and masculinities in this context—especially regarding the caring role of fathers and its impact on children's health and nutrition—and how they intersect with ethnicity, rural poverty, Confucianism, and market changes. She highlights how motherhood and masculinities are negotiated in different ways and their implications for child nutrition.

The chapters in this volume explore numerous relationships between motherhood, mothering, and masculinities from a variety of theoretical perspectives, disciplines, and personal concerns. The authors succeed in drawing attention to social expectations and behaviour at all levels, national, regional, and local across the globe. Several chapters also highlight the significance of international relations, such as the response of Indigenous cultures to colonial or settler encounters, the consequences of war, and reactions to diasporic experiences. Human beings continue to use these contexts in unexpected ways to effect change in their societies.

Endnotes

1. This is a well-known Brazilian proverb that is part of everyday folklore.

Works Cited

Akinware, Margaret. *Child Care and Women's Work in Rural Nigeria.* Report submitted to the Consultative Group on Early Childhood Care and Development. World Bank, 1988.

Bucar, Elizabeth. M. *Creative Conformity.* Georgetown University Press, 2011.

Clark, Gracia. *African Market Women.* Indiana University Press, 2010.

Collins, Patricia Hill. "Shifting the Center: Race, Class and Feminist Theorizing About Motherhood." *Mothering: Ideology, Experience and Agency.* Edited by Evelyn Nakano Glenn et al., Routledge, 1994, pp. 45-65.

Connell, Raewyn. "A Thousand Miles from Kind: Men, Masculinities and Modern Institutions." *The Journal of Men's Studies,* vol. 16, no. 3, 2008, pp. 237-52.

Hearn, Jeff. "From Hegemonic Masculinity to the Hegemony of Men." *Feminist Theory,* vol. 5, no. 1, 2004, pp. 49-72.

Kandiyoti, Deniz. "Bargaining with Patriarchy." *Gender and Society,* vol. 2, no. 3, 1988, pp. 274-90.

Leap, Braden. "A New Type of White Provider: Shifting Masculinities in Mainstream Country Music from the 1980s through the 2010s." *Rural Sociology,* vol. 85, no. 1, 2019, pp. 165-89.

Messerschmidt, James, W. *Masculinities in the Making.* Rowman and Littlefield. 2016.

Olóruntoba-Ojú, Táíwò. "Sexuality Indices in Yoruba Language and Popular Culture." *Sexuality in Africa: Magazine and Monographs,* 2011, www.arsrc.org. Accessed 21 Jan. 2015.

O'Reilly, Andrea. *Matricentric Feminism.* Demeter Press. 2016.

Pearce, Tolá Olú. "Development and Globalization: The Context of Women's Lives in Africa." *University of Missouri Peace Studies Review,* vol. 1, no. 2, 2005, pp. 49-61.

Ratele, Kopano. "Hegemonic African Masculinities and Men's Heterosexual Lives: Some Uses for Homophobia." *African Studies Review,* vol. 57, no. 21, 2014, pp. 115-30.

Semley, Lorelle. *Mother is Gold, Father Is Glass.* Indiana University Press. 2011.

Rich, Adrienne, *Of Woman Born: Motherhood as Experience and Institution.* Bantam Books, 1976.

Rout, Sneha. "Are Indian Mothers Happy?" *The Wire,* 13 Nov. 2018, thewire.in/health/are-indian-mothers-happy. Accessed 4 June 2019.

Santos, Cristina, and Tracy Crowe Morey. "(M)othering the Borderlands: Testimony and the Latina Feminist Group." *Journal of the Motherhood Initiative for Research and Community Involvement,* vol. 4, no. 2, pp. 89-104.

Vagmita, Veeksha. "The Varied Notions of Motherhood." *The Wire*, 7 Mar. 2019, thewire.in/women/the-varied-notions-of-motherhood. Accessed 15 May 2019.

PART I
CULTURAL NARRATIVES

Chapter 1

Motherhood and the Construction of a Regional Hegemonic Masculinity in Southwestern Nigeria

Tólá Olú Pearce

Introduction

This chapter examines the complex relationship between the constructs of motherhood and hegemonic masculinity among the Yorùbá of Southwest Nigeria. This group is composed of several subdivisions who speak a mutually intelligible language and forged a mega ethnic unit during the nineteenth century. By early 2021, the Yorùbá were over forty million in a nation of 211.40 million, thus comprising about 19 per cent of the Nigerian population. My focus is on motherhood and hegemonic masculinity as institutions (Connell and Messerschmidt) as well as on normative expectations and cultural ideals rather than organizational behaviour or mothering experiences (Connell; Rich). I review the expectations embedded in each construct and the impact that each ideal has had on the other. I analyze these issues across the nation's precolonial, colonial (Nigeria was a British colony between 1914 and 1960), and postcolonial periods; most importantly I explore the ways in which the earlier historical periods have had a bearing on present expectations.

The Institutions:
Motherhood and Hegemonic Masculinity

Motherhood

My journey into the study of motherhood began with a collaborative research on female food vendors that started in the 1980s in Ilé-Ifè (1984–1992) and ended in Ìbàdàn (2007–2009), during which time data were collected on various aspects of the women's work, health, and family life.[1] The data for this chapter came from the last phase of the study, in which thirty vendors were asked about the expectations they had of motherhood. I wanted to know, as Yorùbá women, what their beliefs about motherhood were. Their responses, as well as material from secondary sources, form the core of my analysis on the normative expectations regarding the institution of motherhood in Southwestern Nigeria.

Motherhood is influenced not only by the family but also by other social factors, such as religion, education, class, art, and the media, as well as by historical developments. In the pre-colonial period, the Yorùbá had developed kingdoms of various sizes, and family life was patrilineal, patrilocal, and polygynous (Fádípè). The system was patriarchal, but it was different from the Western form. Different forms of patriarchies exist across the globe (Kandiyoti,), and slight variations do exist among Yorùbá subdivisions. Although the Yorùbá emphasized seniority in precolonial times, there still was precolonial gender inequality, and this context was important for motherhood (Emanuel; Fádípè; Pearce, "Dispelling the Myth"). Most women became mothers after having been duly married through recognized matrimonial procedures (Babatúndé). Moving into a husband's extended family compound had implications for the new bride's low status vis-à-vis her spouse and members of his patrilineage.

Nonetheless, the position of mother was highly regarded compared to other statuses within a family, such as daughter, sister, wife, and so forth. Even the venerated status of mother-in-law was dependent on having become a mother at an earlier age. Technically, a woman moved from being an obedient child to a subservient wife and then to the higher status of mother. Within the patrilocal compound, out in the community at large and in reference to the supernatural realm, the term "mother" (ìyá) was a referent for status and/or power as in "Ìyálé" (senior wife), "Ìyálôde" (leader of women in town), and "Àwon Ìyá Wa" (women with mysterious powers or "Àjé"). To alter her low status as wife, a woman had to give birth and become a mother. Her status was further enhanced if she gave birth to a boy. Beyond birthing, mothers were expected to socialize children into accepted practices and cultural values, although daughters were under the control of mothers for a longer period than sons (Fádîpè). Precolonial Yorùbá women also worked as traders, food vendors, farmers, healers, potters, and priestesses, among other roles, and were expected to be providers for their dependents. Although the initial monetary layout for her business was expected to be supplied by the groom, the income generated by a wife from her labour was exclusively hers. These were nonpooling households in which spouses bore household responsibilities separately.

These expectations continued through the colonial period into the postcolonial era. Some members of the educated middle class, particularly the younger generation of charismatic Christians, sometimes now pool resources, but generally women view this as risky in a society where polygyny is still legal. For instance, among the initial sample of 260 food vendors in Ilé-Ifè, none of the married women handed over earnings to a spouse (Kújorè and Pearce). The expectation of an extensive role for mothers continues, as seen from the 2007–2009 study conducted in Ìbàdàn. One participant said, "A mother must bear the expenses of a child. That is what is expected—expenses for school and other things. A mother must behave like a mother." And another asked, "How can an unemployed mother be a good mother?"

These statements indicate that the role of good mother goes beyond that of domestic homemaker; indeed, a bad mother is one who does not take her financial and economic responsibilities seriously. Unfortunately, following the neoliberal economic policies of the 1980s and 1990s, women's financial responsibilities for dependents often increased when their husbands lost jobs in a shrinking formal sector. Both lower-income and middle-class women experienced this increase in responsibilities.

Hegemonic Masculinity

Whereas the focus on motherhood among scholars working on Africa is longstanding, interest in masculinities (not just fatherhood) is relatively new but is rapidly developing. Masculinities are now discussed in the plural; they are viewed as localised, ever changing, and distinct from the focus on biology (Connell; Cornwall; Lindsay, "Money, Marriage, Masculinity"; Morrell et al.; Ratele). While I acknowledge the criticisms levied against Connell's notion of hegemonic masculinity (including her own), it still remains useful here. The idea of hegemonic masculinity (even a regional hegemonic construct) makes sense because of the existence of other masculinities below it, including the subordinated, marginalized, complicit, repressed, dependent, and others. The hegemonic form "embod[ies] *the currently most honored way of being a man*; it require[s] all other men to position themselves in relation to it ... it mean[s] ascendancy achieved through culture, institutions, and persuasion" (Connell and Messerschmidt, 832, my emphasis). Like the institution of motherhood, hegemonic masculinity deals with expectations, norms, and practices that are held up as the ideal in a particular patriarchal gender system. Moreover, like motherhood, learning masculine behaviour begins within the family and continues across other sectors in society. Dean Lusher and Garry Robins argue that the formulation of the hegemonic variant may change but still remain hegemonic in a given society. I want to stress that two issues need to be considered here. On the one hand, there are the assets or components that go into constructing this hegemonic masculinity. Wealth, for example, may be an important component, but it may be defined in terms of land control, ownership of cows, slaves, or money as society changes. On the other hand, these assets are expected to produce a certain type of persona that justifies the way a man presents himself in public and the way he interacts with others. For instance, one might project a certain arrogance, keep aloof, or display generosity as part of this persona. I assert that although certain elements comprising hegemonic masculinity may have changed in Yorùbáland, from the precolonial to the independent era, the style and bearing that go with the persona have not really changed.

Yorùbá masculinity was nurtured in the patrilineal family compound in the precolonial era. Important for men were occupational success as well as having a large compound and a sizeable retinue of wives, sons, their wives, unmarried or returning daughters, visitors, slaves, and grandchildren. Each (lineage or extended family) compound was headed by the baalé or baba ilé (father of the house/compound). Being the head of a sizeable, peaceful, and flourishing compound gave the aging baba some stature. Several family compounds made up a town ward—a larger demarcation in Yorùbá towns controlled by even more powerful men (bálè or baba ilè) than the baalé. Given the long history of territorial invasions and the development of large and small kingdoms, from about 1000 to the mid-1800s (Ejiogu), warriors with large compounds who dominated parts of or entire towns epitomized wealth, success, and control. According to Abôsèdé Emanuel, Ògún—the deity of warfare, fire, and metallurgy, who has remained popular among the Yorùbá to this day—was created as warfare became important in the creation of precolonial kingdoms. Successful Yorùbá towns chose bold leaders who possessed attributes associated with Ògún: "so we should regard Ògún as a deified 'composite hero'" (Emanuel 154). As an ideal, he was associated with success, accumulation, and even fertility. He personified toughness, activity, violence, ruthlessness, but also protection. Warriors who exemplified Ògún were revered, as in the example below:

> Olúyòlé, a warrior from Òyó, arrived in Ibadan in 1829 with a large number of slaves in his train. Having first acquired the minor military title of Aare Ago, he quickly rose to become the Òsì of Ìbàdàn and by 1836, Àlàafor Àtìbà had conferred on him the powerful title of Basòrun (Prime Minister) of the New Òyó Empire. Olúyòlé's extensive household made up of thousands of slaves was the basis of his ambition and power. (Afoláyan 410)

Those at the pinnacle of Yorùbá subgroups were the rulers, chiefs, and warriors who controlled land, wives, and slaves captured during wars and invasions. When the transatlantic slave trade was overtaken by trade in palm oil, cotton, and other products, merchants who were able to acquire land and property along the coast became wealthy. They also acquired wives, labourers, and developed extensive patron-client networks (Mann).

This "big man" image of the regional hegemonic masculinity continued through the colonial period into the independent era. Only the elements or resources used in its construction shifted; the social persona has remained intact. Scholars have chronicled the ways in which Western education (and Christianity) not only allowed younger men to obtain social and physical (household) independence from their elders, but also allowed them to rise in the colonial civil service and in the formal sector (Lindsay; Baden; Adébóyè). Focusing on railway men, Lisa Lindsay writes: "The importance of railway men's economic contributions reinforced prevailing notions that men were considered household heads, even when wives earned income as well" (452).

What is significant here is that with steady income, regular promotions, allowances/benefits, and stable pensions, men could extend the traditional ideals of wealth, status, and control into the modern era. Men no longer needed to become warriors or merchants, nor did they have to be sole breadwinners in the Western sense. Those at the apex of colonial administrative and economic structures simply stepped into the shoes of the British colonials once they left. Olúfúnké Adébóyè recounts the story of Akínpèlú Òbísèsàn, a well-known Ìbàdàn man, who struggled to attain the elite masculinity status during the colonial period, even as he was held back by his lack of education. He was well aware of the assets required and he kept his eye on the prize. Gradually, he secured different appointments that elevated his status, including becoming a judge in a native court. He finally was given a traditional chieftaincy in 1960, the year of independence. Other men leveraged their education and status in Western-style organizations to obtain chieftaincies and other Indigenous positions, thus merging assets from both the Indigenous and Western systems to project the image of the elite or hegemonic masculinity. With education, wealth, a wife or wives, children, and chieftaincies, big men could protect kin and supporters. By writing a letter of introduction or making a phone call to the right person, a big man was expected to help his juniors along. His status was supposed to produce real results for those below; to this day, a big man must display his position.

Mothers and Their Sons

Given the Yorùbá tradition of son preference (Fádîpè), a new bride was expected to give birth to sons to enhance her husband's status and help perpetuate his patrilineage. An infertile woman was traditionally despised, and one who only birthed females was a nuisance (Pearce,

"She Will Not Be Listened To"). The arrival of a son gave (and still gives) a wife a stronger foothold in the husband's family, since Yorùbá women do not themselves become members of the man's patrilineage. I am my father's (born 1915, Lagos) first child. He was said to have joked that this was a sign of weakness on his part. Things did change, however. He went on to have six sons. But the pursuit of sons remains a nightmare for many mothers, since hegemonic masculinity requires having sons. According to Nathaniel Fádîpè, fathers in precolonial times were expected to be especially close to their first son, notwithstanding the fact that mothers bore a heavy economic responsibility for their own set of children (the hearth hold). However, a mother lost control of the disciplining of sons quite early:

> To a large extent owing to fear of resistance, a woman does not attempt to do more than remonstrate with her boys of about the age of twelve and over, when they misbehave themselves in her presence.... If she is a disciplinarian, she might report them to their father. *But she has no recourse to the whip, and consequently is unable to control them,* unless an older male member of the extended family should be near at hand to check any unruliness. (243-44, my emphasis)

The above reference to the whip as a mechanism of control is important, since Fádîpè makes it clear that a man could use the whip on both his children and his wife/wives, an observation surely not lost on a young son. The degree to which mothers lost control over their sons has changed since precolonial days, but growing up in Lagos and Ìbàdàn in the 1950s and 1960s, one was aware of the way mothers often trod lightly when handling their sons—and it wasn't always due to the lack of education in these women, since by the 1960s, women were already becoming teachers, headmistresses, nurses, even doctors and lawyers. No doubt some of the old taboos were in play, even as things were changing. Nonetheless, in a 2012 address to a group of educated mothers in Ilorin, Olúyémisi Abímbólá targeted the problem of son preference that still exists: "A son should not be preferred over a daughter in the home, the son is a brother to his sister, not her head (boss)" (*Women's Empowerment* 6). Clearly, her statement indicates that mothers (and daughters) in many homes still help to define masculinity as something above the feminine. Having delivered a child, her womanhood is not in question, but a mother is also responsible for important aspects of the early socialization of the children, especially her sons.

Given both Fádîpè and Abímbólá's references, what is relevant here is that as a son becomes socialized into the ideals of masculinity, he soon understands the significance of the male children to the security of mothers in their husband's extended family and their status in society at large. Among a Yorùbá subgroup about sixty-four miles from Ilé-Ifè, for instance, the eldest son traditionally inherits the house in which the father had resided, regardless of his birth position or the rank of his mother (first, second, or third wife), even though both male and female children do inherit some property. I witnessed this tradition in the 1990s as well as the horrendous widow rites the women, who were all mothers, went through.

Although a son is dependent on his mother for financial and emotional care, he soon understands the gender hierarchy, the significance of his position vis-à-vis his mother, and her disciplinary powers. Some built in tension therefore exists in this relationship, for while no child wants to bite the hand that feeds him or upset a loving and indulgent mother, he soon realizes that there is a dimension to his birth for which his mother is inordinately grateful. Moreover, socialization into masculinity allows a son, but not his mother, the possibility of striving for hegemonic masculinity.

Nonetheless, the Yorùbá do not specifically abort female fetuses using today's technologies. A woman's financial contribution to family life is significant, and since there is the tradition of female financial independence, her role in the welfare and success of her children is culturally recognized, which is opposite to other cultures in which women work but then hand their earnings over to men or in which they do not receive any separate remuneration for their work in the fields or in the family business. A Yorùbá woman's labour is recognized, particularly by her children. The following response was not exceptional among the food vendors I interviewed in Ìbàdàn: "He (husband) only pays school fees when he has the money. It is the woman who bears the expenses. I bear the expenses." In addition to moral teachings and emotional care, this economic role remains important in the bonding of mother and son. Even within educated middle-class nuclear households, women are expected to maintain financial obligations to children and members of their own natal lineages. Many men who have been able to garner the resources necessary to attain the hegemonic status often recall the financial role their mothers played in their education or movement up the social ladder.

For those who moved from the rural areas and small towns to get a good education or to take up positions in the growing cities after independence, their mothers' efforts remain a source of pride. Images of the long-suffering, obedient wife but financially solvent mother became a constant narrative of husbands. Having left behind familiar local practices and surroundings that supported rural images of masculinity, stories about the mothers of their youth became an important device for controlling educated wives and nuclear households. In 1971, a highly educated male put it to me this way: "What do you expect? Women can have babies. They now hold men's positions [jobs] in the workplace. What is left (for men)?" So the hardworking mother of the past becomes a tool in an attempt to control so-called modern households and to manufacture an acceptable image of femininity for today's professional wife. As a man scales the ladder of hegemonic masculinity, the issues of dominance and control are consciously fought for. Although other factors, such as emotional distance and the threat of "outside" wives play a role, the image of the providing, non-complaining mother is trotted out when masculinity feels challenged. When this icon actually materializes in the form of a live-in or visiting mother-in-law, the issue of control is usually reenforced.

In a patrilineal/patrilocal society like the Yorùbá, a man's mother has immense power within the new household because of the institution of motherhood. Although the venue and structure differ from the past, it is his household, and his mother is technically a mini queen mother. Mother and son reenforce the dominant masculine persona because it serves both their interests. My paternal grandmother (born 1880), who worked hard to assist her children, took out a mortgage on her own house in the 1930s for my father's overseas university education and was purported to have said with regard to my mother, her daughter-in-law: "Òsìsé wà l'ôòrùn, a jo máâje wà ni ìbòòji" (The worker labours in the sun while the one who muscles in to enjoy unearned benefits [reaping what she did not sow] has been lounging in the shade). The more successful a man becomes in society, the more elevated his mother's status. I recall that during the colonial period, sometimes mothers were not addressed by their children's names, as is the tradition. In places like Lagos and Ìbàdàn, Mama Akin, Mama Tòkunbò, or Mama 'Débò affectionately became Mama Doctor, Mama Justice, or Mama Lawyer in the neighbourhood or community at large.

A Man and the Mother of His Children

In aiming for the ideal masculinity, a man needs a wife to bear him sons, and control over both was traditionally undisputed (Fádîpè). His relationship to the mother of his children was and remains complex unless he specifically decided to go thoroughly Western and build a close companionate marriage, which members of his extended family usually resisted. The social dominance exhibited within the community must first be developed in the home. Fádîpè has some choice passages on how husbands controlled wives in the past, with the whip as well as humiliating demands. Emotional distance and bullying were allowed, and polygyny made this easier. From the precolonial times through to the present day, polygyny has morphed into modified arrangements with outside wives, concubines, and sidekicks, who are scattered across town and nation. Legally, a man may have children from all these relationships, since statutory, Indigenous, and Islamic laws operate simultaneously, and polygyny has not been outlawed in Nigeria.

The polygynous home remains hierarchical. In his study of Yorùbá homes on the eve of independence, Mâbògùnje notes the following: "The father is the object of great respect, often verging towards reverence both by the children and even the wives. On a social survey of many villages around Ibadan, for instance, we discovered that apart from the oldest wife, the other wives felt it was beyond them to mention (utter) the name of their husband to us" (28). He also notes that "In most families, in fact, even the first son has greater authority in the house than any of the wives *and sometimes than his mother*" (Mâbògùnje, 29, my emphasis). Such expectations not only support those practices that help cement the father's dominance but also groom sons in the use of authority and pull males away from the control of women. Younger sons who do not have the authority of the first sons watch and learn a thing or two about the ideals of masculinity. Yet the mother is a great source of affection: "Under such circumstances therefore, it is natural to expect that the mother would receive more than her due share of affection. In most cases, she receives nearly all the affection the children can give and, more important, their confidence and secrets" (Mâbògùnje 29).

As can be seen, the emotional bond between mother and children is assumed to be strong, and Fádîpè notes that in the past, a woman had very little expectation of affection from her husband. Although affection may develop, it was not culturally anticipated. Data collected by Janice Oláwoyè et al., in a 1998 multiethnic study, reveal that even at the end of the twentieth century, expectations regarding affection were still low. When asked, without prompting, what a man's responsibilities are to his wife, only 15.7 per cent of Yoruba men in the study mentioned the requirement to meet a wife's emotional needs. Compared to male participants from the other ethnic groups in the study, "it was also found that having authority over one's wife and children was distinctly viewed as an important element of masculinity among the Yoruba men" (Oláwoyè et al. 18).

Nonetheless, similar to sons, fathers, too, are conflicted in the husband-wife dynamic. As he built his own wealth and reputation, a man was traditionally dependent on his wife/wives for the children (i.e., sons) that would uplift his status and for the economic role women play in the lives of children. Then, and today, economically failing wives become dead weight and require too much financial attention. Furthermore, the moral socialization of young children is largely the mother's responsibility, although she generally has a lot of help from extended family members (Fádîpè; Pearce, "Perceptions"). However, she is judged harshly for badly behaved children. Babatúndé put it succinctly using an old saying: "While the mother is most likely to be blamed for every fault in a child, she does not receive the credit for the child's good qualities.... When a child is good, it belongs to the father; if it is bad, it is the mother's (Ti omo ba dara ti baba re, ti oba baje, ti iye re)" (Babatúndé 10).

This saying speaks to the appropriation of maternal labour: pregnancy, domestic childcare, and financial responsibilities. Thus, the tension arising from dependency on and the need to control mothers, clearly stands out. Women who become too powerful, who do not bear children or bear only girls, or who become a financial drain (perhaps due to chronic illness) are a real problem. All four issues expose a woman to being identified as a witch (Àjé), someone with mysterious capacities. Although mythology states that Àjé are powerful, no child wants its mother to be so identified, as this can lead to a strained relationship between the children and their father or his extended family.

These issues, however, draw attention to certain aspects of motherhood. Even though women are elevated by the status awarded to mothers, the institution is without a doubt hemmed in by the particular cultural rules of the group. Fádîpè argues that in precolonial times, some of the stability of marriages came from the fact that children belonged to the husband's lineage (although respect and recognition are due the wife's lineage) and could be held hostage if a wife left her marriage. Even today, mothers are fearful of behaving in a way that allows a man to pronounce the following: "Maa kò e t'omo, t'omo"[2] (I will divorce you and disown your children). Elders could, of course, step in to save the situation and reclaim the children for the patrilineage, but by rebuking a wife this way, one has control over motherhood. Again, the right to beat one's wife is still a male preserve (Oyèdîran and Isiugo-Abanihe; Pearce "Assaulting a Wife"; Voices4Change), her status as a mother notwithstanding. No dispensation is given when after childbirth, the role of mother is added to the status of wife. Although women are believed to be able to overcome problems because of their access to mysterious powers, because they can take on the characteristics of rebellious female deities, like Oya or because women are placated during annual masquerade festivals like Gèlèdè (Abímbólá, "Images of Women"; Awólàlú and Dòpámu; Washington), one needs to ask how much of this mythology actually filters into the daily experience of mothers, since the mother's position is securely structured below that of father in the flow of everyday life (Fádîpè). Women often work hard to elevate the position of their husbands. The narrative below from one of the food vendors in the Ìbàdàn study is not unfamiliar.

A middle-aged mother of five lost her formal sector job as a result of widespread firing following the World Bank and IMF policies in the 1980 and 1990s. Food vending is generally seen as a survival strategy because it requires minimal financial layout. While she was a formal sector worker, she had obtained a government loan: "I used the loan to build a house for my husband. That was my happiest moment. I haven't built mine yet." She specifically said that she did not view the house as her property, since her husband soon married and brought in another wife. Obviously, her former job gave her access to a loan to build the house, which helped raise her husband's status in the community, as he now owns a house. In terms of motherhood, four of her five children are males, the preferred sex. Given the value system, this woman is an all-rounder.

It would be incorrect to conclude that Yorùbá women do not resist patriarchal motherhood. Push back has been the norm. For instance, creation narratives reveal that Òsun, the fertility deity, the Great Mother, retaliated when male deities were disrespectful as they travelled down to earth. Again, prior to colonization, women had their own guilds, associations, and female spokespersons within the community, which they definitely needed. Following colonization, Fúnláyò Ransome-Kuti (Mama Felá) emerged as perhaps the best-known critic of Yorùbá gender relations and is a foremother of today's feminisms in Nigeria. The last two decades of the twentieth century and beyond saw the development of gender research units, women's documentation centres, women's studies departments, and NGOs focused on gender justice, including Women in Nigeria (WIN, established in 1983) and the Nigerian Feminist Forum (NFF, 2008, effectively replacing WIN), which also emphasize the interaction between Indigenous and Western patriarchies and their impact on women (Madunagu). There have been many setbacks but also important breakthroughs. For instance, in March 2019, a female judge in Òyó state broke the usual protocol by pronouncing that any house built during the life of a marriage could not automatically be considered the man's possession upon divorce. I grew up at a time when by custom, women were expected to lay no claim to property acquired through joint effort. The decision of the judge indicates, as suggested by Ìyábò Fágbúlù, that women should become conscious of their worth and promote intragroup identities that do not subordinate the feminine.[3]

Conclusion

This chapter has focused on the way the institutions of motherhood and hegemonic masculinity are intertwined though not of the same standing. Motherhood affords women a high status in Yorùbá society and has implications for power within the community, but it does not have the same structured power as fatherhood within a marriage, nor does it lead to the heights that fathers can reach when they embody this regional hegemonic masculinity. Rather, much that is expected of motherhood is placed at the service of hegemonic masculinity. I have emphasized the importance of the organization of the Yorùbá family as the context in which ideals are learned, and I have noted that the expectations for each have not substantially changed from precolonial times to the present. Traditionally, a few menopausal women were allowed to occupy offices akin to males (Fádîpè; Ratele), and today some women have become highly educated or wealthy, but this has not changed the general status of women. For example, a professorial wife definitely does not have the same standing as her professorial husband either in the home or in the community. On the whole, women are still expected to bear sons who belong to the husband's patrilineage; they continue to be providing mothers and are subject to strong discipline (both verbal and physical) by the fathers of their children. Regarding hegemonic masculinity, the big man persona is still projected, even though the tools or assets used in its construction have changed. That is to say, today's big men (e.g., ranking politicians, educated professionals, pastors of mega churches, and top level military officials) tout the same image as former traditional rulers (Oba), warriors, and merchant princes of precolonial times.

This is not to deny the existence of subregional variants across Yorùbáland. However, it appears that the educated elite (largely located in Lagos, Abéòkúta, and Ìbàdàn), which emerged in the late nineteenth century, sought to establish a Yorùbá collective identity from the disparate subgroups. The educated elite consolidated its power during the colonial era and has remained assertive (Akinjogbìn; Fálolá; Zacheruk). In establishing its position, the educated elite gained definitional control over the requirements for hegemonic masculinity. Basically, this group merged important elements of the traditional construct (e.g., wealth, success, Indigenous titles, control of wives and children, and so forth) with the assets over which it had control (e.g., Western education and titles as well as positions in Western-style organizations—church, military, and state bureaucracy). Thus, a winning formula was crafted comprising of education, status, wealth, traditional titles, control over the household and community recognition, and it lifted the construct to a macro-ethnic level. Interestingly, according to Olúfémi Vaughan, this elite group strove to set the tone for things not only within Yorùbáland but also for Nigeria as a whole. Being a hegemonic male in Nigeria today does seem to run along these lines. The 2015 study on *Being a Man in Nigeria*, reports the following: "'A real man' is one who is married and succeeds in exercising authority over and provides for, wife/wives and children. Men (9 in 10) and women (8 in 10) overwhelmingly concur that women should *obey their husbands in all things*.... This idea of men's dominance over women prevails across regions, genders and ages" (Voices4Change, 23, my emphasis).

Indeed, the study notes that men strongly resist gender equality at the personal level, and female leadership is still problematic. As one Yorùbá participant stated: "[The] eagle was born to fly high to the peak of the sky. The chicken, no matter how you train it, will never fly high to the stage of an eagle. No matter how you train a woman she can never be as good as a man." Women can enjoy the high status of motherhood, but obviously the idea of *woman* still lurks beneath all else, whereas the idea of *man* allows the male to soar to the peak of the sky. Hegemonic masculinity is the ideal that allows you to reach the sky.

Endnotes

1. Data collection for the various aspects of the food vendors' study in Ilé-Ifè was funded by two grants from the Ford Foundation. The final study conducted in Ìbàdàn was funded by a grant from the University of Missouri. The data were collected in collaboration with Ms. O. Kújorè.
2. This statement was supplied by Olúwajù Jameson Pearce.
3. Personal communication with Ìyábò Fágbúlù 3/10/2020.

Works Cited

Abímbólá, Wande. "Images of Women in the Ifa Literary Corpus." *Annals of the New York Academy of Sciences*, vol. 810, no 1, 2006, pp. 401-413.

Abímbólá, Olúyémisi. *Women's Empowerment: An Absolute Necessity for Societal Progress*. Keynote Address, 16th Annual Rhema Chapel Ministers' Wives Retreat. Ilorin, Nigeria, 19-22 April, 2012.

Adébóyè, Olúfúnké. "Reading the Diary of Akínpèlú Òbísèsan in Colonial Africa." *African Studies Review,* vol. 51, no. 2, 2008, pp. 75-97.

Afoláyan, Fúnsó. "Warfare and Slavery in 19th Century Yorubaland." *War and Peace in Yorubaland 1793-1893.* Edited by Adéagbo Akinjogbìn, Heinemann Educational Books, 1998, pp. 407-19.

Akinjogbìn, Adéagbo. "Keynote Address." *War and Peace in Yorubaland:1793-1893.* Edited by Adéagbo Akinjogbìn, Heinemann Educational Books, 1998, pp. 1-6.

Awólàlú, Omosadé, and Adélumó Dòpámu. *West African Traditional Religion.* Onibonje Press and Book Industries, 1979.

Babatúndé, Emmanuel. *A Critical Study of the Bini and Yoruba Value Systems of Nigeria in Change: Culture, Religion and The Self.* The Edwin Mellen Press, 1992.

Baden, Graham. "'Our White Fathers': Patriarchy and Shifting Gender Roles in Colonial Nigeria, 1900-1961." *"Our White Fathers": Patriarchy and Shifting Gender Roles in Colonial...* 13 Jan. 2015, grahambaden.com/.../our-white-fathers-paternalism-and-shifting-gender-roles-in-colonial-nigeria-1900-1961/ Accessed 31 May 2018.

Connell, Raewyn. "A Thousand Miles from Kind: Men, Masculinities and Modern Institutions." *The Journal of Men's Studies,* vol. 16, no. 3, 2008, pp. 237-52.

Connell, Raewyn, and James Messerschmidt. "Hegemonic Masculinity: Rethinking the Concept." *Gender and Society,* vol. 19, no. 6, 2005, pp. 829-59.

Cornwall, Andrea A. "To Be a Man Is More Than a Day's Work: Shifting Ideals of Masculinity in Adó-Òdò, Southwestern Nigeria." *Men and Masculinities in Modern Africa.* Edited by Lisa A. Lindsay and Stephan F. Miescher, Heinemann, 2003, pp. 230-48.

Ejiogu, E. C. "State Building in the Niger Basin in the Common Era and Beyond, 1000-Mid 1800s: The Case of Yorubaland." *Journal of Asian and African Studies,* vol. 46, no. 6, 2011, pp. 593-614.

Emanuel, Abôsèdé. *Odún Ifá.* West African Book Publishers. 1978.

Fádîpè, Nathaniel. *The Sociology of the Yoruba.* PhD dissertation. London School of Economics, 1939.

Fálolá, Toyìn. "Power, Status and Influence of Yoruba Chiefs in Historical perspective. *Yoruba Identity and Power Politics.* Edited by Toyìn Fálolá and Anne Genova, University of Rochester Press, 2006, pp. 161-76.

Kandiyoti, Deniz. "Bargaining with Patriarchy." *Gender and Society,* vol. 2, no. 3, 1988, pp. 274-90.

Kújorè, Olúfémi, and Tólá Olú Pearce. *Street Foods in Ile-Ife: The Preparation, Marketing and Health Aspects of a Small-Scale Enterprise.* Report submitted to the Ford Foundation, 1989.

Lindsay, Lisa. "'No Need...To Think of Home'? Masculinity and Domestic Life on the Nigerian Railway, c1940-61." *Journal of African History,* vol. 39, 1998, pp. 439-66.

Lindsay, Lisa. "Money, Marriage and Masculinity on the Colonial Nigerian Railway." *Men and Masculinities in Modern Africa.* Edited by Lisa A. Lindsay and Stephan F. Miescher, Heinemann, 2003, pp.139-55.

Lusher, Dean, and Robins, Garry. "Hegemonic and Other Masculinities in Local Social Contexts." *Men and Masculinities,* vol., 11, no., 4, 2009, pp. 387-423.

Mâbògùnje, Akin. "The Yoruba Home." *Odù,* vol. 5, 1958, pp. 28-36.

Madunagu, Bene. "The Nigerian Feminist Movement: Lessons from 'Women in Nigeria.'" *Review of African Political Economy,* vol. 38, no. 118, pp. 666-72.

Mann, Kristin. "Women, Landed Property and The Accumulation of Wealth in Early Colonial Lagos." *SIGNS,* vol. 16, no. 4, 1991, pp. 682-706.

Oláwoyè, Janice, et al. "Construction of Manhood in Nigeria: Implications for Male Responsibility in Reproductive Health." *African Population Studies,* vol. 19, no. 2, 2004, pp. 1-20.

Oyèdiran, Koláwolé, and Uche, Isiugo-Abanihe. "Perceptions of Nigerian Women on Domestic Violence: Evidence from the 2003 Nigerian Demographic and Health Survey." *African Journal of Reproductive Health,* vol. 9, no. 2, 2005, pp. 38-53.

Pearce, Tólá Olú. "Assaulting a Wife: Perspectives on Conjugal Violence." *Women's Health Issues in Nigeria.* Edited by Mere N. Kisekka, Tamaza Publishing Company Limited, 1992, pp. 191-202.

Pearce, Tólá Olú. "Perceptions on the Availability of Social Support for Child Care among Women in Ile-Ife." *Child Health in Nigeria*. Edited by Tolá Olú Pearce and Toyin Fálolá, Ashgate Publishing Limited, 1994, pp. 45-57.

Pearce, Tólá Olú. "She Will Not Be Listened to in Public: Perceptions Among the Yoruba of Infertility and Childlessness in Women." *Reproductive Health Matters*, vol., 7, no. 13, 1999, pp. 69-79.

Pearce, Tólá Olú. "Dispelling the Myth of Pre-colonial Gender Equality in Yoruba Culture." *Canadian Journal of African Studies*, vol. 48, no. 2, 2014, pp. 315-31.

Piot, Charles. *Remotely Global*. University of Chicago Press. 1999.

Morrell, Robert, Rachel Jewkes, and Graham Lindegger. "Hegemonic Masculinity/Masculinities in South Africa: Culture, Power and Gender Politics." *Men and Masculinities*, vol. 15, no. 1, 2012, pp. 11-30.

Ratele, Kopano. "Analysing Males in Africa: Certain Useful Elements in Considering Ruling Masculinities." *Journal of African and Asian Studies*, vol. 7, 2008, pp. 515-36.

Rich, Adrienne. *Of Woman Born: Motherhood as Experience and Institution*. Bantam Books, 1976.

Washington, Teresa. *Our Mothers, Our Powers, Our Texts*. Indiana University Press, 2005.

Vaughan, Olúfémi. "Chieftaincy, Structures, Communal Identity and Decolonization in Yorubaland." *Yoruba Identity and Power Politics*. Edited by Toyin Fálolá and Ann Genova, University of Rochester Press, 2006, pp. 177-91.

Voices4Change. *Being a Man in Nigeria: Perceptions and Realities*. Department of International Development, London, 2015.

Zachernuk, Philip. *Colonial Subjects*. University Press of Virginia, 2000.

Chapter 2

Exploring Perspectives on Black Motherhood, Parenting, and Childrearing through Black Social Media Users' Meme Circulation

Kierra Otis and Miriam Araya

> If slavery persists as an issue in the political life of black America, it is not because of an antiquarian obsession with bygone days or the burden of a too-long memory, but because black lives are still imperiled and devalued by a racial calculus and a political arithmetic that were entrenched centuries ago. This is the afterlife of slavery— skewed life chances, limited access to health and education, premature death, incarceration, and impoverishment.... I too am the afterlife of slavery—Hartman 6.

Introduction

Since Black African captives arrived in the Americas on cargo ships, doctors, lawyers, and scholars have been using media outlets to devalue and degrade Black life in order to justify the torture and subjugation of their bodies (Collins). With the advent of social media, Black people have been able to engage in constructing media representations of Black life in an unprecedented way. Today, in what Saidiya Hartman calls the "afterlife of slavery," Black social media users in the United States (U.S.) sometimes participate in undermining Black social life, as we will demonstrate shortly. They often present stereotypes of Black family life without an in-depth analysis of the social conditions that have, to begin with, condemned Blacks to particular social realities. Nonetheless, they have also participated in exposing the various technologies of survival that Black women and families have adopted in order to survive conditions of extreme exploitation and oppression. These mechanisms for survival and desire to thrive can be described as "the untiring practice of trying to live when you were never meant to survive" (Hartman 228). By tracing Black social media users' depictions of memes, one can examine how Black families have been undermined but have also developed mechanisms to survive the current conditions of captivity in slavery's afterlife.

Black people in the U.S. now have significant impact on social media, as their primary mode of communication is their creation and circulation of memes (St. Felix). These communicative devices, which "satirize politics, popular culture and common experiences" (Weise and Kruzman), are a way for Black social media users to offer their perspectives about various topics. Internet memes typically consist of an image from popular culture with some kind of caption or text overlay that describes what the image is depicting. Of particular interest for this chapter is Black users' depictions and discussion of Black parenting, gender, and family life in the U.S. In this chapter, we analyse 145 memes on Black mothers, fathers, and families collected from well-known media platforms between November 2017 and May 2018 in order to answer the following questions. What perspectives do memes from Black social media users offer about Black parenthood, gender, and childrearing? How do these revelations compare with the academic research on the same subjects? What do these comparisons reveal about both Black motherhood and masculinities?

Theoretical Framework and Methodology

Epistemology, the study of knowledge, asks certain questions. How do we know what we know? What is considered knowledge? Who gets to be a "knower" or knowledge producer? In the U.S., the dominant epistemological framework is positivism, which privileges objectivity and detachment rather than lived experience. Patricia Hill Collins argues that Western positivism is harmful because it (a) gives credibility to the most privileged voices and interests (i.e., white, heterosexual, and able-bodied men), (b) subjugates the knowledge of marginalized people as they are scrutinized as too subjective and involved, and (c) forces marginalized groups to use alternative forms of knowledge production and disbursement (251). Black feminist epistemology commits to recognizing alternative knowledge producers and methods of distribution in order to uncover formerly subjugated knowledge. Utilizing a Black feminist framework, this project rejects positivism by taking seriously the situated knowledge Black social media users produce and by analyzing their creation and circulation of memes regarding Black families and Black motherhood, masculinity, and childrearing specifically.

This exploratory project only considers memes created or reposted by Black social media users residing in the U.S. in order to uncover their perspectives on and depictions of Black motherhood, fatherhood, and childrearing. We used the following keywords, hashtags, and search engines to collect memes:

Black mother memes (Google)
Black mom memes (Google)
Black men memes (Google)
Black father memes (Google)
Black family(ies) memes (Google)
Black mothers (Tumblr, Twitter, Instagram)
Black men (Tumblr, Twitter, Instagram)
Black fathers (Tumblr, Twitter, Instagram)
#growingupblack (Tumblr,Twitter,Instagram)
#thanksgivingwithblackfamilies(Twitter, Instagram)
#blackmomsbelike (Twitter, Instagram)
#blackdadsbelike (Twitter, Instagram)
#blackfamiliesbelike (Twitter, Instagram)

Two limitations for collecting memes were immediately apparent. The first was discerning a social media user's race and nationality. We relied on users' profile photos and content (self-identifying as Black or a U.S. resident in a tweet or biography) to determine their race and geographic location. The other limitation was finding the original creator of a meme, which proved to be nearly impossible at times. In order to increase the volume of memes considered in this analysis, we included memes that were created or reposted by Black social media users. After finding a meme related to Black families, we located the social media user who created or posted the meme and assessed their race and geographic location. If the user's demographic information could not be determined or did not meet the criteria of Black and residing in the United States, the meme was not included, as this project focuses on Black families in the United States.

Findings

Figure 1.

Major Themes	# of Appearances in the Collection of 145 Memes
Siblings and Extended Family Members	31 memes
Discipline	31 memes
Conflict	26 memes
Black Fathers as Absent Fathers	11 memes

The collection and analysis of 145 memes from several social media platforms—including Twitter, Facebook, Pinterest, Instagram, and Tumblr—revealed significant discussion surrounding Black parenthood, gender, and childrearing. The most frequently occurring themes include the significant role of siblings and extended family members in Black families, conflict, and discipline. Minor themes include hair, appearance/attractiveness, sports, money, and Black men's relationships with white women.

Black Family Structure—Mothers, Fathers, Aunties, Grandmas, Siblings, and Cousins

In the collection of 145 memes, sixty-four mentioned Black mothers explicitly, forty mentioned fathers, and forty-one mentioned Black families generally without a gendered component. Overall, these memes tell a story of Black families that are predominantly maintained through the Black mothering and communal kinship structures of African Americans. These kinship structures are nonnormative because they do not fit the nuclear colonial family model—the white heterosexual, monogamous couple with their children (Ferguson, "Of Our Normative Strivings"). Many of these kinship structures are believed to predate slavery; they have endured through the horrors of the Middle Passage and chattel slavery and have sustained Black families to date. Part of what is so nonnormative about these families is the vital work and reproductive labour that Black women do to breathe life into Black families.

Figure 2.

| Tumblr user @ mostfamousunknown | Twitter user @Raheem_Martin | Instagram user @i_am_giorgio |

| Twitter user @kallolis | Twitter user @ ronimichelej | Twitter user @alexisprude |

Black Fathers

Of the forty memes directly related to Black fatherhood included in the analysis, over a quarter explicitly characterize Black fathers as absent from their children's lives. Some social media users portray the father as absent from birth. For example, one meme depicts a scenario in which a young child is taking a photograph with his father after meeting him for the first time. Other users offer memes in which the father leaves the child's life later. One meme containing an image of a conventionally attractive woman contains the following caption: "#BlackDadsBeLike I think I'd leave my family for her." With this particular hashtag, Black social media users imply that leaving families is characteristic of Black fathers. Some memes do not say when or why the father left, only that he is gone. For instance, one social media user posted a meme with a photo of an astronaut in outer space and captioned it with "Niggas be like... child support ain't got this address." Although the scenarios are different, these representations of Black masculinity represent men as incapable of and uninterested in caring for their children in physical, emotional, and financial ways. Furthermore, because these memes are created and/or circulated by Black social media users, it tells us that there are Black social media users who may experience and/or represent their fathers as predominantly absent.

The belief that Black fathers are absent fathers is a long-held one, which was most exemplified in the infamous 1965 report from Moynihan: *The Negro Family: A Case for National Action* (Edin et al.). Moynihan argues that "at the heart of the deterioration of the fabric of Negro society is the deterioration of the Negro family" and attributes this deterioration to the prevalence of female-headed households and absent fathers (6-7). The myth of the absent father implies that Black fathers are pathologically absent and leaves opaque the terrors that affect Black male sociality in the afterlife of slavery, including extreme poverty, racial capitalism, mass incarceration, and medical apartheid. Conservatives upheld the report and its racist, misogynistic, classist, and queerphobic underpinnings while Black people—including liberals, sociologists, and feminists—and others denounced it (Mumford). Nonetheless, memes found on social media seem to indicate that despite critiques of the report and growing evidence from social scientists of Black fathers' high involvement in the lives of their children over the last fifty years, the idea persists that Black fathers, particularly unwed, inner-city ones, are pathologically absent (Edin et al.).

The dominant ideology regarding fatherhood in the United States is the "package deal" theory, which posits that a father's involvement and relationship with the child are dependent on his relationship with the mother (Edin et al.). This is significant considering Black children are more likely than white and Latino children to live with single, unwed mothers (Pew Research Center). However, several studies have concluded that Black fathers stay involved in their children's lives through regular visitation and contact even if they do not have a romantic relationship with the child's mother (Mincy and Pouncy; Danziger and Radin; King). Social media memes from Black users argue that Black fathers are predominantly absent fathers, who are neither present in their homes nor in their lives. However, in addition to the information on visitation behaviour presented above, research over the past three decades shows that 31 per cent of Black children live with both parents either in a first marriage or in a remarriage (Pew Research Center). It is therefore possible to argue, as we did in the introduction, that memes on Black fatherhood often undermine the reality of Black social life and encourage longstanding stereotypes.

Black Mothering and the Role of Extended Family

Black social media users depict the presence and role of other family members as an important aspect of childrearing in Black families. Relationships and interactions with siblings, grandmothers, and aunties are all depicted. Representations of sibling relationships feature positive attachments as well as conflict. One example of a positive sibling relationship comes from @_kitadenise, who posted two photos with her younger sister with the caption, "We both beat foster care... Two different backgrounds... now adopted into the same family [and] connected as sisters by heart." This tells us that Black social media users value their relationships with siblings, whether biological, adoptive, or fictive. Social media users also stress the role siblings play in their parents' disciplinary practices. For example, @Bam_Org depicts a scenario in which a parent orders a child to "find [them] a belt," implying a "whupping." Another meme includes a photo from "Little Bill" with three children in the backseat of a car. The caption reads, "I don't care who did it. I'm beatin all ya'll ass when we get home." These representations suggest that there is a shared experience for Black social media users in which sibling relationships are influenced by disciplinary practices of their parent(s). Siblings are sometimes charged with helping parents carry out physical discipline and might have an adversarial relationship with each other. However, at other times, siblings are being disciplined together.

Social media users also represent aunts, or "aunties," as playing an important role in Black families' holiday festivities; they prepare macaroni and cheese, encourage people to help clean up dinner, and/or ask someone to pray. These representations of familial interactions demonstrate a gendered division of labour, as the women of the family are usually the ones cooking, cleaning, and facilitating others' help. The majority of auntie memes included a so-called clapback (responding to criticism with a comeback); the aunt asks a question or makes a comment to the narrator and the narrator responds with a comment about the aunt's personal life. For example, one meme depicts an aunt asking the narrator about a boyfriend and the narrator responds, "You need to worry about your life and your career." The initial questions and comments from aunts demonstrate an eagerness to know about the lives of their family members, whereas the clapbacks from family members demonstrate a desire for autonomy, privacy, or perhaps even inclusivity (as some of these comments can be quite heteronormative).

Black social media users characterize grandmothers as women who are given a rite of place in the Black family: They warrant respect, discipline their grandchildren, enjoy cooking, and care deeply for their families. Social media users appear appreciative of the times their grandmother would prepare food (e.g., "Grandma at the door, when she send everyone back home full,") or "plaster" Vaseline on their grandchildren so they can stay "shiny." These representations demonstrate the significant role that grandmothers have in raising children and the care that Black social media users enjoy around their grandmothers. Another meme includes a grandmother discussing how "God gifted" her with children and grandchildren and how she expects to be gifted with great grandchildren. This meme can be taken to represent the religious arguments that grandmothers might make around one's reproductive decisions. Taken together, these memes on grandmothers show the extent to which Black families take pride in having multigenerational families. Both the institution of motherhood and the behaviour of women, as caretakers, reach their peak through the respect given to grandmothers.

Another important perspective on mothering is the portrayal of complex relationships with siblings and extended family members. Including sibling relationships is important because the "links between sibling negativity and youth adjustment" that researchers have discovered may be even stronger than parent-adolescent linkages (Whiteman et al.). Additionally, Black mothers' reliance on extended family members aligns with previous research on (1) the role strain that accompanies single parenthood, which encourages Black mothers to rely on family members for social support, and (2) surviving components of West African culture stressing collectivism (Mendenhall et al.; Nguyen et al.). This social support consists of "aid, affect, information, and affirmation" (Taylor et al., 148). Developing a larger safety net of extended family members is how Black mothers have had to survive and sustain their families. Although Black social media users do not report on some aspects of the support from extended family members, such as monetary aid or childcare, they put forward images of emotional support and negative interactions.

Conflict

Conflict was the aspect of Black motherhood, fatherhood, and families that Black social media users depict most frequently, appearing in twenty-six out of 145 memes. In most instances, the conflicts portrayed are minor (e.g. small disagreements between parent and child and banter with aunts during family festivities); however, some major conflicts were depicted (e.g. mothers barring fathers from entering the home, and Black men degrading Black women).

The majority of conflicts that were portrayed through the memes relate to food (fifteen memes) and household responsibilities (ten memes). These memes most often feature mothers rather than fathers (see above section on absent fathers), demonstrating that the majority of familial labour is performed by women. Conflict regarding food usually involves a child wanting to eat something other than leftovers or wanting something from outside the home (e.g. McDonald's, the ice cream truck) and the mother refusing. Other food-related conflicts include forgetting to take the frozen chicken out before the mother returned from work, mothers telling their children they have "had enough to eat," and navigating dietary restrictions. Conflict related to household responsibilities usually reveal that mothers expect assistance with household tasks and express frustration over lack of assistance. One meme includes a photo of a Black woman carrying several grocery bags into a house. When asked if she needs help, she responds: "No I got it. I do everything else in this house anyway. Ya'll gone miss me when I'm dead." This type of meme draws attention to the recognition and acknowledgment of frustrations that Black mothers encounter regarding the care of their families. It is labour that is never complete. Other minor conflicts depicted were small disputes, often comedic exchanges. For example, social media user @RGreen_94 posted a photo of Kenan Thompson shrugging his shoulders with wide eyes. The mother says to the child: "You always got an ugly look on your face." The child responds, "People say that I look like you." This meme indicates a particular level of care and playfulness between Black parents, most often mothers, and their children that can be found in the act of childrearing across the globe.

Additionally, our data reveal that academic achievement, activity restriction, and appearance are sources of conflict. These minor conflicts involve exchanges between mothers and children, siblings, and other relatives. For example, one social media user posted a photo of a Black child crying in the backseat of a car. The child says to the mother: "Mom but everybody else..." She responds: "Everybody else ain't my child. I said no." This meme tells us about the difficult situations that arise in parent-child relationships when children have friends who are parented differently. Their parents, Black mothers in this instance, must recall their responsibility to their children.

The negative attitudes that Black men hold towards Black girls and women were a source of major conflict that several (seven) social media users discussed. For instance, @ashleyxkim posted a photo of the model Naomi Campbell looking at something offscreen intensely with the caption, "My face when black guys slander black women, but forget their mothers, sisters, aunts & grandmothers are what? Black." This meme gestures towards the larger issue of misogynoir, the prevalence of misogyny from Black men towards Black women (Bailey). Another user posted a piece from Disney's *The Proud Family*, in which Oscar was telling his daughter she couldn't date until she is married. The social media user captioned the image with, "This is my dad." This meme draws attention to the fact that Black girls often complain that fathers tend to be overbearing. They frequently restrict a daughter's autonomy as a result of their own paternalistic fears about dating, marriage, and heterosexuality. Negative attitudes are also directed towards mothers. For instance in one meme a woman is dancing with four men. The caption says: "I really needed somebody to come get my mama at my wedding dawg, she was outta line. And these dudes ain't my friends no mo'." Unlike the previous meme where fathers police their daughters' behaviours, here the individual scrutinizes the mother's behaviour. Of interest to us is the gendered dimension of the scrutiny between parents and children. Whereas fathers are attempting to control and police the sexual behaviour of daughters, sons feel the need to control the behaviour of their mothers in public. Indeed, in many cultures, motherhood is viewed as the furthest thing from active sexuality, and "inappropriate" dancing becomes a problem.

The way Black social media users depict minor conflict in Black families is consistent with academic research. Scholars have found that Black parent-adolescent conflict often relates to "chores, choice of activities, interpersonal relations, the adolescent's room, schoolwork, time for going to bed and curfew, appearance, and money and spending" (Sematana and Gaines 1453). Most conflicts depicted by Black social media users fit these criteria. However, in addition, major conflicts, including misogynoir, are also taken up, such as the aforementioned incidence of fathers policing their daughters' sexual life and sons policing mothers. One could argue that the authority embedded in hegemonic masculinity affects the parent-child relation-ship, allowing the control of women (including one's mother) and girls.

Discipline

Out of the 145 memes depicting Black families, thirty-one explore discipline and the variety of methods Black parents employ. For the purposes of this chapter, discipline is defined as a "variety of disci-plinary practices" used in order to teach "children to make meaningful life choices" (Adkison-Bradley et al. 198). The disciplinary methods Black social media users show include physical discipline, discussion of unwanted behaviour, shouting or raising one's voice, privilege withdrawal, emphasis on academic achievement, and the monitoring of children's phones. The themes and methods of discipline and punishment are significant for Black families in the U.S., particularly those who are the descendants of enslaved Africans, whose claims to parenthood were secondary to the slave owners' claims of ownership and possession (Roberts).

Nearly half (thirteen) of the memes related to discipline describe physical discipline or corporal punishment, which is defined as "the use of physical force with the intention of causing a child to experience pain, but not injury, for the purpose of correcting or controlling the child's behavior" (Taylor et al., "Perceived Instrumentality" 60). Black social media users often depict scenarios in which public misbehaviour is met with corporal punishment. For example, one meme included a photo of the popular Kermit character and his mother grabbing his neck. The text reads: "#GrowingUpBlack When you was acting up in public and your mama pulled you off to the side to threaten your life." Another example includes a photo of a young, Black woman with a backpack on. The caption says: "When the teacher calls your mom at school and now she has to miss work to come whoop your ass #growingupblack." Each of these memes is featured with the hashtag, "growing up black," and imply that physical discipline is a characteristic of Black mothers, specifically. These memes show that Black children are well aware that their mothers often do not abide by the model of parenting espoused by the larger society. A common phrase that appears in memes related to public behaviour is the phrase "Fix your face before I fix it for you." This focus on what is acceptable behaviour in public can be attributed to the history of surveillance and the undermining of Black parenting during slavery and its afterlives, in which Black families adopted tools to police themselves in the presences of others, especially white people, in order to protect themselves from harm (Roberts). Other misbehaviours warranting physical discipline include a child using the mother's first name and a mother not being able to find her purse. Most of the representations around physical discipline featured Black mothers and their children. These memes could leave viewers with the impression that Black mothers overwhelmingly use physical discipline, for even the most minor offences.

Several memes depict Black parents discussing unwanted behaviour with their children. One meme from the hashtag #HowToughAmIBlack

Edition depicts a mother telling her children that she did not raise them the way they were behaving. Another meme shows a mother discussing how disrespectful her child's generation is. These memes demonstrate Black social media users' understanding of their parent's hopes and disappointments surrounding their behaviour. Again, the conversations overwhelmingly show Black mothers disciplining their children, creating the impression that Black women are the sole disciplinarians in Black families.

Although Black social media users do discuss other methods of discipline in their memes, they emphasize the use of physical discipline or corporal punishment. This is significant, considering that the use of corporal punishment is both prevalent and controversial in the U.S. (Taylor et al., "Perceived Instrumentality"), which is especially true of Black families, where the findings on the prevalence and effectiveness of corporal punishment are uncertain. Concerning the prevalence of corporal punishment in Black families, researchers have found that Black parents prefer to employ physical discipline only when other methods of discipline fail (Taylor et al., "Perceived Instrumentality"; Adkison-Bradley et al.). The intention behind Black parents' employment of corporal punishment is often portrayed as sincere and righteous, with scholars citing the need to keep "children on a path toward responsible citizenship and behavior" (Taylor et al., "Perceived Instrumentality" 69) and adolescence being "a time of increased risk for African American youth" (Adkison-Bradley et al. 203). However, there are those who question its effectiveness. Scholars argue that the negative effects of physical discipline are significant (Taylor et al "Perceived Instrumentality"; Lau et al.; Ferguson "Spanking"). In thinking through Black feminism and abolition, we can also acknowledge how corporal punishment is infused within logics of carcerality and a culture of violence that informed the chattel enslavement of Black Americans and still affect the treatment of Black youth by their parents today in the afterlives of slavery (Davis, *Are Prisons Obsolete*; *Freedom is a Constant Struggle*; Hartman). As noted here, mothering seems to bear the brunt of this depiction.

KIERRA OTIS AND MIRIAM ARAYA

Minor Themes

Other themes that emerge less frequently include hair, appearance/ attractiveness, sports, money, and Black men's relationships with white women. Four memes depict the reality of Black hair through pictures of brushes, hair balls, and (hot) combs. Three of these memes specify that the mother was doing the hair; the fourth depicts a father. Appearance and attractiveness were themes that only appear in memes related to Black men and fathers. For example, one meme includes a photo of a Black man with a hat, sunglasses, and a toothpick. The caption says, "When yo daddy come pick you up for the summer, toothpick a week old #blackfamilies." This resonates with the earlier theme surrounding Black father's absence, with the emphasis on the father's "week old" toothpick, a marker of irresponsibility. Here, masculinity has an air of parental irresponsibility. Sports appear twice; once relates to the way that Black moms watch sports, and the other shows a Black father coming back into his child's life once he learns his son received a basketball scholarship. The juxtaposition between Black mothers and fathers here is particularly clear; the mother is represented as watching the game intently as a way to support her child, whereas the father appears only when money is an option. Money surfaces five more times. Black mothers are depicted as surprising their children with the latest Air Jordan sneakers or giving lunch money to children for school, whereas Black fathers are depicted as wanting every penny of change. Although in many cultures masculinity is tied to the control of money, a negative dimension of that control is suggested in these examples.

Black men's relationships with white women are discussed five times, with two of them depicting the presence of white women at Black family holiday celebrations. One meme contains a photo of Michelle Obama looking at a white woman from the side of her eyes with the caption, "When your brother's white wife says she usually 'prefers to eat healthy.' #ThanksgivingwithBlackFamilies." This comment reflects a prevalent belief among white people that the foods that Black families eat, especially during the holidays, are unhealthy or lack nutrition. Other memes depict Black men expressing contempt for interracial relationships. "The white girl will never love u more than she loves that dog. It'll never work out. Do u even like Starbucks? Can she even fry CHICKEN?" a father says to his son in one meme. This meme demonstrates a recognition of the caretaking work that Black mothers do for their families, including cooking food, and a belief that white women will not or cannot perform this work.

Several themes only appear once or twice in the dataset: a child preferring to take photos with his father over his mother, driving with Black mothers, sassy Black men, #ChristmaswithBlackFamilies, Jesus telling "sis" about her "trash" boyfriend, bedtime stories, playing Uno, drinking Minute Maid juice out of a certain cup, and the war on drugs.

Conclusion

Three major themes were located among Black social media users' creation and circulation of memes on Black families and childrearing: Black family formations, conflict, and discipline. These memetic representations of family structure (i.e., a focus on single mothers, nonresident fathers, siblings, grandmothers, and aunts) subvert Western notions of the nuclear family and demonstrate the importance of extended kinship networks. These portrayals are consistent with the current research on Black families. The majority of Black children live in single households with their mothers; however, their fathers are often still part of their lives (Pew Research Center). Black families have significant contact with their extended family members, usually through the diligence of women keeping families close (Taylor et al., "Patterns of Emotional Support"). These memes, along with scholarly research, make clear that Black women, especially mothers, are expected to perform the labour to maintain strong family ties. The dominant depiction of Black fathers is their absence, demonstrating how masculinity allows them to perform significantly less reproductive, emotional, and affective labour within their families. As in any society, relationships between Black family members can be a source of emotional support or the cause of stress; both are portrayed in Black social media users' memes. Although minor conflicts are normal, the prevalence of conflict can have adverse effects on mental health (Taylor et al., "Patterns of Emotional Support"). Additionally, the use of corporal punishment was the disciplinary method Black social media users' depicted most, although they did not necessarily express attitudes regarding the prevalence or effectiveness of corporal punishment.

These representations of Black families sometimes uphold the familiar pathologizing of Black people and their family formations.

Most of the memes represented mothers in caretaker positions rather than fathers, which gestures towards the long-held belief that Black fathers are pathologically absent and that Black mothers are responsible for the challenges that Black families and communities experience. This dominant misconception about and representation of Black family life fails to consider the enduring effects of chattel slavery and racial capitalism that leave Black people vulnerable to poverty, violence, imprisonment, and debility. However, Black social media users' representations also teach us of the skills that Black families have used to survive, which include (ironically) the care and reproductive labour that Black women provide, a reliance on extended family support, intergenerational familial relationships, affectionate sibling inter-actions, and a sense of humour and playfulness.

Furthermore, the findings have revealed themes and issues that were not able to be taken up in detail in this chapter, such as class, sexuality, and queerness as well as the relationship between corporal punishment, slavery, and carceral logics. Some important questions do remain. How do Black girls and women social media users perceive and depict their families compared to Black boys and men? How do Black trans and gender queer people portray their families? How does class affect Black family life, according to memes? Are there portrayals of queer/LGB Black families in social media memes? What is the relation-ship between corporal punishment, chattel slavery, and carcerality? How do Black children feel about corporal punishment?

Works Cited

Adkison-Bradley, Carla, et al. "Child Discipline in African American Families: A Study of Patterns and Context." *The Family Journal: Counseling and Therapy for Couples and Families*, 2014, vol. 22, no. 2, pp. 198-205.

Bailey, Moya Zakia. *Race, Region, and Gender in Early Emory School*. Dissertation. Emory University, 2013, etd.library.emory.edu/concern/etds/5x2ltg05s?locale=en. Accessed 14 Apr. 2021.

Collins, Patricia Hill. *Black Feminist Thought: Knowledge, Consciousness and the Politics of Empowerment*, 2nd ed. Routledge, 2008.

Danziger, Sandra K, and Norma Radin. "Absent Does Not Equal Uninvolved: Predictors of Fathering in Teen Mother Families."

Journal of Marriage and Family, vol. 52, no. 3, 1990, pp. 636-42.

Davis, Angela. *Are Prisons Obsolete?* Seven Stories Press, 2003.

Davis, Angela. *Freedom Is a Constant Struggle: Ferguson, Palestine, and the Foundations of a Movement.* Haymarket Books, 2016.

Edin, Kathryn, et al. "Claiming Fatherhood: Race and the Dynamics of Paternal Involvement among Unmarried Men." *The Annals of the American Academy of Political and Social Science,* v. 621, January 2009, DOI: 10.1177/0002716208325548.

Ferguson, Christopher J. "Spanking, Corporal Punishment and Negative Long-Term Outcomes: A Meta-Analytic Review of Longitudinal Studies." *Clinical Psychology Review,* vol. 33, no. 1, 2013, pp. 196-208.

Ferguson, Roderick A. "Of Our Normative Strivings: African American Studies and the Histories of Sexuality." *Social Text,* vol. 23, no. 3-4, 2005, pp. 85-100.

Hartman, Saidiya V. *Lose Your Mother: A Journey Along the Atlantic Slave Route.* Farrar, Straus and Giroux, 2007.

King, Valarie. "Variation in the Consequences of Nonresident Father Involvement for Children's Well-Being." *Journal of Marriage and Family,* vol. 56, no. 4, 1994, pp. 963-72.

Lau, Anna S., et al. "Factors Affecting Link Between Physical Discipline and Child Externalizing Problems in Black and White Families." *Journal of Community Psychology,* vol. 34, no. 1, 2006, pp. 89-103.

Mendenhall, Ruby, et al. "Single Black Mothers' Role Strain and Adaptation across the Life Course." *Journal of African American Studies,* vol. 17, pp. 74-98.

Mincy, Ronald B., and Hillard Pouncy. "Baby Fathers and American Family Formation: Low-Income, Never-Married Parents in Louisiana before Katrina." *An Essay in the Future of the Black Family Series,* The Institute for American Values, 2007.

Moynihan, Daniel Patrick. *The Negro Family: The Case for National Action.* Office of Policy Planning and Research, United States Department of Labor, 1965.

Mumford, Kevin J. "Untangling Pathology: The Moynihan Report and Homosexual Damage, 1965-1975." *The Journal of Policy History,* vol. 24, no. 1, 2012, doi: 10.1017/s0898030611000376.

Nguyen, Ann W., et al. "African American Extended Family and Church-Based Social Network Typologies." *Family Relations,* vol. 65, 2016, pp. 701-15.

Pew Research Center. "The American Family Today." *Pew Research Center's Social & Demographic Trends Project,* 17 Dec. 2015, www.pewsocialtrends.org/2015/12/17/1-the-american-family-today/. Accessed 14 Apr. 2021.

Roberts, Dorothy. *Killing the Black Body: Race, Reproduction, and the Meaning of Liberty.* Vintage Books, 1997.

Sematana, Judith, and Cheryl Gaines. "Adolescent-Parent Conflict in Middle-Class African American Families." *Child Development,* vol. 70, no. 6, 1999, pp. 1447-63.

St. Felix, Doreen St. "Black Teens Are Breaking The Internet And Seeing None Of The Profits." *The FADER,* 3 Dec. 2015, www.thefader.com/2015/12/03/on-fleek-peaches-monroee-meechie-viral-vines. Accessed 14 Apr. 2021.

Taylor, Catherine A, et al. "Perceived Instrumentality and Norma-tiveness of Corporal Punishment Use among Black Mothers." *Family Relations,* vol. 60, 2011, pp. 60-72.

Taylor, Robert Joseph, et al. "Patterns of Emotional Support and Negative Interactions among African American and Black Caribbean Extended Families." *Journal of African American Studies,* vol 18, 2014, pp. 147-63.

Weise, Elizabeth, and Diana Kruzman. "What Are Memes—and How Do They Get Kids in Trouble?" *USA Today,* Gannett Satellite Information Network, 9 June 2017, www.usatoday.com/story/tech/news/2017/06/06/what-memes----and-how-do-they-get-kids-trouble/102522244/. Accessed 14 Apr. 2021.

Whiteman, Shawn D., et al. "Sibling Relationships and Adolescent Adjustment: Longitudinal Associations in Two-Parent African American Families" *Journal of Youth Adolescence,* vol. 44, 2015, pp. 2042-53.

Chapter 3

A Feminist Critique of the Representation of Motherhood and Masculinities in Bollywood Cinema: Implications of Gender Violence in the Indian Diaspora

Meghna Bhat

Introduction

The oppression of women in India is not a recent phenomenon. It is, rather, an end product of historical and sociocultural victimization and objectification by religious communities, political bodies, and the colonial state (Menon and Bhasin 66; Narasimhan-Madhavan 400-01). Indian women in the diaspora have also been disproportionately affected by intimate partner violence, including wife battering and domestic violence (Chaudhuri et al. 153; Dasgupta and Warrier 249-50; Raj and Silverman 435). Public debates examining the increasing prevalence of sexual violence in India emphasize the underlying role of Bollywood cinema, especially the way it conveys ideological and stereotypical messages about gender roles and gender relations. These stereotypes contribute to a culture that glorifies abuse, sexism, and oppression against women (Manohar and Kline 234-35; Ramasubramanian and Oliver 334).

Scholars of media and cultural studies suggest that popular culture representations, such as Bollywood films, play an instrumental role in the way audiences may learn from and practice gender norms, roles, and relations in society (Derné 550; Ramasubramanian and Oliver 328). Films also serve as an instrument through which damaging and false ideas of gender inequality, feminism, love, and sexuality are conveyed to children and adolescents (Derné 548). Topics discussed in this chapter are drawn from a larger study that examined Bollywood films using thematic film analysis and gender-specific focus groups.[1] This chapter examines the depiction of motherhood and masculinity in twenty-six Bollywood films.[2] Critiquing these representations through a feminist lens contributes to a deeper understanding of the ways in which women and men are positioned and inserted into patriarchal structures that span time and location (Menon viii).

The Indian film industry, reportedly the largest in the world, produces between fifteen hundred to two thousand films every year in more than twenty languages (Jain et al. 9). This number includes both Bollywood cinema and regional films produced and released in India. Indian movies have risen in popularity, with increased production of films and billion-dollar profits not only in India but overseas as well (Jain et al.). The portmanteau term "Bollywood" merges the word "Bombay" (presently known as Mumbai) with "Hollywood." Bollywood films primarily use Hindi as the spoken language and address a wide variety of genres and themes.

Bollywood moviegoers are ubiquitous in India and abroad, and they represent populations from all walks of life, across age, gender, socio-economic status, caste, and geographical residence. Thanks to the globalization and digitalization of mass media, Indian cinema not only is popular in India but also appeals to the audiences across the world, especially among non-resident Indians (NRIs) and foreign populations ("Bollywood's Expanding Reach" para 1). This chapter explores and reviews Bollywood Hindi films from 1957 to 2018, spanning six decades. However, a majority of the analyzed films (65 per cent) were released between 2001 and 2018.

The Social Construction and Representations of Women

The social construction and representations of women in Bollywood Indian films play a critical role in the way women are being treated in both local and diaspora Indian communities—especially when it comes to women's roles, screen time in the films, as well as the depiction of their choices, bodies, relations with men, sexuality, and desires. Hence, I argue that it is important to study the images and roles of women in films to gain a contextual understanding of motherhood. Bollywood films reflect decades of rigid expectations and policing of women in India, especially related to the idea of compulsory motherhood (Reissman 112). Consider this example from the 2001 film *Chori Chori Chupke Chupke* (*Secretly and Silently*): "Aurat ke ek nai teen janam hote hain...pehla jab vo kisiki beti bankar is duniya mein ati hain...doosra jab vo kisiki patni banti hain aur teesra jab vo maa banti hain" [A woman has got not one but three births. One is when she comes to the world as a daughter to someone, second when she becomes a wife to someone and third is when she becomes a mother]. As the film dialogue above suggests, in traditional Indian culture, a woman's life and identity are not complete until she has a husband in her life and then at least one child, if not more. As a result, women are expected and required to obey these cultural norms and intergenerational practices without questioning. This quality of obedience without challenging cultural practices resonates with the principles in Confucianism, an ancient Chinese tradition. According to Hyun-Joo Lim and Tina Skinne, Confucianism can be described as "supporting the belief that a 'natural' hierarchy is the fundamental means to achieve all human relationships and generate harmony to all of society" (3).

Similarly, societal expectations along with the historical and cultural context of gender roles in India are reflected in the onscreen representations and different roles men and women play in Bollywood cinema (Mathur 66). Representations of women in popular culture, whether films or television series, have been largely influenced by the definitions of "Indian culture," which have been framed and rigorously promoted by Hindu cultural and political movements in India (Vishwanath 41) and are strongly rooted in casteism. The emergence of the dominant Hindu ideology not only fostered monocultural traditional pro-Indian values, the concept of maintaining family legacy and honour, and the promotion of nationalist and patriotic identities and sentiments through Bollywood films, but also showed women in traditional and subordinate roles (Vishwanath).

The film *Mother India* (Fig. 1) caught the attention of the world in 1957 and featured as its protagonist a strong yet self-sacrificing and assertive mother. This Oscar-award nominee for best foreign language film glorified the title character as an ideal and virtuous Indian woman and moral goddesslike mother (Mathur 66–67). Motherhood in India and its cinematic depictions have often been equated with Hindu Indian goddesses, thus bearing resemblance to the "devi maata" (mother goddess) (Mathur).

Figure 1. A promo poster of the film *Mother India*
(Picture Credit: Ziya Us Salam, 2010)

Even as women have been glorified and adored for their sacrifices and traditional (silent) heroism in Bollywood films (Mathur 67), womanhood and motherhood have also been represented synonymously with victimhood in Indian films. These onscreen representations often suggest that ideal women are those who have quietly and heroically endured and survived oppression and violence and have sacrificed their choices and life for their husband and families. Portraying submissive, sacrificing, and silent women as representative of heroic victimhood not only projects patriarchal and misogynist values but also reinforces and promotes problematic images of the ideal Indian woman (Bhat 119-20).

Other maternal characters were played by the late veteran actress Nirupa Roy, known for her onscreen roles as the "beemar aur bebas maa" (unwell and helpless mother) of leading male protagonists. In films like *Amar Akbar Anthony* (released in 1977) and *Deewar* (*Wall*) (released in 1975), she was depicted as unconditionally loving, hard-working, helpless, poor, disabled or physically weak, self-sacrificing, as well as a submissive widowed mother. In short, Nirupa Roy and other onscreen maternal characters in Bollywood films framed and suggested what an ideal Indian mother looks like.

Another example of the suffering and helpless widowed mother eagerly waiting for her son(s) to take revenge is the actress Rakhee star-ring in both these films *Karan Arjun* (1995) and *Ram Lakhan* (1989). The Indian mothers in these films were depicted as either widowed, poor, or helpless in order to be glorified for their sacrifices and strength. Idealizing and valorizing the good wife and mother are symbolized by the widowed mother wearing a white saree. This image may have emerged from the Hindutva notion of womanhood.

Motherhood in India is a contested, complex, and nuanced site of gendered performance because a woman's worth, societal approval, and utility are likely to depend on her choice of whether or not to have children (Maji para. 5; Philipose para. 1). These complex versions of mothering are often falsely represented, or they are presented as one-dimensional and oversimplified representations of motherhood in Bollywood cinema.

A few Hindi films released in the 1980s depict traditional Indian notions of mothering but also question and challenge Indian family and motherhood. For example, the 1982 film *Masoom* (*Innocent*) (Fig. 2) investigates changes experienced by the Indian family, thus challenging the simple, traditional, one-dimensional notions of marriage, mother-hood, and relationships. Indu, a happily married wife and mother of two young daughters, is distraught and hurt when her husband informs her that his illegitimate son, Rahul, will have to live with them in their home. This film not only examines the issue of infidelity in relationships leading to extramarital affairs and the underlying preference for a son, but also follows Indu's emotional and conflicted journey between her roles as a wife and mother (Singh 98-99). Rahul reminds Indu of her husband's infidelity and her shattered dreams of marital bliss, but she is expected to forgive him and graciously accept Rahul as her son. Even though the film chronicles Indu's conflict, *Masoom* has a happy ending for the audiences, as Indu accepts Rahul as her own child, thus protecting the sanctity of marriage and resulting in a happy family (Singh). Yet a few questions remain. What if Indu was not ready to accept Rahul as her child and forgive her husband for being unfaithful? Would the audience still relate to Indu, or would they hold her accountable for a failed marriage and broken family? Would the husband have forgiven Indu and accepted an illegitimate child from her extramarital affair?

Figure 2. Poster of the film *Masoom (Innocent)*
(Picture Credit: Gupta, 2018)

Another film that speaks about infidelity in marriage is the 2000 film *Astitva* (*Identity*). In this film, Aditi admits that she had an extramarital affair with her music teacher. Additionally, the music teacher, not Aditi's husband, is the biological father of her only son. Angered by the betrayal that has shattered their notions of her as a chaste mother and wife, Aditi's husband and son verbally humiliate a very apologetic and guilty Aditi in front of their family and friends. The film concludes with an unapologetic Aditi leaving her house, husband, and grown up son behind, but not before reprimanding them for their male chauvinism, gendered policing, and double standards against her. She begins a journey of self-discovery outside her marriage to establish her own identity.

Whether it is Indu in *Masoom* or Aditi in *Astitva*, they both question and doubt their commitment to their marriage and to motherhood, but the men in these stories who have committed adultery are not shamed or questioned about their (lack of) commitment. Examples of how women like Indu and Aditi are socially perceived and treated through the lens of motherhood, especially the nuances and complexities, reflect in Nivedita Menon's argument. According to Menon, three different aspects in the biological experience of motherhood can be identified due to advances in reproductive science and technology (47). Whereas Indu is expected to play the social mother (rearing and bringing up the child), Aditi has already played all the traditional biological roles of being the egg donor, the gestational mother, and the social mother (Menon).

Women in India have been fighting against the patriarchal system to maintain a balance between their family life and career. Even though working women have become increasingly visible in the workforce and a wide range of blue-collar and white-collar industries, the sexual division of labour in the family and household remains unequal (Maji para. 3; Menon 11). Like most cultures, women in India and in the Indian diaspora are applauded for doing it all: taking care of their children, husband, in-laws, and parents while working outside the home. These expectations often come at the expense of women's physical and mental health and long-term wellbeing. Bollywood films that depict a modern and independent woman's preference to focus on her career and work instead of getting married or wanting to be a mother tend to portray these desires as associated with the negative effects of Westernization on Indian culture.

Furthermore, Hindi films portray young girls or women having a child out of wedlock as being un-Indian, since it implies premarital sexual relationships (Manohar and Kline 236). Contradictory messages about unwed mothers or out-of-wedlock pregnant women are conveyed through Bollywood cinema. The lead character, Sonia, in the 2001 film *Aitraaz* (*Objection*) is depicted as an aspiring career-oriented model who wants to be a famous supermodel at any cost. When Sonia realizes she is pregnant with her lover's child, she decides to abort, as motherhood would ruin her career goals and dreams. This decision is later used as a reason to assassinate her character in court, even though she is on trial for falsely accusing her subordinate of sexual harassment. Similarly, many Hindi films depict women's decision to not opt for motherhood (and focus on a career, identity, or life) as adopting anti-Indian Western values and culture, and most importantly, these choices are portrayed as disappointing and unnatural.

The 2001 film *Lajja* (*Shame*) depicts Vaidehi an immigrant woman living in New York, who is constantly abused and assaulted by her husband. After Vaidehi realizes she is pregnant, she feels her and her unborn child's lives are in danger, and she finally gathers the courage to run away to India to seek help and support. Leaving abusive relationships and partners is often a complex and challenging process for immigrant women. Factors that must often be considered include fear of being deported, fear for her own and her children's safety, fear of losing her children to the system, and lack of financial security (Bhat 174). According to Soma Chaudhuri et al., "the 'patriarchal bargain' can be used to explain how women's choices and solutions to leave and break the pattern of abuse when they are in the U.S. is largely influenced by gendered norms and societal expectations" (144). Vaidehi's decision to stay in the abusive marriage may occur more often than we know in South Asian immigrant communities (Raj and Silverman 435).

Most Hindi films focus on the protective mother-son relationship and the troubled mother-in-law versus daughter-in-law dynamics; few films have shed light on the mother-daughter relationship. An exception is the 2016 film *Nil Battey Sanatta* (*Good for Nothing*) that depicts a deeply moving relationship between Chanda, a school dropout working as a house maid, and her school-going daughter Apeksha. The mother encourages and inspires her daughter to study well in school, thus empowering her despite their social class and economic status (Maheshwari para. 9).

Women in Bollywood films have been represented as pitted against each other to the extent of committing abuse and violence, especially in the role as a mother-in-law. In a deeply patriarchal culture, women end up isolating and abusing other women both in reel and real life, thus highlighting the complex layers of harassment and violence committed against women by women. Cases of marital and domestic violence, including dowry harassment against women in India and the South Asian diaspora, are often documented as perpetrated by in-laws (Bhat 167-68).

(Re)Defining Motherhood

The role of mothers and portrayal of motherhood in Bollywood cinema have seen a gradual yet visible transformation in terms of the messages conveyed to the audiences. The 2008 film *Dostana* (*Friendship*) depicts an Indian mother who finds out her son is gay and is living with his partner. But the story suggests these men are only pretending to be gay to continue staying in the same apartment as roommates with a young and beautiful woman. Despite being disappointed at first, the mother is shown as lovingly accepting her gay son and his partner.

The following three Bollywood films suggest how the image of the Indian mother is changing and beginning to represent different demographic sections of the population, thus providing viewers complex and multicultural meanings of mothering. First, in the 2015 film *Dil Dhadakne Do* (*Let the Heart Beat*) (Fig. 3), Ayesha, a young and successful businesswoman but unhappy in an arranged marriage, confides in her mother about facing marital issues and being unhappy. Her mother, Neelam, dismisses and trivializes her daughter's marital struggles and unhappiness with the response: "Every marriage has problems." Neelam's minimizing of her daughter's dysfunctional marriage is rooted in her own feelings of insecurity and stagnancy in her own thirty-year marriage with her husband. When Ayesha's husband and her own mother suggest that their marital problems will go away when they have children, this unhelpful advice is rooted in restrictive and patriarchal gender roles. Furthermore, when Ayesha mentions to her parents that she wants a divorce because she is miserable in the marriage, instead of listening and sympathizing, her parents reprimand her, justifying how their family honour will be affected by her divorce with the cliched response: "Log Kya Kahenge?" [What will people say?].

Figure 3. A still from the film *Dil Dhadakne Do*
(Picture Credit: Dharmani, 2015)

In the 2017 film *Tumhari Sulu* (*Yours Sulu*), Sulochana is a happy, unapologetic, and cheerful wife as well as an ambitious homemaker and a doting mother to her son. Although she is excited about the little joys in her day-to-day-life such as winning small contests in her community, she dreams of being a working woman. Her older sisters and father constantly belittle and criticize her for not doing anything with her life, so Sulu decides to take up the job of a local radio jockey who talks in a sensual voice and provides relationship advice for a late-night radio show. Even though Sulu's husband, Ashok, is depicted as encouraging and supportive, he succumbs to their family pressure and policing about the shame she is bringing to their family. For example, he starts worrying about "what will people say?" about Sulu and the kind of listeners she is gathering for her late-night radio show. When Sulu's adolescent son goes missing, she feels guilty for missing out on her role as a mother and after her son is safely found, Sulu decides to quit working. Although the story happily ends with Sulu continuing to be a radio jockey with the support of her husband, this distinctive film centres on the aspirations, dreams, conflicts, and challenges of middle-class urban wives and mothers. In short, Sulu being shamed about the nature of her work and Ayesha in *Dil Dhadakne Do* being criticized for her desire to get a divorce both stem from troubling patriarchal notions about how women are responsible for preserving family honour.

In most Bollywood films, motherhood has been largely represented from the Hindu family's perspective, usually overlooking the role of Muslim women as mothers or motherhood in Muslim communities. In the hard-hitting film *Chandni Bar* (2001), Mumtaaz is a young Muslim orphan and former bar dancer who marries a gang leader and has two children. After her husband dies in a police encounter, Mumtaaz resumes her work as a bar dancer and a sex worker to pay her dead husband's overdue loan to ensure the continuation of her children's education and to keep them away from the gritty world of sex work and crime. Despite Mumtaaz's painstaking efforts to educate her teenage children and protect them from her and her husband's less-than-savoury careers, her young daughter turns to dancing in the bar to support her mother's income while her son, who is raped in the detention centre, ends up shooting his perpetrator. The film ends with Mumtaaz's painful and heart-breaking reaction to her son killing another person and the realization that her daughter had become a bar dancer. At no point in the film is Mumtaaz's motherhood visibly questioned or criticized. Instead, the film highlights how as a single parent she cannot protect her children.

Portrayals of women as stepmothers and their maternal respon-sibilities have been vilified or misrepresented in some films, either as antifamily vamps or antagonists, or as modern independent women devoid of any maternal feelings or care. For example, the 1992 film *Beta* (*Son*) and the 2002 film *Dil Hai Tumhara* (*My Heart is Yours*) portray stepmothers as angry, bitter, resentful, greedy, and devoid of maternal feelings. But in the 2003 film *Kal Ho Na Ho* (*Tomorrow May Never Come*), Jaya Bachchan, a stepmother, is portrayed as loving, nurturing, and protective of her younger stepdaughter, who is the product of her deceased husband's infidelity. Bollywood films over the past two decades have started portraying more complex, multilayered, and nuanced notions of motherhood in relation to marriage, family, and violence as well as its implications on audiences in India. But how are Indian fathers depicted in Bollywood films and what are the implications and influences of these portrayals on the images of masculinity?

Bollywood Portrayals of Pitaji (the Father)

A majority of films represent the Indian father as the patriarch, the man of the household, and the one who makes the important decisions. The patriarch's decisions may even include the son's education and career, the daughter's marriage and choice of partner, the daughter-in-law's freedom to work as well as her ability to be a mother. When an entire genre of Bollywood films in the past depicts the Indian mother as demure, submissive, helpless, and having no agency, the Indian father typically falls on the other end of the parenthood spectrum.

The representation of the father in Bollywood cinema varies depending on whether the character is portrayed as having sons or daughters. For example, in one of the most popular and commercially successful films in 1995—Dilwale Dulhaniya Le Jayenge (DDLJ) (The Big-Hearted Will Take Away the Bride)—the patriarch of the family, Baldev Singh, is a successful small business owner and first-generation immigrant settled in the United Kingdom; he is a proud Indian, husband to a traditional Indian wife, and father to two young daughters. An angry and disappointed Baldev is depicted ordering his family to pack their belongings to permanently move to India after realizing his older daughter, Simran, has fallen in love with another man as opposed to the arranged alliance approved by him in India. Even though the film focuses on the romantic aspect of Raj and Simran's love story, Baldev's wife and daughters have no agency or voice to present their views to object to or refuse his orders in any way during the film. A similar example of the powerful and controlling patriarch is the role of Yashwardhan Raichand in the 2001 film Kabhi Kushi Kabhi Gham (Sometimes There's Happiness; Sometimes There's Sadness). When Yashwardhan, a wealthy successful tycoon and a strong believer in family traditions, disowns his older adopted son, Rahul, for marrying Anjali, a poor girl outside their social circle instead of the girl of Yashwardhan's choice, the film centres on the sentiments and experiences of the immigrant Indian diaspora. Similar to the previous example, Yashwardhan's wife and Rahul's mother, Nandini, is portrayed as submissive, having no voice, and despite her maternal yearning and longing to see her son Rahul, she dutifully obeys her husband.

Bollywood Hindi films have also been called out for focusing "on men and their conflicts, their dreams, their aspirations, their tragedies, their revenge, their desires and their heroism" (Sharma 52). Men depicted in Bollywood—particularly fathers, such as Baldev Singh and Yashwardhan Raichand—reflect male authoritarian hegemony, which plays a critical role in portraying the type of women approved by men; these types of women are often deeply embedded in patriarchal norms and reinforced through the male gaze (Mathur 66).

Similarly, in the 2000 film *Astitva* (*Identity*), Aditi's husband, the patriarch Shrikanth Pandit, does not even realize how controlling and misogynistic he is or the impact that his behaviour has on his and Aditi's son, Aniket. Examples of his controlling behaviour include Aniket and Shrikant not allowing the women (Aniket's fiancée or Aditi) to work, Shrikant opening Aditi's personal mail without her permission, and Shrikant sexually assaulting Aditi or not caring for her feelings. Aniket's resentment and anger towards his mother, Aditi, appears to be a reflection of what he may have learned from Shrikant, even if he is not Aniket's biological father. The pride that Shrikant initially feels towards Aniket being his son gradually dissolves as he realises Aniket is the product of his wife's infidelity. In the film *Dil Dhadakne Do* (2015), Anil Kapoor is a father and an entitled wealthy man; he wishes for his son to also become a visionary businessman and take over his business. He does not, in contrast, validate or appreciate his daughter's keen sense of entrepreneurship, evidenced by her own successful business venture. Even in Hindi films that focus on the Indian diaspora, such as *Pardes* (*Foreigner*), Amrish Puri represents another wealthy, entitled patriarch, and business tycoon, who convinces his foreign-born Indian son to marry a traditional, simple, and ideal Indian girl so his son can adopt and appreciate their Indian cultural values. Men depicted in these Bollywood films—such as Shrikant from *Astitva* (2000) or Baldev Singh from *DDLJ* (1995)— underline men's preference that their daughters (or sometimes sons) and/or wives obey a father's/husband's every wish and expectation. Otherwise, the family will be shamed because of their wife's or children's rebellious acts or mistakes, thus affecting the family's honour.

Additionally, the disturbing prevalence of "honour killings" in India is visibly and starkly represented in a few Bollywood Hindi films,[3] such as *Lajja* (Shame) (2001), *NH10* (National Highway 10) (2015), or *Aakrosh* (Anger) (2010). Honour killing—a means to control women's autonomy, body, sexuality, and choice to love and marry someone they want—is usually perpetrated against young men and women having partners belonging to different castes, social status, religions, and so forth (Krishnan). There are quite a few Bollywood films that may not overtly show honour killings but depict community and family members', especially the fathers', desire to separate the young couple in love and possibly kill the partner of their son or daughter. For example, past Hindi films—such as *Qayamat Se Qayamat Tak* (From Doom till Doom) (1988) or *Ek Duje Ke Liye* (Made for Each Other) (1981) and more recent films such as *Ishaqzaade* (Rebel Lovers) (2012)—portray the leading protagonists as young couples in love with each other, who hail from completely opposite backgrounds (e.g., upper/lower caste, rich/poor, Hindu/Muslim, and north Indian/south Indian). When they are kept apart by fathers and family members and forced to marry someone else against their will, such young couples are depicted as not having any alternative but to kill themselves—a worrisome theme that is glorified for its romantic ending drawn from the Romeo and Juliet saga.

Although Bollywood films have long depicted controlling, conservative, and misogynist men and fathers, recent films indicate a progressive shift in how men are represented, especially pertaining to their roles as fathers. Bollywood films—such as *Piku* (2015), *Bareilly Ki Barfi* (Bareilly's Sweet) (2017), *Queen* (2014), and *Khoobsurat* (Beautiful) (2014)—depict parents, especially fathers, as less controlling or patriarchal, more peaceful in demeanor, and most importantly, as their daughter's confidante and friend. This type of daughter-father relationship may not be perfect but is refreshing in terms of representing a less gendered perspective of parenting and fatherhood. For example, *Piku* (2015) highlights the struggles of Piku, a young, strong, and unapologetically unattached woman, who is a successful architect. The film follows her conflicts, role, and journey as the only caretaker for her old and grouchy father—a liberal man who stands up for his daughter's right to choose or engage in any kind of relationship with men and live her life without any judgment.

A similarly supportive father appears in the 2014 film *Queen,* which highlights the story of Rani, a young girl from a small city, who is jilted by her fiancé a day before their wedding and decides to embark on her honeymoon trip to Paris by herself. Even though her parents are initially reluctant about her odd decision and concerned for Rani's safety, her parents are shown to be encouraging and supportive. Having the parents' support, especially for girls and women, plays an important role in their empowerment in India, and Rani's parents in this film represent a preview of what nonpatriarchal, nonmisogynistic, multi-dimensional, and multilayered levels of parenting could look like. If onscreen and offscreen representations and constructions of mother-hood in India and abroad are perceived as biological, onscreen and offscreen portrayals of fatherhood lean towards social parenting. Certain decisions—such as working while parenting, securing child-care from a nanny or from daycare centre, and breastfeeding versus using formula milk—are often imposed on the mothers.

These public narratives about motherhood when compared to fatherhood can vary depending on the gender of the child and on whether the parents have similar gendered expectations of, or exert similar pressure on, their children. However, what are these onscreen and offscreen representations of masculinity, including those of fatherhood? How do these constructions of masculinity in Bollywood films affect gender violence, especially the interpretations of the Indian diaspora? These are important questions that need to be further explored and require an in-depth analysis of additional Bollywood Hindi films. In the past decade, there has been a gradual yet visible progressive transformation in how masculinity is portrayed and enacted through Bollywood cinema. The next section takes a brief look at these narratives.

Conclusion: Shift towards Healthy Masculinity

Films offering examples of healthy masculinity without the saviour syndrome and taking away the focus from women provide us with a glimmer of hope about the shifting trends in gender roles and gender relations. Hence, it is important to recognize the ways in which men are portrayed as sensitive, empathetic, respectful, and as an ally to women in Bollywood films. For example, films such as *Mary Kom*

(2014), a sports biopic about the first female Olympian boxer from India, depict Mary's husband as a supportive ally, companion, as well as a nurturing husband and father to their twin children while she trains for her boxing competitions. Second, the 2015 film *Dil Dhadakne Do* (*Let the Heart Beat*) portrays Sunny's character as respectful and proud of the accomplishments by his former love interest, Ayesha. Sunny also points out to Ayesha's misogynistic husband that just because men might claim to be progressive does not mean that women need permission from men to work, pursue their dreams, or achieve their career goals. Films like these reflect a healthy example of men as "compassionate and understanding" (Jain and Rai 12), who do not use their power and control to resolve conflicts or dominate women. Whether film viewers are Indians living in India or abroad as a part of the diaspora, it is important to consider the ways these representations of motherhood and masculinity influence global audiences.

This chapter used a feminist lens to question and challenge heteronormative, patriarchal, and culturally imposed yet normalized representations of motherhood and masculinity through an analysis of twenty-six Bollywood Indian films. Bollywood cinema has shifted from portraying only traditional, one-dimensional, limited, unrealistic, and stereotypically gendered roles of mothers and fathers to deeper, more complex, and multilayered depictions of these two identities. Even though the co-constructions and portrayals of motherhood and masculinity may appear progressive and promising in more recent Bollywood films, I have to caution that these depictions are often far from perfect. Portrayals of gender in Bollywood cinema may have come a long way, yet they are not there yet in terms of having nontraditional, nonheteronormative, healthy, realistic, and complex representations of gender roles and identities. This lack of overall progressiveness becomes significant when considering Bollywood cinema's impact on audiences and the implications for the prevention of gender violence. Since Bollywood films are seen by Indians all over the world, it is important to highlight the fact that Indians in the diaspora do not escape gender depictions in these films and may still be affected by their underlying messages. One's location outside India may be strongly influenced by the constant exposure to ideas and ideals coming from the Indian subcontinent.

In summary, global representations of motherhood and masculinity in popular culture, including Bollywood cinema, influence the social construction, shaping, and enactment of these important distinct identities. However, the roles of those who identify as mothers or fathers are still inextricably linked, especially in India and the diaspora, as these critical identities are crucial to the cultural development of individuals and the nation.[4]

Endnotes

1. As part of my doctoral dissertation completed in 2017, I conducted film screenings followed by gender-specific focus group discussions. One of the two Bollywood films *Lajja* (2001) and *The Dirty Picture* (2011) was shown to each of the groups. The purpose of the study was to examine gender differences in how this group of the Indian diaspora (located in the larger metropolitan Chicago areas) interpreted onscreen images of violence against women in Bollywood cinema.

2. In this chapter, the term "Bollywood films" is used interchangeably with the terms "Bollywood cinema" and "Hindi films".

3. I have watched these Bollywood films that show honour killings and/or highlight the significance of family name and honour, but they are not analyzed here for their images or specific content, as this subject requires a separate in-depth consideration. These films are excluded from the total count of Bollywood films that have been analysed and discussed in detail.

4. I am grateful to Dr. Aimee Wodda for her timely and thoughtful assistance in refining this chapter and to Sneha Bhat and Nayana Bhat for their helpful critique as Bollywood cinephiles.

Works Cited

Bhat, Meghna. "Violence Against Women in Bollywood Cinema: Exploring Gender Differences in the Indian Diaspora." 2017. University of Illinois at Chicago, PhD Dissertation.

"Bollywood's Expanding Reach." *BBC News.* 3 May 2012, www.bbc.com/news/world-asia-india-17920845. Accessed 14 Apr. 2018.

Chaudhuri, Soma, et al. "Marriage Migration, Patriarchal, and Wife Abuse: A Study of South Asian Women." *Violence Against Women*, vol. 20, no. 2, February 2014, pp. 141-61.

Dasgupta, Shamita Das, and Sujata Warrier. "In the Footsteps of 'Arundhati': Asian Indian Women's Experience of Domestic Violence in the United States." *Violence Against Women*, vol. 2, no. 3, 1996, pp. 238-59.

Jain, Neeraj, et al. "Indywood, The Indian Film Industry." *Deloitte*, www2.deloitte.com/content/dam/Deloitte/in/Documents/technology-media-telecommunications/in-tmt-indywood-film-festival-noexp.pdf. Accessed 12 July 2017.

Derné, Steve. "Making Sex Violent: Love as Force in Recent Hindi Films." *Violence Against Women*, vol. 5, no. 5, 1999, pp. 548-75.

Dharmani, Lokesh. "The Good, The Bad or The Ugly: What Dil Dhadakne Do Was Really About!" *Masala*, 2015, www.masala.com/the-good-the-bad-or-the-ugly-what-dil-dhadakne-do-was-really-about-198261.html. Accessed 21 Aug. 2019.

Gupta, Naveen. "Masoom (1983): The Ultimate Heart-Strings Tug!" *The India Saga*, 2018 /theindiasaga.com/review-corner/masoom-1983-the-ultimate-heart-strings-tug. Accessed 7 July 2019.

Jain, Jasbir, and Sudha Rai, eds. *Films and Feminism: Essays in Indian Cinema*. Rawat Publications, 2015.

Krishnan, Kavita. "'Honour' Crimes in India: An Assault on Women's Autonomy," *Al Jazeera*, 2018 www.aljazeera.com/indepth/opinion/honour-killings-india-assault-women-autonomy-180314090856246.html. Accessed 10 Mar. 2019.

Lim, Hyun-Joo, and Tina Skinne. "Culture and Motherhood: Findings From a Qualitative Study of East Asian Mothers in Britain." *Families, Relationships and Societies,* vol. 1, no. 3, 2012, pp. 327-43.

Maheshwari, Laya. "Commentary: Bollywood's Feminist Potential Falls Short." *Chicago Tribune*, www.chicagotribune.com/news/opinion/commentary/ct-bollywood-feminism-dangal-20170416-story.html. Accessed 12 April 2018.

Maji, Sucharita. "Motherhood and The Work Life Balance." *Feminism in India,* Oct. 17 2017, feminisminindia.com/2017/10/17/motherhood-work-life/. Accessed 14 Apr. 2018.

Manohar, Uttara, and Susan L. Kline. "Sexual Assault Portrayals in Hindi cinema." *Sex Roles,* vol. 71, no. 5-8, 2014, pp. 233-45.

Mathur, Vrinda. "Women in Indian Cinema: Fictional Constructs." *Films and Feminism: Essays in Indian Cinema.* Edited by Jasbir Jain and Sudha Rai, Rawat Publications, 2015, pp. 65-71.

Menon, Nivedita. *Seeing Like a Feminist.* Penguin UK, 2012.

Menon, Ritu, and Kamla Bhasin. *Borders & Boundaries: Women in India's Partition.* Rutgers University Press, 1998.

Narasimhan-Madhavan, Deepa. "Gender, Sexuality and Violence: Permissible Violence against Women during the Partition of India and Pakistan." *Hawwa,* vol. 4, no. 2-3, 2006, pp. 396-416. EBSCO *host,* doi:10.1163/156920806779152237.

Philipose, Pamela. "Book Review: To Be a Mother or Not: Are Indian Women any Closer to Having the Choice?" *Scroll.in,* 2017, scroll.in/article/854017/to-be-a-mother-or-not-are-indian-women-any-closer-to-having-the-choice. Accessed 14 Apr. 2018.

Raj, Anita, and Jay G. Silverman. "Immigrant South Asian Women at Greater Risk for Injury From Intimate Partner Violence." *American Journal of Public Health,* vol. 93, no. 3, 2003, pp. 435-37.

Ramasubramanian, Srividya, and Mary Beth Oliver. "Portrayals of Sexual Violence in Popular Hindi Films, 1997–99." *Sex Roles,* vol. 48, no. 7-8, 2003, pp. 327-36.

Reissman, Catherine K. "Stigma and Everyday Resistance Practices: Childless Women in South India." *Gender and Society,* vol. 14, no. 1, February 2000, pp. 113-135.

Ziya Us Salam. "Mother India (1957)." *The Hindu,* 2010, www.thehindu.com/features/cinema/Mother-India-1957/article16836460.ece. Accessed 10 July 2019.

Singh, Veena. "Towards the Radicalization of the Indian Family." *Films and Feminism: Essays in Indian Cinema.* Edited by Jasbir Jain and Sudha Rai, Rawat Publications, 2015, pp.94-105.

Vishwanath, Gita. "Saffronizing the Silver Screen: The Right-Winged Nineties Film." *Films and Feminism: Essays In Indian Cinema.* Edited by Jasbir Jain and Sudha Rai, Rawat Publications, 2015, pp.39-51.

Chapter 4

How the Principles of Matristic Societies Can Provide More Flexibility on Mothering, Motherhood, and Masculinities

Katharine I. Ransom

Introduction

In a globalized world, where many marginalized groups are feeling more oppressed and fearful than in previous years, it is imperative to look to other cultures and societies to learn how issues that stem from sexism, racism, homophobia, and inequality can be addressed. One source of ideas could lie in the inner workings of matristic and matrilineal societies. These societies often experience more peace, wellbeing, and economic growth than societies that limit women's economic and social choices (Göettner-Abendroth). The differences between the genders and the generations are respected and honoured in matriarchies, but they are never served to create hierarchies, as is common in patriarchy (Göettner-Abendroth). These societies create distinctive ways of mothering, motherhood, and masculinities, which can be explored through caretaking and labour roles, art, community organization, economic choices, and religious worship. These principles can be applied to today's strict gender roles to help find more personal peace and balance. This chapter will start with a brief discussion of the terminology, followed by a historical account of matristic societies and how matristic principles have shown up in various religious and spiritual movements. In addition, it will provide a brief economic analysis of the benefits of this way of life. The chapter will conclude with an interdisciplinary discussion of how gender differences and gender roles in matristic societies can offer alternative ideas for gender relations.

From Matriarchal to Matristic

Most scholars, specifically those in anthropology, do not use the term "matriarchy" to describe a female-centred society. However, there are two notable researchers, Peggy Reeves Sanday and Heide Göettner-Abendroth, who reclaim the term in a way that honours how some of these societies define themselves. In this context, a matriarchy is not a social structure in which women are in control. Rather, matriarchal cultures are characterized by shared leadership between men and women that results in political harmony, social balance, and emotional wellbeing. In matriarchal societies, the mother is the central figure, nurturing is a primary value of all members, and the earth is seen as sacred (Göettner-Abendroth). According to Göettner-Abendroth: "The matriarchy paradigm ... goes beyond all the various western feminisms that tend to remain captive to the European/western way of thinking. It is not confined to the situation of women and does not foster an essentialist antagonism between women-in-general and men-in-general" (xix).

Göettner-Abendroth classifies the Khasi in Northeast India, the Newar in Nepal, the Mosuo in Southwest China, the Minangkabau in Indonesia, the Trobriand islanders of Melanesia, the Arawak of South America, the Kuna of Central America, the Hopi and Iroquois of North America, the Nayar, Pulayan, and Parayan of South India, the Bantu in Central Africa, the Akan of West Africa, and the Tuareg of North Africa as Indigenous matriarchal societies. There are many societies that are matrilineal or matrifocal that do not have the characteristics of matriarchal societies.

The most comprehensive term, which seems to be well accepted, is the one coined by Marija Gimbutas. She called these societies "matristic, not matriarchal, because matriarchal always arouses ideas of dominance and is compared with the patriarchy" (237). She continues: "But it was a balanced society[;] it was not that women were really so powerful that they usurped everything that was masculine" (Gimbutas 237). For Gimbutas, matristic means combining matrilineal, matrifocal, and egalitarian in the sense that the sexes complement each other (Marler, 72). This chapter will employ the term "matristic" when the research does not specifically state a society is matrilineal or matrifocal.

The History of Matristic Societies

It is thought that matristic societies originated in East Asia and spread through waterways as agricultural societies. Some believe they date as far back as the Palaeolithic Age, ranging from 2.6 million years ago to 10,000 BCE. Gimbutas believes that the majority of these societies diminished during the Iron Age (600 BCE to 1000 CE), when personal property became more widespread and patriarchal tribes took over. Women were the most likely inventors of agriculture and the ones who domesticated animals. Carol Christ argues: "Women were the primary food gatherers and food preparers in Palaeolithic societies, so they noticed the relation between dropped seeds and the green plants that grow. Because women had responsibility to care for human babies, they may have been the ones to care for the abandoned young of wild animals" (53).

Archaeological findings have been collected and catalogued on the collective identity of Indo-European cultures from the Neolithic (10,200 BCE to 4,500 BCE) to the Chalcolithic (4,500 BCE to 3,000 BCE) period, which is known as the Copper Age. This matristic area, which some scholars call "Old Europe," extends from the Aegean and Adriatic seas, including the islands, as far north as Czechia and Slovakia, Southern Poland, and Western Ukraine (Gimbutas). Between 7,000 BCE and 3,500 BCE, the inhabitants of this region developed a much more complex social organization than their western and northern patriarchal and patrilineal neighbours, involving craft specialization and the creation of religious and governmental institutions (Gimbutas). The matristic societies in Old Europe independently discovered the use of copper and gold for ornaments and tools, appear to have created a rudimentary form of written language, and developed arts, technology, and social relationships (Gimbutas). These societies showed no evidence of organized warfare and left behind thousands of artefacts, such as a rich legacy of painting, pottery, sculptures, and figurines, all connected to goddesses and gods, who were at the centre of a rich religious life (Reed and Starhawk).

A recent study from researchers at the University of Cambridge is the first to compare the bone strength in prehistoric women to those of living women. Previously, there were some data from living men, but there were no collected data on the bone structure of modern women to provide a comparative dataset. This research is important because men and women do not build bone in the same way in response to repeated physical strain and stress (Macintosh, Pinhasi, and Stock). When researchers look at living people and athletes, and their level of activity is known, they can link characteristics in their bones to those activities. The researchers compared the bones of prehistoric women to those of women who had been on the Cambridge University rowing team, since they wanted athletes from a sport that targeted the arm muscles and was very repetitive. After the comparison, it was discovered that these Bronze Age (3,000 BCE to 600 BCE) women had arms that were 9 per cent to thirteen percent stronger than those of female rowers and thirty per cent stronger than nonathletes of any gender (Macintosh, Pinhasi, and Stock). The researchers believe processing grain and farming by hand is what caused this impressive muscle mass (Macintosh, Pinhasi, and Stock). There would not have been plows yet, and they would have had limited tools to help alleviate the intensity of work. A culture in which women are the ones who do much of the agricultural work today can be found in the south of China.

The Mosuo people in the Yunnan and Sichuan provinces of China, close to Tibet, are a matrilineal culture, which has resided there since, at least, the mid-thirteenth century. Most of the inhabitants practice "walking marriage," in which a woman can be with a man for as long as she chooses, and the culture does not seem to experience issues with rape or illegitimate children (Lugu Lake). Women are in charge of farming, trade, household decisions, and businesses. Young men interviewed in a recent film on the Mosuo state that they do not work as hard as the women because their traditional roles as traders have been replaced by capitalism, their roles as information gatherers have been replaced by television and internet, and their roles in negotiating disputes have been replaced by the government (Christ). Historically, Mosuo food production was derived from small-scale agriculture and animal husbandry; they grew crops such as highland buckwheat, barley, potatoes, corn, and garden vegetables and raised pigs, chickens, and other animals for consumption or other uses, such as trans-portation, hauling, and ploughing (Matteson et al.).

Children belong to and reside within their mother's household, and any child residing within a household has access to its land and resources (Matteson et al). When the father is not a co-resident, the mother's brothers occupy a central role in the household structure; along with women in the family, they take responsibility for disci-plining, caring for, and supporting children of the matrilineage (Matteson et al.). Although Mosuo fathers are not always physically present in the household of their children, they still support the monetary, educational, and emotional needs of each child.

Whereas patriarchal Western societies tend to abuse nature, the egalitarian matristic Minangkabau of western Sumatra base their worldview on the principle of growth in nature. The Minangkabau believe that women who nurture growth in children and rice exemplify the good within nature (Christ). Women are the stable factor in Minangkabau life. Descent is drawn through the female line, and both the big house, where extended families live, and the land that surrounds it are passed down through the female clan (Christ). Peggy Sanday highlights the following: "The youthful male energy of sons is associated with raw physical energy, which is treated as disorderly and immature until shaped by the teachings of the authoritative mother and channelled by the activities of the male who follows and administers the dictates of the adat. [The] Adat is ... the force that modulates human passions and emotion" (36).

In contemporary Minangkabau culture, women are the stable element in the family and uphold the traditional rituals of the adat, whereas men articulate the meaning of adat during rituals and adjudicate disputes between adat, Islam, and the government (Christ). The household and parenting structure of the Minangkabau differ in several ways from the nuclear family that is typically seen in Western households; for one, women who are not mothers can participate in shaping young men. Other non-conforming gender roles are also found in contexts where mothers are worshipped.

In *Transgender Warriors*, Leslie Feinberg wanted to find information on trans expression and discovered abundant evidence on male-to-female trans women priestesses, who played an important role in the worship of the Great Mother (40). Feinberg argues the following: "Our earliest ancestors do not appear to be biological determinists. There are societies all over the world that allowed for more than two sexes, as well as respecting the right of individuals to reassign their sex. And transsexuality, transgender, intersexuality, and bigender appear as themes in creation stories, legends, parables, and oral history" (43).

Although this goddess is called the Great Mother, is it likely those who worshipped her viewed this deity as intersexual, a being in whom the sexes had not yet been split (Feinberg 40). This information is paramount for the liberation of those in the LGBTQ community because one can see that, historically, the preferences and lives of others do not have to be determined by outside power structures. Feinberg states the following: "In these early societies, most men hunted while most women developed a division of labour in large centres of production and shared responsibility of childcare. Women didn't rule *over* men the way men dominate women in patriarchal society. There were no signs of Pharaohs and emperors, queens or presidents, who lived in luxury while others toiled in squalor" (42). More information on this historical perspective could be empowering to the trans movement; it could validate their feelings, since our ancestors participated in these gender and sex changes. Although these trans individuals were priestesses and went through castration to become so, there might have been men who opted to live a transgender life without being leaders in spiritual or religious practices. This decision could be for several reasons, but, perhaps, some of these men enjoyed childrearing more than the women in their family and chose to change their outward appearance to represent their desires.

Matristic Revisionings in Religion and Spirituality

Gimbutas found, restored, described, and photographed tens of thousands of relics from Old Europe over her lifetime of work. She concluded that these relics were from societies that were matrilineal in nature; they prospered far longer than the warring patriarchal tribes that followed, due to their cooperative and Earth-based religious and spiritual practices. A goddess, not a male god, was revered and worshipped throughout the Neolithic period in European history. According to Gimbutas:

> The "Fertility Goddess" or "Mother Goddess" is a more complex image than most people think. She was not only the Mother Goddess who commands fertility, or the Lady of the Beasts who governs the fecundity of animals and all wild nature, or the frightening Mother Terrible, but a composite image with traits accumulated from both pre-agricultural and agricultural eras. During the latter she became essentially a Goddess of Regeneration, *i.e.* a Moon Goddess, product of sedentary, matrilineal community, encompassing the archetypical unity and multiplicity of feminine nature. She was giver of life, and all that promotes fertility, and at the same time she was the wielder of the destructive powers of nature. The feminine nature, like the moon, is light as well as dark. (152)

There is a need for something different when women across the world relate to the sentiments described by Gloria Anzaldúa: " [A] woman does not feel safe when her own culture, and white culture, are critical of her; when males of all races hunt her as prey" (42). It is important to look at motherhood, mothering, and masculinities in expanded ways that include more than housework and childrearing because the solutions need to be intersectional and transnational. One way women have been breaking down the strict gender definitions, on a personal level, is through the removal or change in gender of the divine. Shug says the following: "My first step from the old white man was trees. Then air. Then birds. Then other people. But one day when I was sitting quiet and feeling like a motherless child, which I was, it come to me: That feeling of being a part of everything, not separate at all.... I think it pisses God off if you walk by the color purple in a field somewhere and don't notice it" (qtd. in Walker 103-104). Shug is reimagining and recreating the divine, so it makes more sense to what she sees and what she believes. This is also happening within the goddess movement.

Leah Novak states: "I began to experience the Divine Feminine in the hills, the ocean, and the landscape. At first, she spoke through sand

and rocks, flowers and animals; later she spoke through visions and memories of earlier lives" (1). Much of the reimagining of the divine is also earth based, as it is impossible to live on a planet that is destroyed. Earth is the original and pervasive mother to all that was and will be.

These principles can be seen in other religions and cultures throughout geographic locations and history, but there are some religions that have more definitive female beings that are worshipped:

> *Isanaklesh,* the Apache deity, is a leading religious authority for most women. She exemplifies compassion, balance, knowledge, harmony, power, *diye,* ultimate spiritual strength. Apache women and men can come to her whenever necessary for their own well-being and special needs as well as for the needs of the community, because she is seen as the perfect example of virtue and strength for the culture.... Women in this tradition have always had influence and have worked toward a balanced sense of power within the culture. (Talamentez 131)

It seems that the goddess is important for women and men to take a step away from religious and spiritual practices steeped in patriarchal structures. Each person's experience of the goddess will vary because we are the singular owners of our experiences and memories, but those who practice some form of goddess worship or spirituality feel more connected to life and the divine. Even those who do not have a spiritual or religious practice may find comfort that there are female-centred options for spirituality.

Matristic Revisionings of Economic Systems

Research that is rooted in economic analysis is not, usually, considered in the discussion of matristic societies. This sort of economic research enhances the conversation because it provides empirical and statistical analysis that shows the economic benefits of matristic social struc-turing. In several of these studies, matrilineal societies are compared to patriarchal societies; the patriarchal societies are also patrilineal. It is likely some of these authors used the term "matrilineal" to avoid entering the debate on matriarchies. Although these societies are matrilineal, Göettner-Abendroth also classifies them as matriarchal.

In "Gender, Competitiveness, and Socialization at a Young Age:

Evidence from a Matrilineal and a Patriarchal Society," Steffen Anderson and colleagues were interested to learn if girls and boys have biological differences in competitiveness as they age, or if the phenomenon is based on societal pressures. They conclude that fifteen-year-old girls are significantly less likely to compete than boys around the same age, and they observe a strong gender gap in patriarchal societies. Although their findings support the idea that societal differences have an impact on competitiveness, socialization may act along with biological forces in determining the difference between the matrilineal and patriarchal societies around puberty.

In "Do Women Supply More Public Goods than Men? Preliminary Experimental Evidence from Matrilineal and Patriarchal Societies," Anderson et al. explore whether women produce more public goods than men by conducting experiments within three different societies in Northeast India: a matrilineal Khasi village and two patriarchal Assamese villages. First, fewer people are free-riders—those who do not contribute anything to the public good—in the matrilineal society compared to the patriarchal ones. Second, public good provision is higher in the matrilineal society. Third, this higher level of provision is due primarily to male rather than female differences in contributing to the public good. These results support the idea that matrilineal and matrifocal societies are more communal and beneficial to the individual.

In "Gender Differences in The Dictator Experiment: Evidence from The Matrilineal Mosuo and the Patriarchal Yi," Binglin Gong, Huibin Yan, and Chun-Lei Yang wanted to learn how gender-specific economic and social activities differ as they relate to gender and social preferences. They conclude that Mosuo men are much more generous than Mosuo women, which has not been seen in any of the other studies using the dictator experiment. In some other studies, the researchers found that women were more generous than the men, and some found that the women were equally as generous as the men. The results of this research are significant because they show that men are not biologically predetermined to generous behaviour.

In "If You're happy and you know it: How Do Mothers and fathers in the US Really Feel about Caring for Their Children?", Rachel Connelly and Jean Kimmel discuss whether women in the United States really do enjoy childcare more than men. The authors use in-depth econometric analysis of several datasets to determine whether women receive more pleasure from childcare than men do, and they discuss why these perceptions have pervaded society. Connelly and Kimmel use time-diary data information in three ways. First, they use descriptive statistics and ad hoc regressions to describe the gender differences in time use and emotions experienced during those activities. Then, they extend the definition of child caregiving time to include time spent with the children present. Finally, they construct an aggregate measure of wellbeing, an unpleasantness index (U-index), which determines the percentage of time devoted to activities that are experienced as un-pleasant.

Connelly and Kimmel conclude that women in the United States do not enjoy childcare more than men and found that men enjoyed the responsibility more than women (29). They suspected that women in patriarchal societies are more likely to be seen as better caregivers and are expected to perform more childcare duties due to cultural norms and difficulty maintaining executive level positions after having children (Connelly and Kimmel 29). However, their research did not focus on the reasons why this phenomenon occurs, and they suggest there need to be comprehensive measurements for happiness to understand why women do not enjoy childcare as much as men (Connelly and Kimmel 30). These economic studies are an important start to conversations around mothering, motherhood, and mas-culinities in matristic cultures. The authors seem to find empirical benefits to living in this kind of society, and other economic phil-osophies support these behaviours and beliefs.

Although some economic researchers and many feminist economists explore gender differences and disparities—such as the greater cost to women who either choose to or must work in both the home and in the labour force—very few have applied Western economic theory to matristic societies. Genevieve Vaughan uses her knowledge of economic systems, Western thought, and Marxism to explore what she calls the "maternal gift economy": "[A] birth mother, relative or entire village must give free to young children, who cannot pay back. This free giving is the basis of a maternal economy that existed before the market economy, which is based on exchange.... In fact, free maternal giving is the original economic model for all genders" (1). Gifting creates mutuality and trust, whereas exchange is ego oriented and adversarial, creating separation and competition (3). Gifting is concentrated on satisfying the needs of others, whereas exchange economies are focused on using the satisfaction of the needs of others to satisfy the exchanger's own needs (3).

In capitalism, the gift economy still exists in the domestic sphere, especially in childrearing. In some rural and Indigenous communities, as well as in some surviving matristic societies, the gift economy is the basis of the socioeconomic system (Vaughn 1). In capitalist patriarchy, however, people of the male sex are given a social gender role that is antimaternal and antigift. Patriarchy and capitalism have now merged into a structure in which the urge to dominate permeates the market, motivating a desire to grow wealth at the expense of many (Vaughan 1). According to Vaughan, "this is done by taking the free gifts of all: of Nature, of workers (Marx's 'surplus value') and of women's free reproductive labour. Thus, the market is a parasite on the gift economy" (1). By emphasizing the positive importance of the free maternal economy, both women and men can understand themselves differently as "homo donans" (the giving being) rather than just homo sapiens or homo economicus. The host can recognize the parasite and liberate itself (Vaughan 1).

Conclusion

In this chapter, the discussion crossed disciplines to give a multifaceted view of matristic societies to show how gender differences and gender roles can be approached from a variety of perspectives. Looking beyond patriarchy, the chapter focused on matristic societies as proof that mothering, motherhood, and masculinities are not fixed based on biology but can change depending on circumstance and the individual. Mothers in matristic societies want their sons, as well as their daughters, to be happy and to feel important and valuable; thus, women make special efforts to ensure that everyday life celebrates the contributions of males as brothers, husbands, and fathers to the family (Christ). These concepts are vital to explore because in modern Western cultures, a shift is taking place in which traditional male roles are not as secure as they used to be, and women are having fewer children due to the rise in family planning and fertility issues. It is vital to look beyond what is typically thought of as mothering and who can take on the role as a mother. Western society needs to find room to value men as nurturers, protectors, caregivers, and creators.

Works Cited

Andersen, S., et al. "Do Women Supply More Public Goods than Men? Preliminary Experimental Evidence from Matrilineal and Patriarchal Societies." *The American Economic Review,* vol. 98, no. 2, 2008, pp. 376-81.

Andersen, S. "Gender, Competitiveness, and Socialization at a Young Age: Evidence from a Matrilineal and a Patriarchal Society." *The Review of Economics and Statistics,* vol. 95, no. 4, 2013, pp. 1438-43.

Andreoni, J. "Warm-Glow versus Cold-Prickle: The Effects of Positive and Negative Framing on Cooperation in Experiments." *Quarterly Journal of Economics,* vol. 110, no. 1, 1995, pp. 1-21.

Anzaldúa, G. Borderlands: La Frontera. Aunt Lute, 2012.

Connelly, R., and J. Kimmel. "If You're Happy and You Know It: How Do Mothers and Fathers in the US Really Feel about Caring for Their Children?" *Feminist Economics,* vol. 21, no.1, 2014, pp. 1-34.

Christ, C. *Rebirth of the Goddess: Finding Meaning in Feminist Spirituality.* Addison-Wesley, 1997.

Christ, C. "Women and Men in 'Egalitarian Matriarchy.'" *Feminism and Religion,* 2018, feminismandreligion.com/2018/05/14/women-and-men-in-egalitarian-matriarchy-by-carol-p-christ/. Accessed 3 Nov. 2018.

Feinberg, L. Transgender Warriors. Beacon Press, 1996.

Gimbutas, M. *The Gods and Goddesses of Old Europe: 7000 to 3500 BC Myths, Legends, and Cult Images.* University of California Press, 1992.

Göettner-Abendroth, H. *Matriarchal Societies: Studies on Indigenous Cultures Across the Globe.* Peter Lang Publishing, 2012.

Gong, B., H. Yan, and C. Yang. "Gender Differences in the Dictator Experiment: Evidence from the Matrilineal Mosuo and the Patriarchal Yi." *Experimental Economics,* vol. 18, no. 2, 2015, pp. 302-13.

Macintosh, A. A., R. Pinhasi, and J. T. Stock. "Prehistoric Women's Manual Labour Exceeded That of Athletes through the First 5500 years of Farming in Central Europe." *Science Advances*, vol. 3, no. 11, 2017, p. eaao3893.

Marler, Joan. "The Beginnings of Patriarchy in Europe: Reflections on the Kurgan Theory of Marija Gimbutas." *The Rules of Mars: Readings on the Origins, History and Impact of Patriarchy.* Edited by Cristina Biaggi. Knowledge, Ideas & Trends, 2005, pp. 53-75.

Mattison, S. M., B. Scelza, and T. Blumenfield. "Paternal Investment and the Positive Effects of Fathers among the Matrilineal Mosuo of Southwest China." *American Anthropologist*, vol. 116, no. 3, 2014, pp. 591-610.

Novak, R. L. *On the Wings of Shekhinah: Rediscovering Judaism's Divine Feminine.* Quest Books, 2008.

Reed, D., and Starhawk. "Signs Out of Time: The Life of Archaeologist Marija Gimbutas." *YouTube*, 2004, www.youtube.com/watch?v=S_b4zRlV_po. Accessed 34 May 2018.

Sanday, P. R. *Women at the Center: Life in a Modern Matriarchy.* Cornell University Press, 2002.

Talamentez, I. "Images of the Feminine in Apache Religious Tradition." *After Patriarchy: Feminist Transformations of the World Religions.* Edited by Paula M. Cooey and William R. Eakin. Orbis Books, 1991, pp. 131-145.

Vaughan, Genevieve. "The Economy of the Maternal Gender." *Seminário Internacional Fazendo Gênero 11 & 13th Women's Worlds Congress*, 2017, www.wwc2017.eventos.dype.com.br/resources/anais/1525978268_ARQUIVO_FINALTheEconomyoftheMaternalGender.pdf. Accessed 16 Apr. 2021.

Walker, A. "God Is Inside You and Inside Everybody Else." *Weaving the Visions: New Patterns in Feminist Spirituality.* Edited by Judith Plaskow and Carol Christ. Harper and Row, 1989, pp. 101-04.

PART II
ETHNOGRAPHIC RESEARCH

Chapter 5

Healing Foundational Wounds in Sons and Mothers: From Womb Envy to Asymmetrical Generativity

Cheryl Lynch Lawler

Introduction

When I think about motherhood, mothering, and masculinities, I do so as a feminist psychoanalyst who has practiced for thirty years and as one who is engaged in academic activism towards the goal of transforming self and world. In my daily psychotherapy practice, I see the overlap between psyche and culture in which unresolved conflicts and distortions within the wider culture manifest as intrapsychic dilemmas in individual lives and relationships. As these conflicts are metabolized and resolved within individuals, they then are in a position to facilitate evolutionary changes within the culture.

Psychoanalytic theory is known for providing useful tools for understanding the internal colonization of the psyche by the culture (Oliver). These theories help to "elucidate the processes through which the social etches itself on the psychic on both the individual and the collective level" (Saketopoulou 280). Yet psychoanalytic theory is itself a product of Western culture, inheriting its errors and blind spots. Given the authority it is granted, psychoanalytic theory must be held to account for its originary errors in order that it "can be made truer to a complete understanding of personality and gender formation" (Kittay 385). In this chapter, I am interested in using a deconstructive psychoanalytic method against psychoanalytic theory to interrogate its ambivalent relationship with the concept of womb envy. Although the concept of womb envy can be interrogated from multiple perspectives, this work will be limited to the mother and son relational field as a potential site for cultural change.

My Western worldview is informed by being a United States citizen educated in Western systems of thought and steeped in its culture. However, in bringing a critical feminist lens to errors in the originary foundation of Western thought, including psychoanalytic theory, I position myself as an outsider within Western androcentric culture. Using a deconstructive, critical feminist method, I will show how womb envy and Western oppositional consciousness are co-constitutive and how together they guarantee the continuation of both a culture of matricide (Irigaray, "The Bodily Encounter with the Mother") and a culture of toxic masculinity (Sexton).

A Contextual History of Oppositional Consciousness

Although the oppression of women has received much attention in feminist theory, the particular oppression of mothers has received much less theoretical attention from feminists (O'Reilly) and the cultural wounding of boys and men even less (hooks). Given that feminist theory in its emancipative spirit is attentive to the emancipation of every person, it is resonant with the message of Dr. Martin Luther King when he stated that "Until all of us are free, none of us are free." Emancipation for all must also include sons and their mothers, whose relationships are often marred by the oppositional consciousness endemic to Western culture. Emancipation here involves the freedom to create life-sustaining relationships that are grounded in our ontological connection-in-difference, which entails freedom from oppositional consciousness. Emancipatory relationships are not achievable in a culture founded on oppositional consciousness.

Oppositional consciousness continues to undermine our lived

relationships with one another, including relations in academic scholarship, regardless of our best attempts to subvert or move beyond it (Keating). Oppositional consciousness is anti-relational; rather, relations forged in its shadow are determined by a sacrificial logic in which one is defined against an other, who is deemed to be deficient (Caldwell; Lawler-Lynch, "Desire at the Threshold"). The underlying dynamic of oppositional consciousness is a hierarchical binary, in which, for example, the feminine is defined as the "non-masculine" (Irigaray, *Je, tu, nous* 20) and as the denigrated other of the privileged term—rather than on its own terms as a positive asymmetry (Stoller). A relationship grounded in the positive asymmetry between mothers and sons subverts another Western binary pairing, which views relationship and emancipation as oppositional in the sense that to be in a relationship is to be tethered and not free. In a culture that values autonomy above all, relationships are to be eschewed. In this sense, positive asymmetry opens to a nonsacrificial, relational logic of sexuate difference between mothers and sons, which can be characterized as an emancipatory relationship in that one does not have to sacrifice relational connection in order to be, and continue to become, one's distinctive and authentic self. One is only free to become more fully one's authentic self as a self-in-connection. In the spirit of an emancipatory relationship between mothers and sons, it is my objective in this chapter to propose a model that views the son's early identification with the mother as a natural developmental phase in which the son can negotiate his procreative sexuate difference from the mother while maintaining connection-in-difference.

The concept of sexuate difference as introduced by Irigaray (*Key Writings*), in contrast to sexual difference, is about cultural and relational identity and not sexual preference. Sexuate difference is what has been repressed and thereby abolished in Western culture, as Western man "did not work out his maternal beginning but put it into the unthought background of his story and his history" (Irigaray *Key Writings* ix). Sexuate difference has to do with being and becoming a woman and a man in a relational and cultural sense (Bostic; Grosz; Hill; Irigaray, *Key Writings*; Jones), yet it does so through an insistence on undoing the opposition between being and embodiment.

The opposition between body and being is at the root of Western bifurcating either/or logic that sees the body as purely inert matter. The concept of sexuate difference creates an intervention into the form-matter distinction relied upon by much of poststructuralist feminism —a distinction that is being challenged on many fronts, including new materialist feminism (Barad; Hird; Kirby) and feminist critical realism (Gunnarsson), each of which is prefigured by the Irigarayan concept of sexuate difference. The concept of sexuate difference, along with the concept of positive asymmetry, provides a theoretical framework for reconceiving relations between mothers and sons, not as oppositional, but in terms of what I designate "asymmetrical generativity," which can be understood through both deconstructing and reimagining the concept of womb envy as it has been postulated in psychoanalytic theory.

The conceptualization of womb envy, first articulated in psycho-analytic theory in the 1920s, has met with considerable resistance (Jaffe), repression rising from unconscious male narcissism (Lax), suppression (Stevens), and "relative silence" (Bayne 154). Because the concept of womb envy asserts an intrinsic and enviable positivity to maternal-feminine identity, it has been met with the same antagonism and bias that characterizes androcentric Western thought, itself founded on cultural matricide (Irigaray, "The Bodily Encounter with the Mother").

Due to the resistance encountered when approaching the concept of womb envy in Western psychoanalytic thought, a deconstructive and psychoanalytic methodology is necessary to expose its contribution to Western oppositional consciousness. However, in order to transform the concept of womb envy, a creative movement is also required. Thus, a further methodological lens found in a creative hermeneutic of love (Irigaray, "The Return"; Sandoval) can create an opening towards the mutual transformation of self and other as well as self and world. A creative hermeneutic can facilitate an evolutionary transmutation of the oppositional consciousness that often accompanies mother-son dynamics by offering a different conceptualization leading towards a more authentic relational dynamic between mothers and sons. A hermeneutic of love beckons a return to the logic of the middle voice, which was characteristic of preoriginary consciousness in the West prior to the setup of a metaphysics of oppositional logic around the time of the pre-Socratics (Irigaray, "The Return"). With the loss of the logic of the middle voice, both the bridge leading to self-reflection and the bridge to the mysterious internal world of the other is lost, creating a tragic culture "mediatized by exteriority" in which the self and the other become overly objectified (Irigaray, "The Return").

The logic of the middle voice "expresses the relation in two or between two; two who are different" (Irigaray, "The Return" 271). The middle voice mediates between self and other, self and world, creating a threshold for mutual transformation of self and other, self and world (Sandoval 155). In its self-reflexivity that returns one to their inner world, the middle voice creates an appreciation for the sanctity of the inner world of the other who remains beyond appropriation. When the self and other are objectified, which is the tendency in a world that has lost access to the middle voice, the hidden depths of subjectivity are diminished. A return to the middle voice provides a framework for reconceiving the (m)other in a ternary role, which I refer to as "a(M) other logic (of love)" (Lynch-Lawler, "A(M)other Logic (of Love"). In a(M)other logic (of love), differences in procreative generativity may be lifted from the repressive barrier that is sustained by Western op-positional consciousness, which ultimately is an externalizing and objectifying consciousness. A return to a conceptualization of the middle voice creates a threshold between sons and mothers that allows both difference and connection to be conceived. Given that the oppositional dynamic found in mother-son relationships is paradigmatic of Western bifurcating logic, its reconceptualization has the potential to transform Western consciousness.

Since Western oppositional consciousness cannot find a way beyond its own logical roots, a further non-Western creative hermeneutical lens is useful. Ta'wil, a hermeneutical process derived from the ancient Sufi mystical philosophy of Ibn' Arabi, refers to the use of creative imagination, whose function is to return phenomena to their "true reality" (Corbin 208). Ta'wil offers an interpretative lens that is relational, nonhierarchical, and creative, insisting that truth "must always be un-veiled, re-vealed, disclosed" (Heath 207). Ta'wil is related to a Sufi hermeneutic of love, the himma, meaning the "creative power of the heart" (Corbin 220). Through the action of creative love, a threshold emerges that can foster and sustain asymmetrical difference between the self and the other, a difference-in-relation in which neither self nor other is cannibalized.

Together, ta'wil and the himma open perceptive capacities that, like the middle voice, have been left to atrophy in Western rational and oppositional logic. These hermeneutical lenses, each in their own way, allow the use of creative imagination in opening a nonoppositional conceptual space between mother and son, which has been repressed in Western discourse. By opening a conceptual threshold, these hermeneutics of love and creative imagination can subvert the logic that grounds womb envy and which subtends Western oppositional consciousness. This threshold can open to a love that is evolutionary. It can allow love to emerge as connection-in-difference within the asymmetrical generativity that is shared between mothers and sons. The creation of a conceptual space for two who are different yet connected may be extended outwards into the larger culture and transmute the very foundation of a Western logic predisposed towards sacrificial othering.

There are perhaps multiple tributaries that feed Western oppositional consciousness; however, this chapter is undertaken in a redemptive spirit towards revealing, healing, and transmuting an underexplored wound at the root of Western culture that originated in ancient Greek mythology and is reflected in psychoanalytic theory—womb envy (Bayne; Keller; Kittay, "Womb Envy"; Shabad). I propose that a reclamation of the concept of womb envy as a natural developmental passage achieved in relation with rather than in opposition to the mother will enable an evolution of Western consciousness. In regarding the son's primordial closeness to and identification with the mother as part of a natural developmental trajectory, sons are given a way to integrate their so-called feminine identifications with the mother and to negotiate their sexuate difference as a positive asymmetry in a way that fosters their capacity to love across difference

Using a creative hermeneutic of love, I explore an alternative developmental trajectory for negotiating sexuate difference between mothers and sons that does not involve severing and antagonistic identifications. This alternative developmental trajectory is grounded in the concept of asymmetrical generativity, which contributes to the transformative work of remedying one of the roots of both toxic masculinity and the denigration of the maternal-feminine found in unresolved womb envy.

The History of a Concept: Womb Envy

Womb envy was first conceptualized in psychoanalytic theory by Karen Horney, as it arose from clinical experience with men in analysis. It is defined as "envy of pregnancy, child-birth and motherhood, as well as of the breasts" (Horney 330). Horney was subsequently ostracized by the predominantly male psychoanalytic discipline (Maroda), yet many others have corroborated her clinical findings (Bettelheim; Boehm; Brunswick; Eschbach; Jacobson; Jaffe; Klein; Kubie; Lax; Semmelhack et al.). Envy is a painful experience, often involving "the angry feeling that another person possesses and enjoys something desirable—the envious impulse being to take it away or to spoil it" (Klein 6). If not acknowledged and metabolized, envy can lead to debilitating symptoms. It can become a festering wound that undermines one's capacity to relate to the world and to others lovingly and in a spirit of mutual becoming.

Disavowed envy of women's procreational capacity is at the heart of Western oppositional consciousness and has permeated Western systems of thought as far back as pre-Socratic Greek philosophy. In ancient Greek philosophy, the maternal-feminine was conflated with body and nature and relegated to the outside of culture (Irigaray, *In the Beginning*). Womb envy is blatant in cultural matricide as recorded in ancient mythological cycles, in which is found an inversion of maternal procreation, often achieved through violence, as male gods usurp maternal gestational and birth-giving capacities for themselves (Keller; Lawler). Womb envy is manifest in the erasure of the procreative mother in the creation stories of the monotheistic religions, including Judaism, Roman Catholicism, and Islam (Semmelhack et al; Shabad). Being outside the philosophical discourse that was being set up, the maternal-feminine was defined in abstentia only as its (m)other, as that against which the philosopher raised their discursive edifice. The maternal-feminine was interred as the mute, unacknowledged ground of Western civilization.

Feminist psychoanalytic theory derived from clinical experience has found that, despite feminism, the maternal-feminine is imagined as the denigrated other as evidenced in the analyses of both men and women (Birksted-Breen; Elise; Krausz; Lawler-Lynch, "Orestes with Oedipus"; Rose; Weiland), thus reflecting the cultural devaluation of women and mothers. Although it is typically the child's wish to have and to be everything (Kubie), and for the "boy's earliest wishes to be both his mother and his father" (Diamond 1100), maternal identifications are often compromised by the cultural devaluation of mothers as it is filtered through cultural and familial relationships (Lawler, "Orestes with Oedipus").

The cultural devaluation of the mother manifests in the formation of masculine subjectivity, which is often structured against rather than in relation to the maternal-feminine (Irigaray, *Key Writings*; Lawler, "Orestes with Oedipus"; Stone, *Feminism, Psychoanalysis, and Maternal Subjectivity*; "Against Matricide") as its other (Irigaray, *Speculum of the Other Woman*; "The Return"). In place of a concept of the maternal-feminine rendered on its own terms as a positive asymmetry, there are "twin poles of idealization and a defensive scorn and denigration ... [as] she who must to some degree be left, or more forcefully abjected or killed off, in order that 'the subject' ... can emerge unscathed" (Baraitser 5). Even though consciously a son may forcibly disidentify through a process that may involve denigration, alternating with overvalorization of the mother, in their inner world, they still harbour this unintegrated pairing, which as long as it remains unresolved will infuse all subsequent relationships where it can manifest in a multitude of ways. One of the ways it shows up clinically in my practice is in male masochism. These men identify with the internalized and denigrated maternal image and seek self-sabotage and ways of humiliating themselves. Identification with the denigrated maternal image can also manifest as a form of sadism in which the other is devalued and humiliated. Overall, these identifications create problems in fostering intimacy, since one person in a given relationship, whether it be the self or the other, is assigned the role of the denigrated. While one may alternate roles with subsequent partners, the oppositional and sadomasochistic paradigm remains in place.

As I have shown, identification with the mother is natural for all children, requiring a process of individuation. This process is further complicated for the son, who must metabolize his inability to gestate life inside his own body, unlike his mother. The son's individuation from the mother need not turn into envy. For example:

> The imitative behavior of the three-year-old boy who stuffs a pillow or a puppy under his shirt and upon releasing it announces that he has given birth need not yet be *envious*. It is when he

realizes that this power will never be his and that despite wo-man's devalued status and his own membership in the dominant sex, he still desires to have these powers, that this desire can turn to envy. It is when the boy perceives his incapacity as a wound to his narcissism that the desires and curiosities are transformed to envy, and the behavior it gives rise to has a cutting edge. (Kittay, "Mastering Envy" 141)

The recognition of this procreative difference, which sets a natural limit to an otherwise undifferentiated sexuate identity (Fast), is often traumatic for sons, creating a "narcissistic wound" (Lax 135). Here I am reminded of a clinical situation I once supervised:

A three-year-old boy was brought for treatment around the time of the birth of a new sibling. The presenting problems were that the boy had begun soiling himself and had also become aggressive towards his mother and other children. During a session of play therapy in which the boy soiled himself and was able to talk about it through the play characters, his therapist learned that having noticed his mother's periodic bleeding, he felt that his soiling made him "just like mom." It was further disclosed that prior to the onset of these behaviours, he had been told that, as a male, he would not be able to have babies, like his mother. This had made him very sad, as he struggled with not only his procreative limitation but also his fear that he was destined to lose her and her love altogether, fearing that he was different and therefore deficient. After working through the grief about his procreative limitation, he was enlightened by the therapist about the capacities of his body. He had not known that his body would eventually be capable of cocreating life through the sharing of semen. He was delighted to learn this and said, "Oh, so I have life in me too?" The soiling ceased with the working through of the grief, and the treatment ended with the boy having come to terms with being differently embodied. He was helped to grieve his inability to have and to be everything and found joy and pride in his own capacities as a male.

In a follow-up session with the parents, the therapist learned that the boy was actively assisting in the care of his younger sibling while also exhibiting healthy narcissistic pleasure in his own body, which he said was "special too." The fact that this boy's maternal uncle also modelled caregiving responsibilities with both of his children helped to further consolidate a healthy identity that included a sense of both difference and connection.

As the above vignette illustrates, sexuate differentiation of sons from mothers need not become an unresolved narcissistic wound leading to womb envy. However, due in part to the cultural devaluation of mothers and mothering inherent in Western culture, this psychic wounding often remains unconscious and therefore inaccessible to transformation. Here, the son's developmental impasse is seen as a psychic reflection of an unconscious cultural dynamic in which envy and devaluation are closely correlated (Lerner) and in which the pain of envy must be denied via devaluation of the object of envy. For how can one envy what has been rendered deficient and radically other? Yet when such painful feelings are left without pathways for healthy resolution, they manifest in less than optimal psychic and emotional health for individuals and society. The intensity of these disavowed feelings and the resulting psychic wounds create a susceptibility to "fragile, rigid masculine identity and narcissistic psychopathology" (Diamond 1099). This form of toxic masculinity can ripple and negatively affect relationships between fathers and sons, especially when the father's own narcissistic wounding has not been healed. What often occurs is that a father attempts to overcome his own narcissistic fragility through sadistic rivalry with his son, which creates a double wounding for the son. This situation clinically presents a dilemma for the sons of these fathers, who feel they are presented with a no-win scenario: Either they compete with the father (and other men who stand in for the father) in a zero-sum game in which they are either the victor who humiliates or the loser who is humiliated, or they abnegate their maleness altogether. Through the therapeutic process, these men are most often able to pick up the struggle and revision for themselves what it means to be a man in this world and, in a quite revolutionary sense, transform the world one by one. This therapeutic work can be understood in light of a hermeneutic of love in which there is a mutual transformation of self and world. Likewise, as a process of ta'wil it returns them to their true selves where they can reconnect with their himma, the creative power of their heart. These therapeutic pathways allow men to creatively imagine a more authentic sense of themselves as only part of a positive asymmetry in which identity is both distinct and connected. More will be said about this further on, but suffice it to say that left without a healthy pathway for resolution, narcissistic wounding continues to ripple, thereby contributing to a culture of opposition.

Although there have been numerous papers written on female envy, there is a paucity of papers on male envy. This is attributed to an unconscious "resistance [that] is supported by ... prevalent social stereotypes" (Lax 118-19). Given the universality of birth as a "non-trivial event" and although "everyone has a mother ... it would be stunning if this were not important, everywhere" (Stevens 291). Yet the significance of birth, and even of the pregnant female body, has been sorely lacking in psychoanalytic theory (Balsam).

Much has been accomplished by feminist psychoanalysts in deconstructing Freud's "mythic ... concept of femininity" (Kittay, "Rereading Freud" 385), yet there remains a powerful underlying current that leads to the reinscription of oppositional gender dynamics. Given that psychoanalytic theory "remains the most cogent account of the development of human personality" (Kittay, "Rereading Freud" 385) and one that for better or worse continues to leak into other academic disciplines and into the culture, it must be held to account for its role in the perpetuation of suboptimal gender patterning. To further this aim, it is useful to turn a critical analytic lens backwards in time to gain perspective on how Freud's own blind spots, which reflect the misogynistic culture of his time, continue to cast their shadows on the current historical time in regard to the concept of womb envy.

Womb Envy in Psychoanalytic Theory

In a critical reconsideration of Freud's famous paper on Schreber (Freud, "Psychoanalytic Notes"), in which Freud attributes Schreber's mental condition to a father complex and castration anxiety, he overlooks Schreber's wish to give birth as accompanying his fantasy of being inseminated by a father God (Macalpine and Hunter). Perhaps, Freud's repressed pregnancy envy kept him from a deeper analysis of Schreber's case (Stevens). Likewise, Freud's analysis of little Hans (Freud, "Analysis of a Phobia") clearly demonstrates the boy's iden-tification with the mother's capacity to give birth. When Hans's father states, "You know quite well that boys can't have children," Hans replies, "Well, yes but I believe they can all the same" (Freud, "Analysis of a Phobia" 94-95).

This primary identification with the mother is validated by object relations theorists who have shown that children of both sexes form initial identifications with the mother and her life-giving capacity. As stated above, this primary identification poses an often difficult psychological and emotional hurdle for the males, who must negotiate their sexuate difference from their mother and reconcile their own incapacity to gestate life and give birth. This is exemplified in the clinical vignette presented above and also by the analysis of little Hans, who in an attempt to negotiate this difference creates his own imaginary children with regard to whom he states, "I was their Mommy before. Now I am their Daddy" (Freud "Analysis of a Phobia" 96-97).

It seems that the attempt towards the negotiation of sexuate difference—so clear in the struggles of little Hans—was not something that Freud was able to acknowledge. For Freud, the feminine was viewed as the "dark continent" in psychoanalytic theory (Freud, "Femininity"), perhaps indicating both his denial and his repression of sexuate difference. Given this, it is perhaps not surprising that for psychoanalytic theory in his wake, womb/pregnancy envy has been the victim of "repression of no small dimensions" (Stevens 276), remaining the dark continent of the dark continent.

Given that the other side of womb envy is the devaluation of women (Bayne; Lerner), the resistance to deepening the understanding of these dynamics risks not only the psychological and emotional health of boys and men but the health of the culture as a whole. The cultural devaluation of the maternal-feminine—accompanied by the cultural prohibition placed on men that insists that they sacrifice their early identifications with the procreative mother—forecloses a healthy pathway for resolving the wounding disappointment of their procreative difference from the mother. Left to fester in the subconscious, this developmental foreclosure fosters destructive envy and the devaluation of the maternal-feminine, thereby perpetuating an ongoing cycle of misogynistic and matricidal cultural dynamics. Not only do these dynamics have dire consequences for intimate relations and for the capacity to love across difference, but they also ripple outwards and reinforce an oppositional consciousness in which the sacrificial relationship with the mother, now the (m)other, negatively affects all relationships with the other.

Sacrificial Relations: The Faulty Logic of Forced Gender Symmetry

As noted above, repressed and unresolved womb envy is a contributing factor in Western oppositional consciousness, which is secured by a faulty logic of sacrifice found in the practice of othering. Othering occurs in the context of binary thinking, in which the concept of difference is confined to mere opposition and enforced complementarity rather than in terms of connection-in-difference. However, the most insidious feature of this form of logic is that it is inherently hierarchical and restrictively symmetrical. In each pair of contraries, only one is privileged at the expense of the other, which is defined as its other and not on its own terms. This was illustrated above when discussing the ways in which unresolved womb envy led to an internalized dynamic of alternating devaluation and overvalorization that infused relations between the self and the other. Now I want to further discuss the ramifications of this dynamic for gender identity.

Individual consciousness of self and gender identity that emerges within Western sacrificial logic is truncated, given that it is forced into artificial bifurcating categories that have arbitrarily assigned universal human qualities to an either/or classification—that is, masculine or feminine. These universal human qualities, now classified as masculine and feminine, are further transcribed onto male and female embodiment. The uniqueness of each individual is potentially compromised by a system that asks individuals to disavow certain qualities deemed to be the province of their socially designated other. In this sense, it leads them away from the deeper authenticity of their being found in the process of ta'wil, which reveals a truer depth and breadth of being and becoming.

In order to unveil and reveal the deeper truth of their being, the process of disavowal of otherwise universal human qualities needs to be separated conceptually from the necessary process of negotiating the ontological trauma of human limitation regarding one's procreative capacities. In Western societies the two are often conflated, leaving the young male without an adequate framework for metabolizing the disappointment of generative difference from the mother while simultaneously integrating an ongoing sense of connection-in-difference via mutual sharing of those qualities they have in common as sentient human beings. For instance, if young men are expected to disavow aspects of their authentic nature, such as the capacity to nurture, simply because they may arise within the identificatory field formed with the mother and are socially coded feminine, they are thereby kept from full self-expression. This unnecessary sacrifice of valued qualities of the authentic self can accentuate an already present, and very natural, womb envy, making it more difficult to resolve. In fact, the psychodynamics around disavowed and unresolved womb envy contribute to a culture that undervalues nurturing (Semmelhack, et al.)

As I have noted, unacknowledged envy is most often manifested as the devaluation of the object of envy, thus contributing to hierarchical binary relations in which the identity of the privileged one is founded at the expense of the other. For example, the devaluation of so-called feminine qualities is accompanied by the defensive overvaluation of those qualities socially coded as masculine. This defensive overvaluation often manifests as narcissistic exhibitionism in males. What is often overlooked is the sense of loss and insecurity that subtends much of male exhibitionistic and narcissistic displays. For example, implicit within the Western stereotype of the independent and self-made man is a compensatory disavowal of envy in the form of the devaluation of women (Bayne). The significance for males of being born from a woman with whom they do not share that capacity has led to "the male quest for significance in the eyes of the cosmos" (Shabad 76), which is found in multiple origin stories of male self-creation and superhero fantasies. That these fantasies and origin stories convey an unsustainable omnipotence adds to the challenges a son faces in establishing a healthy sense of self that houses a full array of human attributes, such as emotional and physical strength, vulnerability, knowledge and uncertainty, self-dignity, and respect for others.

When devaluation of the mother occurs, there is no conceptual space within which sons are able to negotiate what it means to be a limited human being—to be not-all—and to thereby come to appreciate the mother in terms of their asymmetrical difference. Recognition of asymmetrical generativity can set a limit to the very lonely, solipsistic narcissism and create a threshold space within which to form a more authentic and integral sense of self in-connection-in-difference. Otherwise young males are cast out as lonely warriors left to navigate an increasingly toxic culture. A culture of toxic masculinity is made all the more toxic through a wounding that becomes multigenerational, as fathers transmit their own psychic and cultural wounds onto their sons in yet another, perhaps even darker continent beneath the dark continent beneath the dark continent.

The father-son story is "practically nonexistent" (Chodorow 262) for Freud and for psychoanalysis, but it is beginning to be addressed in feminist psychoanalytic theory. Father-son dynamics are not unrelated to the trauma of unresolved womb envy on the part of a father, in which these dynamics contribute to a culture of sacrificial relations. For example, if the father has developed narcissistic grandiosity as a defense to compensate for the narcissistic wounding he experienced and did not resolve, then he is more likely to create a toxic rivalry with his own son and/or other junior males. With humiliation being the other side of narcissism, the senior male often resorts to rivalrous humiliation of the junior male. Such "humiliation-generated wrath is an under-cited, under-noticed organizing theme in masculinity, male development and the inner object world of men" (Chodorow 267); it completes a cycle of sacrificial relations that fan out into the culture as a whole.

Asymmetrical Generativity: Towards a(M)other Logic (of Love)

Although currently in the United States there is avid discourse around so-called toxic masculinity (Sexton) as it affects women, there is little discussion around the psychic and emotional toxicity that this version of masculinity poses for young boys and men. As I have shown, toxic masculinity is an integral feature of a culture that is founded on unresolved womb envy and oppositional consciousness. Even though men are the apparent beneficiaries of Western patriarchal systems, they are also oppressed by being born into its oppositional structure in which "the very practices which construct men's capacity to oppress women ... work by systematically harming men" (New 730). When males in Western capitalist societies are inhibited from the full expression of a whole range of universal human qualities and are told at the same time that men are bad (New 739), the stage is set for their psychological and emotional damage, which can only reinforce cultural toxicity, resentment towards women, sado-masochistic relations, and what I am seeing much more often in my practice—male masochism.

Masochism is especially prevalent in my clinical practice among younger males who were raised in a culture that is increasingly feminist. They have internalized a sense of being bad just because they are male, which often manifests in self-hatred and self-destructive behaviours. In agreement with Chodorow, I view this tragedy as the next horizon for feminism. For if all we manage to do is to invert an unjust system of privilege and a mere reversal of those who are to be denigrated, then we remain imprisoned in Western oppositional consciousness. As AnaLouise Keating passionately admonishes, it is the time for interconnectivity. It is time for a new paradigm.

There remains a glaring discrepancy between the social power granted to men in Western culture and the psychological and emotional cost of being cast as the bearers of this power, which takes much more than it gives. It leaves men internally split between a socially constructed ego, which gains its status by becoming increasingly autonomous, and a nascent and more authentic self that is at its core a self-in-connection. When the asymmetrical generativity of the mother and son relationship remains unthought, as it is in Western oppositional culture, the son's authentic self-in-connection remains likewise undeveloped, given that it is inconsistent with the ego formed through the hierarchical and oppositional logic of the one and its other.

If masculinity is in crisis, then with that crisis, there is opportunity for transformation. In fact, as a concept, masculinity in Western culture is seen to be moving towards a new developmental level in which male subjects are acknowledging their own ambivalence around the roles they have been assigned, "making it imaginable to experience genuine sorrow for all that one is not" and to relinquish the defensive sense of invincibility that has served as a disguise for real human vulnerability (Saketopoulou 279). In this rupture, there is the opening for a genuine encounter with the mother in terms of both asymmetrical sexuate difference and in the sharing of qualities that belong to every human being regardless of differences in procreative capacities. Perhaps even more exciting is that men are reappropriating the concept of masculinity as it has been given and revisioning and embodying a more authentic, sustainable, and even joyful sense of what it means to be a man (Baldoni; Betcher and Pollack). It is in this spirit that I offer the following model.

In contrast to a model that understands male sexuate differentiation from the mother as an either/or and all or nothing oppositional disconnection, I propose a model that honours the son's identification with the mother as a natural developmental experience arising within their relationship, and here I am part of a chorus (Applegarth; hooks; Jaffe; Kittay, "Mastering Envy"; Lax; Rank; Ross). These early identifications with the mother can provide a relational bridge that can facilitate a more optimal negotiation of their asymmetrical sexuate difference which, when kept in context, is seen to be only one aspect of the relational field they continue to share.

The optimal negotiation of sexuate difference does not have to become the narcissistic wounding that creates pathological womb envy; instead, it can open a new threshold space of connection-in-difference. It is within this space of connection-in-difference that males can begin to revision and revalue the other side of a positive asymmetry that belongs to them and is theirs to evolve and to embody. In resolving the fact of their natural limitation with regard to procreative generativity, they are free to create a truly sustainable and positive concept of masculinity—not that of the wounded, competitive, and lonely warrior but as a vital part of the human community.

I have argued that by grounding sexuate difference in a concept of asymmetrical generativity, a threshold is opened that can transform Western consciousness, whose foundation rests on the defensive denial of sexuate difference. The denial of sexuate difference provides the organizing principle of oppositional consciousness, which began with the erasure of the maternal-feminine along with the body and nature— all three of which, body, nature, and mother, were cast outside as the others of Western discourse sustaining the disavowed ground of Western consciousness. I now want to further suggest that this denial persists in the erasure of the body in feminist poststructuralist theory, which views the body as inert matter, as a blank material substrate for the performativity of discourse (Butler). In fact, social constructivist and deconstructive feminist attempts to undo Cartesian binary dualism—which grounds such oppositional frameworks as culture and nature, body and mind—end up creating the opposite; by granting agency only to culture and mind, while maintaining a concept of nature and the body as blank slates for cultural inscription, they repeat the binary logic they set out to deconstruct (Kirby). The repetition of binary thinking is most apparent in Judith Butler's description of materiality as what is an effect of so-called cultural norms of sex, which Butler claims have the power to "materialize the body's sex [and] to materialize sexual difference" (2). This is but another tragic expression of a sacrificial and hierarchical binary in which the body and nature are cast as the devalued others of culture.

Gunnarsson views the Butlerian abjection of the body as an "*epistemic* ... [and] *linguistic* fallacy," which conflates reality and repre-sentation, Lena Gunnarsson notes that certain "biological realities," such as men's inability to gestate life within their bodies, when construed by Butler as politically exclusionary is logically "bizarre [in that it overlooks] the possibility that certain discursive exclusions may correspond to causally effective boundaries in *being*" (26-27). For Gunnarsson, then, to grant that bodies are situated in social reality does not negate the ontological being of the body. Likewise, Luce Irigaray's model of sexuate difference conceives the body as having its own ontological being that is not inert but generative and "actively self-shaping" (Jones 177). An example of the body's agency is the placental economy between mother and fetus in which is found "actively self-shaping matter that can bear otherness within and that is replete with form-giving powers" (Jones 176). What is even more exciting is the research on chimeric cells, which migrate from fetus to mother, settling in various organ systems, where they are found to have a therapeutic effect. This "recent biological science of gestational cell transfer ... has the potential to bring renewed attention to issues of relationality between pregnant women and fetuses, both as bodies and as subjects" (Kelly 252). Here again, the ontological reality of the body is seen to be both actively self-organizing and relational as the developing body of the fetus actively gives of its cells to the mother who is giving it life. Chimeric cell migration provides a lovely illustration of connection-in-difference and the culture that inheres in the body itself—a body that is itself a culture of relationality.

In contrast to the either/or binary logic, which places the body as an inert object and subject to cultural directives, a dialectical approach to the relationship between culture and body conceives of these two levels of reality—these two registers, culture and body—as distinct from one another yet related and mutually informing of one another in a relationship of "unity and difference" (Gunnarsson 77). The human is conceived as that which emerges at the intersection of nature and culture, as both nature and culture in a relationship of "consubstantiality," in which the body already is culture (Kirby 230). If the body already is culture, then it is a culture that has been left in a state of dereliction. The culture that the body already is has not been spoken. To begin to "speak corporeal" (Irigaray, "The Bodily Encounter with the Mother" 43) is not to merely invert the hierarchical binary that placed the body as the derelict other of the mind by placing the body in a position of privilege and culture as its derelict other—but to recognize the unity-in-difference of these two registers that comprise us as human beings. We are that consubstantial threshold wherein two distinct yet always related realities comingle and go on becoming.

The consubstantiality of nature and culture that we as human being are returns us to the threshold of asymmetrical generativity in which it is possible to cultivate this bridge between nature and culture beyond a hierarchical binary logic of the one and its other. Given that the two do not exist within a sacrificial logic of the one, there is no threshold between the one and its other within which to think genuine difference without sacrificing connection. I posit the mother and son relationship as a prime place to begin to construct a language and a logic that hold the tension between difference and connection. In granting predis-cursive agency and culture to the human body and the asymmetrical difference found in the procreatively sexuate bodies of mothers and sons, we are able to establish a logic of "at least *two*" (Irigaray, *I Love to You* 37), which subverts the insidious hierarchical binary logic of the one and its other. Here it is important to note that in my use of Irigaray's concept of "at least *two*," a threshold is sustained within which many other forms of difference may express themselves.

The creation of a culture of at least two creates a threshold for another, ternary, consciousness to emerge, supplanting the hierarchical binary logic of the one and its other. If we are to engender another, a(M)other, logic (of love), then "what we need to discover is how *two* can be made which one day could become a *one* in the third which is love.... If the *one* of love is ever to be achieved, we have to discover the two" (Irigaray, *An Ethics of Sexual Difference* 66-67). Love has been left in a state of virtual dereliction by being defined within the parameters of this sacrificial logic of the one. Respect for the mother with whom one shares valued personal characteristics, while also recognizing their sexuate difference as being beyond appropriation, creates an opening for a mutually transformative, generative hermeneutic of love to emerge. The threshold space which I have referred to as asymmetrical generativity, cotended by a mother and a son, provides a healing paradigmatic shift in an oppositional culture that has forever set them, mothers and sons, at odds with one another—forcing them to sacrifice the sacred connection that was theirs in the beginning.

The threshold space of asymmetrical difference, if conceptualized in Western thought, has the potential to reopen the closure of the middle voice that began with the advent of Western logical systems. Like the Sufi concept of *ta'wil,* the threshold space opened within asymmetrical difference returns mothers and sons to their preoriginary beginning, to the time before the foundational wounding that set them forever at odds with one another. Asymmetrical generativity is a transformative concept that opens the *himma,* the creative power of the heart, which when aligned with creative imagination allows the revisioning of a future horizon that is nonsacrificial. The concept of asymmetrical generativity is resonant with Chela Sandoval's concept of a revolutionary hermeneutic of love in that it imagines that love comes to be in a middle space between two who are different and that in that middle space of love, something new can become. As a revolutionary hermeneutic of love that sustains a middle space for connection-in-difference, the concept of asymmetrical generativity holds the potential for undoing binary oppositions that ground the dominant logic of the West, which, I submit, is most painfully embodied in mother-son relations, making it a powerful centre from which to subvert sacrificial logic and to creatively imagine an evolutionary horizon for love across difference in Western culture. For "we always love across difference(s), if we really love" (Bostic 608).

As embodied males and females, we are clearly not-all. With this acknowledgement, that we are only part and not the whole of sexuate human being, we are able to embrace and express the many universal human qualities that are not limited by being limited, and together we begin to create a nonoppositional culture that is grounded in our interconnectedness. This is the cultural moment when interconnectivity provides the next horizon beyond intersectionality (Keating). Genuine interconnectedness is not possible in a sacrificial dynamic in which difference is reduced to a hierarchical binary of the one and its other, which is the relational logic found in Western oppositional consciousness. Rather, what I have referred to as asymmetrical generativity acknowledges a threshold space between two, mothers and sons, in which neither is defined in terms of the other but in recognition of natural, ontological limit with regard to procreative generativity found in the culture that is inherent in the body. This is fostered through a loving recognition of embodied, procreative limitation, which can sustain a cultural and relational threshold space wherein we can begin to create a nonsacrificial way of relating to one another. Nonsacrificial relating has the potential to subvert the hierarchical binary logic that underwrites a culture of sacrifice and opens to what I refer to as underwriting a(M)other logic (of love).

Conclusion

If the maternal-feminine forms the repressed unconscious of Western consciousness, as that "which is censored by the logic of consciousness" (Irigaray, *This Sex Which Is Not One* 73), then womb envy can be understood as the repression that subtends the repressed beneath Freud's infamous dark continent, in which he viewed a concept of the feminine as residing in an unfathomable realm. I have shown that unresolved womb envy informs the sacrificial logic that fans out into all relationships and is a contributing factor to an oppositional consciousness.

In what has been a masterful inversion of the power of maternal procreative capacity, the god of discourse was born out of the philosophers' self-inflicted wound—womb envy. It is a wound still awaiting healing. Feminist theory has shown clearly how girls and women suffer from oppressive devaluation in Western androcentric culture. Yet the less obvious oppression that boys and men suffer in patriarchal culture remains undertheorized. It remains to account for the tremendous psychic and cultural pain that boys and men endure as a result of having to disavow universal human qualities such as nurturing and tenderness because they are classified as feminine in order to take a position as a man in such a culture.

In (re)membering the maternal-feminine culture on its own terms and not as merely the other of (Western) culture, a logical limit to a purely androcentric and patriarchal culture is established, creating the possibility for an evolution of consciousness and of love. I have argued that for love to thrive a threshold is needed that preserves the integrity of the other in their asymmetrical difference. I have located one such threshold in the asymmetrical generativity between mothers and sons.

Asymmetrical generativity is grounded in the consubstantial relationship between the nature and culture that we are. In the corporeal culture of human embodiment, a(m)other logic exists that awaits cultivation. The inherent cultural logic of the human body has the potential to transmute oppositional consciousness in a paradigmatic shift from the logic of the one and its other to a culture of at least two. This new paradigm holds the potential for those in the West to accede to a capacity for loving across difference. This is a cultural achievement that, for the West, is yet to come.

Works Cited

Applegarth, Adrienne. "Origins of Femininity and the Wish for a Child." *Psychoanalytic Inquiry*, vol. 8, no. 2, 1988, pp. 160-76.

Baldoni, Justin. "Why I'm Done Trying to Be 'Man Enough.'" *YouTube*, uploaded by Justin Baldoni, December 6, 2017, www.ted.com/talks/justin_baldoni_why_i_m_done_trying_to_be_man_enough. Accessed 16 Apr. 2021.

Balsam, Rosemary H. "The Vanished Pregnant Body in Psychoanalytic Female Developmental Theory." *Journal of the American Psychoanalytic Association*, vol. 51, 2003, pp. 1153-79.

Barad, Karen. "Posthumanist Performativity: How Matter Comes to Matter." *Material Feminisms*. Edited by Stacy Alaimo and Susan Hekman. Indiana University Press, 2008, pp. 120-54.

Baraitser, Lisa. *Maternal Encounters: The Ethics of Interruption*. Routledge, 2009.

Bayne, Emma. "Womb Envy: The Cause of Misogyny and Even Male Achievement?" *Women's Studies International Forum*, vol. 34, 2011, pp. 151-60.

Betcher, William, and William Pollack. *In a Time of Fallen Heroes: The Re-Creation of Masculinity*. Atheneum, 1993.

Bettelheim, Bruno. *Symbolic Wounds: Puberty Rites of the Envious Male*. The Free Press, 1954.

Birksted-Breen, Dana. "Unconscious Representations of Femininity." *Journal of the American Psychoanalytic Association*, vol. 44, Spring

1996, pp. 119-32.

Boehm, Felix. "The Femininity-Complex in Men." *International Journal of Psychoanalysis*, vol. 11, 1930, pp. 444-69.

Bostic, Heidi. "Luce Irigaray and Love." *Cultural Studies*, vol. 16, no. 5, 2002, pp. 603-10.

Butler, Judith. *Bodies That Matter.* Routledge, 1993.

Caldwell, Anne. "Transforming Sacrifice: Irigaray and the Politics of Sexual Difference." *Hypatia*, vol. 17, no. 4, 2002, pp. 16-38.

Chodorow, Nancy J. "From the Glory of Hera to the Wrath of Achilles: Narratives of Second-Wave Masculinity and Beyond." *Studies in Gender and Sexuality*, vol. 16, 2015, pp. 261-70.

Corbin, Henry. *Alone With the Alone: Creative Imagination in the Sufism of Ibn' Arabi.* Princeton University Press, 1998.

Diamond, Michael J. "Masculinity Unraveled: The Roots of Male Gender Identity and the Shifting of Male Ego Ideals Throughout Life." *Journal of the American Psychoanalytic Association*, vol. 54, no. 4, 2006, pp. 1099-1130.

Elise, Dianne. "Primary Femininity, Bisexuality, and the Female Ego Ideal: A Re-Examination of Female Developmental Theory." *Psychoanalytic Quarterly*, vol. 66, 1997, pp. 489-517.

Eschbach, Cheryl L. "Toward an Understanding of Womb Envy: Developmental and Clinical Perspectives." *Jealousy and Envy*. Edited by Leon Wurmser and Heidrun Jarass. Analytic Press, 2008, pp. 49-74.

Fast, Irene. "Women's Capacity to Give Birth: A Sex-Difference Issue for Men?"*Psychoanalytic Dialogues*, vol. 4, no. 1, 1994, pp. 51-68.

Freud, Sigmund. "Analysis of a Phobia in a Five-year-old-boy." *The Standard Edition of the Complete Works of Sigmund Freud, Vol. 10.* Edited by James Strachey. Hogarth, 1955 (1909), pp. 5-149.

Freud, Sigmund. "Femininity." *The Standard Edition of the Collected Works of Sigmund Freud, Vol. 22.* Edited by James Strachey. Hogarth, 1968 (1933), pp. 112-135.

Freud, Sigmund. "Psychoanalytic Notes on an Autobiographical Account of a Case of Paranoia." *The Standard Edition of the Complete Works of Sigmund Freud, Vol 12.* Edited by James Strachey. Hogarth, 1955 (1911), pp. 9-82.

Grosz, Elizabeth, and Luce Irigaray. "Sexuate Identity as Global Beings Questioning Western Logic." *Conversations*. Edited by Luce Irigaray. Continuum, 2008, pp. 123-37.

Gunnarsson, Lena. *The Contradictions of Love: Toward a Feminist-Realist Ontology of Sociosexuality*. Routledge, 2014.

Heath, Peter. "Creative Hermeneutics: A Comparative Analysis of Three Islamic Approaches." *Arabica*, vol. 36, no. 2, 1989, pp. 173-210.

Hill, Rebecca. "The Multiple Readings of Irigaray's Concept of Sexual Difference." *Philosophy Compass*, vol. 11, no. 7, 2016, pp. 390-401.

Hird, Myra. "Feminist Matters: New Materialist Considerations of Sexual Difference." *Feminist Theory*, vol. 5, no. 2, 2004, pp. 223-32.

hooks, bell. *The Will to Change: Men, Masculinity and Love*. Atria Books, 2004.

Horney, Karen. "The Flight from Womanhood: The Masculinity-Complex in Women, as Viewed by Men and Women." *The International Journal of Psychoanalysis*, vol. 7, 1926, pp. 324-39.

Irigaray, Luce. *An Ethics of Sexual Difference*. Translated by Carolyn Burke and Gillian C. Gill, Cornell University Press, 1993.

Irigaray, Luce. *I Love to You: Sketch for a Possible Felicity in History*. Translated by Alison Martin. Routledge, 1996.

Irigaray, Luce. *In the Beginning, She Was*. Bloomsbury, 2013.

Irigaray, Luce. *Je, tu, nous: Toward a Culture of Difference*. Routledge, 1993.

Irigaray, Luce. *Key Writings*. Continuum, 2004.

Irigaray, Luce. *Speculum of the Other Woman*. Translated by Gillian C. Gill, Cornell University Press, 1985.

Irigaray, Luce. "The Bodily Encounter with the Mother." *The Irigaray Reader*. Edited by Margaret Whitford. Blackwell Publishers, 1991, pp. 34-52.

Irigaray, Luce. "The Return." *Rewriting Difference: Luce Irigaray and the Greeks*. Edited by Elena Tzelepis and Athena Athanasiou. SUNY Press, 2010, pp. 259-72.

Irigaray, Luce. *This Sex Which is Not One*. Translated by Catherine Porter. Cornell University Press, 1985.

Jacobson, Edith. "Development of the Wish for a Child in Boys." *Psychoanalytic Study of the Child*, vol. 5, 1950, pp. 139-52.

Jaffe, Daniel S. "The Masculine Envy of Woman's Procreative Function." *Journal of the American Psychoanalytic Association*, vol. 16, 1968, pp. 521-48.

Jones, Rachel. *Irigaray: Towards a Sexuate Philosophy.* Polity Press, 2011.

Keating, AnaLouise. *Transformation Now: Toward a Post-Oppositional Politics of Change.* University of Illinois Press, 2013.

Keller, Catherine. *From a Broken Web: Separation, Sexism and Self.* Beacon Press, 1986.

Kelly, Susan Elizabeth. "The Maternal-Foetal Interface and Gestational Chimerism: The Emerging Importance of Chimeric Bodies." *Science as Culture*, vol. 21, no. 4, June 2012, pp. 233-57.

Kirby, Vicki. "Natural Convers(at)ions: Or What if Culture Was Really Nature All Along?" *Materialist Feminisms*. Edited by Stacy Alaima and Susan Hekman. University of Indiana Press, 2008, pp. 214-36.

Kittay, Eva Feder. "Mastering Envy: From Freud's Narcissistic Wounds to Bettelheim's Symbolic Wounds to a Vision of Healing." *The Psychoanalytic Review*, vol. 82, no. 1, 1995, pp. 125-58.

Kittay, Eva Feder. "Rereading Freud on 'Femininity' or Why Not Womb Envy?" *Women's Studies International Forum*, vol. 7, no. 5, 1984, pp. 385-91.

Kittay, Eva Feder. "Womb Envy: An Explanatory Concept." *Mothering: Essays in Feminist Theory*. Edited by Joyce Trebilcot. Rowman & Allanheld, 1984, pp. 94-128.

Klein, Melanie. *Envy and Gratitude.* Basic Books, 1957.

Krausz, Rosemary. "The Invisible Woman." *International Journal of Psychoanalysis*, vol. 75, 1994, pp. 59-72.

Kubie, Lawrence S. "The Drive to Be Both Sexes." *Psychoanalytic Quarterly*, vol. 80, no. 2, 2011, pp. 369-439.

Lynch Lawler, Cheryl. "Orestes with Oedipus: Psychoanalysis and Matricide." *Thinking With Irigaray*. Edited by Mary Rawlinson et al., SUNY Press, 2011, pp. 13-37.

Lynch Lawler, Cheryl. "Desire at the Threshold: 'Vulvar Logic' and Intimacy between Two." *Engaging the World: Thinking with Irigaray.*

Edited by Mary C. Rawlinson. SUNY Press, 2016, pp. 233-64.

Lynch-Lawler, Cheryl. "A(M)other Logic (of Love): Languaging the Corporeal Culture of Placental-Maternal-Chimeric Relations." *Gender and Women's Studies,* vol. 3, no. 1, 2020, pp. 1-15.

Lax, Ruth. "Boy's Envy of Mother and the Consequences of the Narcissistic Mortification." *Psychoanalytic Study of the Child,* vol. 52, 1997, pp. 118-139.

Lerner, Harriet E. "Early Origins of Envy and Devaluation of Women: Implications for Sex Role Stereotypes." *Bulletin of the Menninger Clinic,* vol. 38, no. 6, 1974, pp. 538-553.

Macalpine, Ida, and Richard A. Hunter, editors. *Memoirs of My Nervous Illness.* Translated by Ida Malcapine and Richard A. Hunter, W.W. Dawson and Sons, 1955.

Maroda, Karen. "Gender and Envy." Review of *Gender and Envy.* Edited by Nancy Burke. *Psychoanalytic Review,* vol. 87, no. 2, 2000, pp. 310-314.

New, Caroline. "Oppressed and Oppressors? The Systematic Mistreatment of Men." *Sociology,* vol. 35, no. 3, 2001, pp. 729-48.

Oliver, Kelly. *The Colonization of Psychic Space: A Psychoanalytic Social Theory of Oppression.* University of Minnesota Press, 2004.

O'Reilly, Andrea. *Matricentric Feminism.* Demeter Press, 2016.

Rose, Jacqueline. "Of Knowledge and Mothers: On the Work of Christopher Bollas." *Gender and Psychoanalysis,* vol. 1, no. 4, 1996, pp. 411-28.

Saketopoulou, Avgi. "Diaspora, Exile, Colonization: Masculinity Dislocated." *Studies in Gender and Sexuality,* vol. 16, 2015, pp. 278-84.

Sandoval, Chela. *Methodology of the Oppressed.* University of Minnesota Press, 2000.

Semmelhack, Diana, et al. "Womb Envy and Western Society: On the Devaluation of Nurturing in Psychotherapy and Society." *Europe's Journal of Psychology,* vol. 7, no. 1, 2011, pp. 164-86.

Sexton, Jared Yates. "America's Toxic Masculinity." *New York Times,* 13 Oct 2016, p. A25.

Shabad, Peter. "Of Woman Born: Womb Envy and the Male Project of

Self-Creation." *Jealousy and Envy: New Views about Two Powerful Feelings.* Edited by Leon Wurmser and Heidrun Jarass. The Analytic Press, 2008, pp. 75-90.

Stevens, Jacqueline. "Pregnancy Envy and the Politics of Compensatory Masculinities." *Politics and Gender.* Edited by K. Dolan and A. M. Tripp. Cambridge University Press, 2005, pp. 265-96.

Stoller, Silvia. "Asymmetrical Genders: Phenomenological Reflections on Sexual Difference." *Hypatia*, vol. 20, no. 2, Spring 2005, pp. 7-26.

Stone, Alison. "Against Matricide: Rethinking Subjectivity and the Maternal Body." *Hypatia*, vol. 27, no. 1, 2012, pp. 118-38.

Stone, Alison. *Feminism, Psychoanalysis, and Maternal Subjectivity.* Routledge, 2012.

Weiland, Christina. *The Undead Mother: Psychoanalytic Explorations of Masculinity, Femininity and Matricide.* Rebus, 2000.

Chapter 6

Achieving Womanhood through Motherhood? A Phenomenology of the Experience of Mothering for the Hijras[1] in India

Stuti Das

Introduction

Early in the year 2017, Vicks, a cough and cold medicine manufactured by Procter & Gamble, released an ad in India featuring Gauri Sawant, a well-known hijra activist and her adopted daughter, Gayatri. The advertisement narrates the story of Sawant's own journey of adopting and raising her daughter. In a TEDx Hyderabad talk titled, "Main Maa Hoon" ("I Am a Mother"), Sawant, speaking of her daughter, says, "She has completed the woman in me." A. Revathi, a well-known hijra activist from Bengaluru, India in her book, *A Life in Trans Activism* writes: "I knew I couldn't have biological children. But I could give my love and affection to these three girls. After all, isn't motherhood all about being nurturing and caring?" (37). In *Mona's Story*, an essay on Mona Ahmed, a hijra from Delhi, India, Urvashi Butalia writes about how Ahmed "yearned to experience motherhood—it was the only way for a woman to be complete." These stories of hijra mothers in the media give rise to several important questions. In the public eye, motherhood among the hijras—female-identified, male-bodied individuals—may seem contradictory, but how and why has motherhood gained significance for them? While for the hijras themselves motherhood may facilitate ways to articulate their chosen gender identity, to what extent does the notion of hijra motherhood signal a reconceptualization of the dominant mainstream ideas about mothering and about the connections between biological sex and the mother identity among the broader public?

The experience of motherhood and mothering practices among the hijras have not yet been dealt with adequately within sociological literature (Reddy). Consequently, this chapter attempts to shed light on this issue through exploring the following questions: first, the meanings placed by hijra persons on the phenomenon of motherhood, which is considered in mainstream culture as strictly a feminine prerogative; second, the role of motherhood in resolving and minimizing the dissonance between hijra persons' sense of their own gender as females and their material bodies and in consolidating and negotiating a feminine gender identity; and third, whether hijra persons' performances of motherhood pose a challenge to mainstream cultural ideologies of motherhood or reflect an attempt to adhere to an image of hyperfeminine womanhood.

Who Are the Hijras? Hijra Community, Structure, and Recognition

The Hijras are a religious subculture of female-identified, male-bodied individuals in the South Asian countries of India, Pakistan, Nepal, and Bangladesh (Nanda; Hossain). The religious character of this subculture derives from the community's allegiance to a combination of Hindu and Islamic beliefs and practices.

The Hijra community has an elaborate organization of membership, hierarchy, and responsibility. As female-identified persons, hijras take female names, dress in female clothing, wear their hair long, and enact a feminine gender performance (Reddy; Vanita). Although some do, not all hijras undergo the ceremonial castration after joining the community; accordingly, they are classified into akwa (noncastrated males) and nirvana or nirvan sultans (castrated males) (Reddy; Vanita; Goel, "Beyond the Gender Binary"). The latter enjoy a greater degree of prestige as compared to the former within the community as they are seen as possessing the strength necessary to denounce worldly pleasure and acquire seniority, so much so that one comes to be considered as a "real hijra" only after the operation (Reddy).

Membership of the Hijra community is attained by "putting a rit" (rit is the symbolic act of initiation) in any one of the gharanas, or houses, into which the community is organized, and this can take place only under the ceremonial sponsorship of a senior hijra who comes to be the initiate's guru, with the initiate becoming the latter's chela. This ritual marks the hijra's formal membership within the community and signifies authenticity and commitment to the hijra identity. Additionally, it also endows the initiate with izzat, or respectability, within the community. However, there are also individuals who declare themselves as a hijra without putting a rit in any of the houses. But those who have a rit in a hijra house are accorded a higher status as compared to those without a rit (bina ritwale). During the initiation process, the chela is given a female name by her guru. As part of the process, the chela is required to pay a certain sum of money to the guru as a fee which identifies her as the chela of the guru and gives her the right to work in the latter's name (Reddy).

Several scholars have highlighted the prominent place occupied by motherhood within the hijra kinship and social structure. In addition to the guru-chela (master-disciple) relationship, which constitutes the cornerstone of the hijra social structure and is modelled on the mother-daughter relationship, hijras also establish ma-beti (mother-daughter) relationships among themselves (Reddy).

Although the Hijras have a long history in South Asia, it is only recently that they have gained recognition by the Indian state. On April 15, 2014, in the National Legal Services Authority (NALSA) v. Union of India judgement, the Supreme Court of India acknowledged a diverse and plural transgender population that includes several community groups spread across India. Among the host of identities that were accorded legal recognition, Hijra is just one; others include Aravanis and Tirunangis, Kothis, Jogtas and Jogappas, Shiv Shaktis, and Kinnar (Kavi). Describing transgender "as an umbrella term for persons whose gender identity, gender expression or behavior does not conform to their biological sex," "persons who do not identify with their sex assigned at birth, which include Hijras/Eunuchs" who "do not identify as either male or female," "persons who intend to undergo Sex Re-Assignment Surgery (SRS) or have undergone SRS to align their biological sex with their gender identity in order to become male or female," that is, "transsexual persons," and "persons who like to cross-dress in clothing of opposite gender, i.e. transvestites," the Supreme Court of India recognized transgender persons as the "third gender" and ordered that their fundamental rights under Part III of the Indian Constitution be protected.

Methodology

This study is a phenomenology of the experience of mothering among the hijras. Phenomenology "describes the meaning for several individuals of their lived experiences of a concept or phenomenon" (Creswell, 57). Within this approach, I chose to adopt interpretative phenomenological analysis (IPA) for the purpose of this study. Rooted in phenomenology and hermeneutics, IPA places emphasis on the subjective experience of individual actors in order to gain an insight into how they make sense of their experience (Dearden). Between December 2017 and April 2018, I conducted in-depth, face-to-face interviews with eleven individuals associated with the Hijra community in Hyderabad, India, in various capacities. The interviews were then analyzed to identify the various convergent and divergent themes emerging from them in order to arrive at the major themes governing the narrative. In this chapter, I use the results of my analysis, combined with insights gained from extant literature on the Hijra community in India, to present a coherent account of the phenomenon of motherhood among the hijras.

Among the eleven individuals I interviewed, six are currently members of the Hijra community. Three had been part of the community at some point in their lives but decided to renounce their membership later, as community regulations made it difficult for them to pursue their own career goals. One is a transgender woman closely associated with the community, and one is a male-born gender fluid person, who shares close ties with the community through their activism. All of my respondents are part of the mother-daughter relationship as either mother or daughter or both. Snowball sampling was used to select the respondents. All names have been altered to anonymize the participants.

The Place of Motherhood within the Hijra Social Structure

It is commonly perceived that hijras are people without kin ties, but this is far from the truth. In fact, hijras place considerable premium on kinship networks and articulate the relationships that they establish with other members of the community using female kinship terms, as is generally the case in South Asian societies. For example, within the community, hijras "call one another nani (grandmother), dadnani (great grandmother), mausi (mother's sister) ... or amma or ma (mother)" (Saxena 55). These relationships play a crucial role in the way hijras construct and articulate a sense of self (Reddy).

Kinship among the hijras is based on the noncentrality of biogenetic connections (established through either blood or marriage), wherein the notion of "caring" is centred around the temporal and spatial dimensions of "being there." Although, in many ways, these notions symbolize resistance to the heteronormative ideas of family (Goel, "The Lifestyle"), kinship patterns among the hijras also display significant resonance with normative familial arrangements and participate in the reinscription of hegemonic principles (Nanda; Reddy). Kinship bonds among the hijras can assume three forms: the guru-chela relationship, the mother-daughter relationship, and the jodi (bond) with a husband (Reddy). However, the hijra notion of family accommodates only the first two types of bonds.

The guru-chela relationship, besides incorporating economic dimensions and mirroring that of a master and a disciple, is modelled on the parent-child relationship and is often viewed as a substitute for the family relationships that the hijras have renounced. Just like a parent-child arrangement, this relationship incorporates elements of care, obedience, loyalty, and respect (Nanda). My respondents, however, told me that the guru-chela relationship is one of a mother-in-law and daughter-in-law. Furthermore, the authority vested in the guru and the obligatory nature of the relationship renders it a formal nature, and the guru is looked upon as an authoritarian figure.

The mother-daughter relationships within the Hijra community include those that exist between a hijra and her dudh beti (literally "milk daughter"). Hijras generally establish dudh beti relationships with chelas of other hijras with whom they would like to form an alliance. The procedure involves the symbolic enactment of the nursing ritual, which Gayatri Reddy describes as follows:

> The *dudh ma* (mother) sits cross-legged and pulls up her blouse while holding her *beti* (daughter) in her lap, as any nursing mother would. She then pours some milk, using a cup held over her breast, into the mouths of the prospective *betis*, thereby sealing this relationship with "her" milk. To further seal the bond thus forged, each of the prospective *dudh behans*[2] pricks her finger and lets a few drops of blood flow into the cup of milk, which is then shared by all of them, mother and sisters. (165)

Hijras perform all the duties expected of a mother towards her daughter for their dudh betis. In turn, the dudh betis are expected to respect and serve their mothers. However, this arrangement has no significance in tracing lineage within the hijra social structure, which is traced along the guru-chela relationship. Despite this, mothers generally tend to be more affectionate towards their daughters than towards their chelas.

However, not all hijras are in a position to have a dudh beti because the rituals involved in establishing this relationship tend to incur considerable expenditure. Rohini, one of the respondents, who is also mother to a hijra daughter, elaborates: "It is a very expensive affair which is entirely borne by the mother. It is quite similar to the actual sending away of a daughter to her in-laws' house with dowry. So the mother has to give the daughter clothes, jewellery, items of daily use, and so on."

Although the economic involvement does act as a major deterrent to hijras forging the dudh ma-dudh beti relationship, many also want to avoid it because of the differential treatment the presence of such a relationship might give rise to. As Chandrika, a former member of the Hijra community, who is mother to ten members of the community and an eight-year-old adopted son, says: "I don't have any dudh beti, nor am I dudh beti to anybody. One can have only one dudh beti. In that case, my other daughters might accuse me of giving preferential treatment to my dudh beti. I don't want to discriminate among my children. I want to treat all of them equally."

However, even those who are unwilling or unable to forge this relationship do, in fact, establish mother-daughter relationships with members of the community. Jyothika, who is both a hijra guru and hijra mother, explains the difference between the two: "The main difference is that a dudh beti cannot change her mother, whereas the other daughters can leave you if you get into a big fight or something. Plus, a dudh ma can have only one dudh beti, and the reverse is also true—a dudh beti can have only one dudh ma. But one can certainly have multiple mothers or more than one daughter." In the latter instance, there are no rituals involved, and a hijra can call anyone from within or outside the community her mother(s). Commenting on the nature of this relationship, Chandrika says that: "The community mother-daughter relationship is just like a regular mother-daughter relationship."

Crucial to the idea of motherhood among the hijras is the notion of support. As Saurav, a male-born gender fluid individual who identifies as a trans person and is also the godchild of another of my respondents, Vimala, tells me:

Trans communities often have a sense of loneliness that they experience as they are away from their families. For example, I have not yet come out to my parents, even as I identity myself as gender fluid. So what happens with us is that a lot of us are quite removed from our homes, and we are looking for support all around. We also learn to understand family as beyond biological parenthood. Once you understand there is somebody to support, guide, and understand you better and who is a good friend, you end up building familial relationships. So Vimala is my godmother, and I call her mausi [mother's sister or aunt] because she has certain issues with me or anybody calling her mom. But she calls me her daughter mostly; that's how it is between us. I don't have to explain to her anything about my identity, of how I'm a transgender, and so on. She is somebody who is undergoing the same thing. She has been out as a transgender person for a much longer time and has faced the violence that comes with it. She has experience in tackling and navigating these situations. She has been a great support, and I can confide in her without having to explain myself so much. She has guided me in a lot of things. She has helped me clarify a lot of questions I had about my identity and some of my self-reflections on trans politics. Although we live far from each other, we have been in constant touch.

Reddy notes that hijras usually nurture a strong fantasy of giving birth and nursing children. Underlying this attachment is the belief that motherhood and womanhood are intrinsically connected. For instance, Jyothika tells me the following:

> I think motherhood is a very important part of being a woman. It's crucial for a woman's honour. I believe that all women must become mothers. Who else will take care of them in their old age otherwise? Also, if you do not become a mother, people might think you are infertile or that you have some other problems. I got a mother who loves me and takes care of me, but more importantly, treats me like a daughter. I feel that my gender identity is better expressed in this relationship.

Sonali, a former member of the Hijra community, adds the following:

> Motherhood comes naturally to women. Men may not have as strong a desire to have a child. They usually have other priorities. Motherhood is important for women. Many women cannot experience biological motherhood. But there's no difference between one's biological child and an adopted child. I am capable of providing support and care just like a biological mother. I don't think a man can do it. But I can because I am a woman.

However, such views are not universal. For instance, Vimala, a transgender rights activist who was briefly part of the Hijra community, is dismissive of the patriarchal imperative for women to become mothers: "I definitely don't go with the idea that you're not a complete woman unless you're a mother. That's nonsense. If you like it and enjoy it, take it up, and do a good job with it." In a similar vein, Radhika, a transwoman who is mother to several members of the Hijra community, notes the following:

> I don't like to construe the term "mother" in terms of gender. If we do that, then we are restricting the ability to care for a child only to women. This is not right. Motherhood should not be confined to any particular gender. However, I'm not denying the concept of womanhood. There is a physical aspect to that concept. But we all have different journeys and experiences of

womanhood, and that is different from motherhood. To me, motherhood is unconditional love, and any person capable of offering that sort of love can qualify as a mother. Confining motherhood to a few genders especially based on biology, I feel, is patriarchal.

All of my respondents viewed the experiences of mothering and of being mothered as playing a key role in affirming their feminine gender identity, and interestingly, this was true not only of those who believe that women should be mothers but also of those who think that motherhood needs to be freed from the confines of any specific gender. As Sonali explains:

Motherhood is an important part of a woman's life, and one's womanhood is expressed fully on attaining motherhood. Motherhood has definitely enhanced my womanhood. With my biological mother, I shared a mother-son relationship. It didn't matter how I identified myself, for her I am her son. So I couldn't share what I was going through with my biological mother because I was afraid she wouldn't support me. And, in fact, she didn't support me. She didn't stop my brothers from hitting me. My family still thinks that they are right, whereas my community mother understood me completely. She cared for me, supported me, and looked after my wellbeing. She got me the clothes I wanted to wear and the food I wanted to eat. She loved me more than my biological mother did. I was able to fully express my feminine side to her. She understood me completely because she had been through all of that too. Before I met her, I did not know what a mother's love is. My community mother treated me like her own daughter. She was proud of me because I look and behave so feminine. I always say that one mother gives birth, and the other mother [community mother] gives birth to our feminine side.

Similarly, Chandralekha, a hijra sex worker who is also mother to three hijra daughters, highlights the following: "Motherhood is very important to me. I don't think my life as a woman would have been complete if I were not a mother. Every time I see a child being fed and loved by the mother, I feel in me an innate desire to be a mother just like that. I think this motherly instinct or desire is there in every one of us in the Hijra community. Maybe, this is because we are women inside."

Chandrika adopted her sister's son four years ago when his parents were undergoing severe financial difficulties. The child is being brought up by his biological mother, but it is she who provides for him:

> I adopted him as an independent trans woman after I had exited the community. Motherhood is extremely important to me because I feel ... 100 per cent [a] woman because I am a mother. I forget everything else when I see my son. I pay him surprise visits. He WhatsApps me his report card, his drawings, his pictures when he wears new clothes. Because of him, I am being able to experience motherhood like any other woman. I believe that I'm living my life as a complete woman now. If I had my own child, I would have given the same amount of love. This experience has made me extremely patient. You would not know how to be as caring if you are not a mother. I feel that if you want to be a woman, you must be able to do everything that a woman does. Motherhood occupies the central place in making you feel like a woman.

Vimala, who thinks that the association of motherhood with womanhood is entirely a patriarchal construct, is, however, of the view that if she were to experience motherhood herself, it would help her feel more feminine:

> For me, the question of adopting a child does not even arise under the present circumstances. There is a lot of chaos in my life now. My father is terminally ill, and I have a lot of debt. By the time all this has been taken care of, I will be much older. I have too many things on my plate now, and I am too stressed out. A child will only be an added burden. That is no way to raise a child. A child raised that way will always resent me. But, I mean, if it were like in the old movies where three women raise a child and the child grows up not knowing who the biological mother is, I would want to consider it. If two or three trans women volunteered, I could raise a child with them. It would definitely help me feel more feminine. I just don't think I can be a single

mom and be all responsible. There will be no fun in my life then. Motherhood is a lot of work. It's like another life altogether.

Likewise, Radhika is against the idea of motherhood being confined to any particular gender. And when I ask her if she thinks her role as a mother has an impact on her gender identity says as follows: "Yes, the fact that so many people think of me as their mother does make me feel feminine, even though I have not given birth to anybody. My daughters make me feel happy and satisfied."

At present, in India, there are many barriers, including legal ones, for trans women to experience adoptive parenthood. But as I could gather from my respondents, their thoughts on adoptive motherhood are heavily mediated by the stigma attached to their hijra identity. As I stated earlier, Chandrika's adopted son lives with his biological mother. The reason, she says, is this:

> I didn't want my son to face any discrimination because of my identity. But he is my son, and I know it in my heart. He also calls me mummy and loves me more than his biological mother. But I don't want people to say, "Iska ma hijra hain." [His mother is a hijra.] So I asked my mother to keep him in the family only, and that I would take care of all his expenses. But we stay close by so I can visit him whenever I want to. The stigma is still very much there in our society, and the price we have to pay as a result is huge. I don't want him to face all this.

On being asked about her thoughts on adoption, Jyothika offers the following:

> I can never carry a child. As for adoption, there will be problems when the child grows up. It will only make me sad then. But if our society did not discriminate against us, I would have definitely thought about adoption. I would have adopted a kid because I think like a woman. I want to have a husband, kids, in-laws to take care of, and when I get old, I would want my children to take care of me. My heart would be joyous just to hear someone call me ma [mother].

Negotiation with Masculinities

As a transgender identity that cannot be incorporated within a neat binary conception of gender, the Hijra role poses a challenge to conventional notions of gender in many ways and, thus, embodies a subversive potential. However, as part of a society that is premised on a dichotomous understanding of gender, hijras also have to deal with and negotiate this binary. As a result, in many ways, the Hijra role displays certain conformist elements. For instance, given the mainstream understandings of motherhood within the context of heterosexual marriage or marriagelike relationships, the hijra aspiration for motherhood can imply participating in a reinscription of the normative ideals of femininity. Another way to ascertain the extent to which the Hijra role incorporates conformist and subversive elements would be to look at how, as embodiments of a trans-feminine identity, they negotiate and deal with masculinities. In order to gain insights into this issue, we need to look at the coordinates that the hijras themselves use to map various gender and sexual identities. Prior to this, however, it would be useful to look at what constitutes hegemonic masculinity in India.

Masculinity encompasses the social and cultural identity constructs—that is, the qualities and behaviours that are typically associated with being biologically male within a given culture or subculture (Oakley). There exists more than one model of masculinity (Collinson and Hearn), and although some masculinities are accorded honour and recognition, others are stigmatized and marginalized. In this context, R.W. Connell has proposed the concept of hegemonic masculinity to refer to the configuration of practices "that occupy the hegemonic position in a given pattern of gender relations" (76) in a given setting and at a particular time shores up the "legitimacy of patriarchy" (77). In the Indian context, intricately linked to the issue of hegemonic masculinity are the conditions of the emergence of postcolonial masculinities (Dasgupta and Gokulsing). The Victorian regulation of sexual mores during the British regime in India resulted in the "minoritization of queer sexualities" (Dasgupta and Gokulsing 10). Consequently, homosexuality came to be viewed as a threat to masculinity. Since then, what has come to constitute hegemonic masculinity in India, despite the emergence of new and alternative models of masculinity in response to economic and cultural changes, is an apparent "muscular manliness" (Banerjee; Srivastava; Jain;

Dasgupta and Gokulsing). Here, muscularity and masculinity are joined, and muscular manliness becomes characterized by self-control, discipline, confidence, martial prowess, military heroism, hetero-sexuality, and rationality (Basu and Banerjee).

Recounting the categories that the hijras themselves use to organize their social universe, Reddy notes that for them the central axes of sexual and gender identity are based on bodily practice as well as on sex/gender performativity, rather than anatomy. Underpinning this framework of understanding gender, which Reddy terms as "the koti model of same-sex sexuality" (214), is the act of penetration in sexual intercourse and the performance of gendered work. Accordingly, all sexually active or adult individuals are categorized into three identities: kotis, panthis, and narans. Naran is a generic term encompassing all women regardless of age and marital status. Panthis are men who look like, act, and dress like men and are the penetrators in sexual encounters. Kotis, in contrast, are the receptive partner in a sexual performance, who claim to be "like women" in the things they desire and engage in (such as so-called women's work) and who describe themselves as those who desire panthis.

Matthew Stief describes panthis as relatively male-typical individuals who have a bisexual pattern of viewing time and self-reported sexual attractions, stating that the word has "meanings comparable to 'sissy' or 'butch' in American English" (75). However, Paul Boyce argues that panthis do not constitute a "self-identifying, coherent constituency" (178); rather, it is a term that koti-identified individuals use to refer to seemingly more masculine men, particularly prospective sexual partners.

Koti, in contrast is not a singular term; rather, it is an umbrella term for a range of nonmutually exclusive identities that can be arranged into a hierarchical order based on factors such as evaluations of authenticity, idealized asexuality, sartorial preference, kinship patterns, religious practices, norms of respectability, the centrality of the body in self-conceptualization, and class differences. These identities include the following: hijras, or the catla (sari-wearing) kotis, kada-catla (non-sari-wearing) kotis, zenana kotis, jogins, siva-satis, AC/DCs, or "alternating" koti/panthis, and berupias, or hijra impersonators. Within this hierarchical system, the Hijra identity occupies the top position by virtue of the higher degree of authenticity enjoyed by them (an attribution of the kinship ties that they establish), their apparent lack of sexual desire, their greater degree of visibility, and the respectable status enjoyed by them in the past, for instance, in the Delhi Sultanate and the Mughal courts, where they held positions of eminence.[3] Additionally, hijras constitute the most visible dimension of the koti identity.

Being the receptive partner of a panthi constitutes an important aspect of the hijra identity, and having a panthi, or husband, is something that is desired by the hijras, but many would deny this in an attempt to epitomise the hijra ritual/asexual role. Although the hijras are notorious for being aggressive with men in general, they are usually docile and relenting when it comes to their husbands, even when being subjected to violence and abuse by them. Hijras' panthis also engage in heterosexual encounters and many of them have their own families comprising of their cis-woman wife and children.

As mentioned earlier, the relationship between a hijra guru and her chela is one of a mother-in-law and daughter-in-law. Many hijras accommodate their amorous or marital alliances within the framework of this arrangement to realize their desire to be part of a structure that closely mirrors a heteronormative family. Thus, as Sonali tells me: "The guru is like the chela's mother-in-law. So the chelas' husbands become our sons." Similarly, Chandrika notes: "I have good and loving relationships with my chelas' husbands. They call me mummy. I try to resolve their problems if they ask me to and even counsel them when needed. It's just like a regular family."

However, these relationships do not enjoy any formal recognition within the community, as there is no room for cisgender male-identified men or non-koti identities within the hijra social structure. As Radhika tells me, "The hijra havelis [households] are all-women spaces." However, she also acknowledges the desire among many hijras for a family:

There is an overwhelming desire among many of them to have something like a heteronormative family. However, what they end up creating is not legally binding, nor is it acknowledged by the community. But it carries important social bearings for them, all the more so when you are from a marginalized background. If I have a male partner who I can refer to as my husband, people are more likely to treat me as a regular woman.

For many hijras, their daughter's partner is like their son-in-law. As Jyothika narrates: They [her daughters' partners] are my sons-in-law, and I treat them just as normal in-laws would. They call me ma [mother] and I call them beta [son]. We are all just one big family." Similarly, the mother's partner is looked upon as a father figure. As Sonali tells me: "I used to address my mother's husband as papa [father], and he would treat me just like his own daughter. It's like any other family. We all love each other and understand each other. We resolve conflicts peacefully as well." Likewise, Chandrika tells me: "My husband is like a father to my daughters. They are a little shy around him, just as daughters tend to be around their fathers. He is very friendly with them, even more than me."

Amorous and marital relationships also have important implications with respect to the gender identity of the hijras. As Reddy notes, being the receptive partner of a panthi constitutes an important aspect of the hijra identity. In this context, Vimala explains the following: "I don't know about affirming my gender identity, but it could, say, when I'm with a man who tells me I'm better than a woman or something similar, it would make me feel good and reinforce the fact that I am a woman. But this is not an essential requisite, just an add-on. There have been bouts of time when I was without a male partner, but I still felt like a woman even then." Similarly, Deepthi tells me about how her life with her husband when both of them were living together in Mumbai made her feel "completely like a woman": "He worked outside; I stayed in. I cooked for him and had a maid to clean the house. We were like a regular family. He was the man, and I was the woman. I had always wanted to be a woman, and after marriage, I felt really happy because I felt completely like a woman." Likewise, Chandralekha tells me:

> I have a lot of male partners and I share good relationships with all of them. I can share everything with them and they can do the same with me; it is a love relationship. Among them, I have placed only one man as my husband in my mind. We do not have a registered marriage. I wish to forever maintain this relationship. It is very important to me. It makes me feel like a woman.

However, not everyone articulated a similar view. Given the ubiquity of intimate partner violence within this community, many harbour an ambivalent attitude towards men. As Radhika notes: "Men have no role in this community. They are like tourists who visit and go. There is no sustainable relationship possible with men. There is a lot of intolerance and violence in these relationships. Usually, the trans woman is the earning member in the relationship and takes care of the man. The man is in it mostly for monetary benefits. It can get very exploitative."

Hence, Chandralekha, despite acknowledging how her relationship with her male partners helps affirm her feminine gender identity, says that she does not want to maintain any relations with the partners of her daughters or those of her chelas:

> We are distrustful of men in general. But some gurus do treat their chelas' husbands as their own sons. It is different with different people. It's all according to your way of thinking. But strictly speaking, there is no place for any such relationship within our community. Men can't come in between the relationship of a mother and daughter or a guru and chela. They can have relationships with my daughters or chelas individually. All my daughters have husbands. But I don't have any relations with any of them. They are not entertained inside my house. We don't forge relationships like that of a regular family here; we don't want to.

Conclusion

For trans-feminine individuals who experience multiple levels of marginalization, the Hijra community organization not only provides a powerful network of support but also helps them in giving expression to their feminine gender identity. In facilitating the latter, the emphasis is not so much on the individual right to freedom of expression but in the embeddedness of identities in kinship networks. For instance, Neelima, a hijra sex worker, who is both a mother to a hijra daughter and a daughter herself of another member of the community, points out how she has been able to experience life as a sister, daughter, mother, and wife as part of the community and how, through these roles, she has been able to live as a woman. "I have got everything," she says.

Therefore, while at many levels, the hijra identity subverts conventional ideas of gender, at others, it displays prominent tendencies to reinscribe the dominant normative order within its various modes of articulation and expression. For instance, underlying the hijras' proclamation of a feminine gender identity is a clear transcending of biology. In this manner, the hijra identity, as a transgender identity that cannot be incorporated within a neat binary framework, poses a challenge to conventional notions of gender. In many ways, this challenge serves to expose the socially constructed character of essentialist thinking and destabilizes essentialist interpretations of gender (Koyama). Simultaneously, however, in a number of ways, particularly through the sartorial and performative practices with the help of which Hijras attempt to resemble ciswomen as closely as possible—and through the assumption and execution of feminine gender roles in accordance with the normative standards of femininity—they are also engaged in a reinscription of the normative ideals of femininity. Additionally, the notion of womanhood that members of the community subscribe to clearly reflects an internalization of heteronormative ideas about gender roles. The most prominent among such conformist tendencies among the Hijras is the notion that motherhood is a woman's prerogative—an idea that also makes the phenomenon a facilitator of feminine gender identity for many members of the community.

Viewed through the lens of mainstream feminist perspectives, which tend to evaluate heteropatriarchal conceptualizations of femininity as negative, such efforts come across as an attempt on the part of the Hijras to attain hyperfeminine womanhood. Given their marginalized position in society, and the constant interrogation of the authenticity of their identity, the hijras' aspiration for motherhood does help to explain their insistence on conforming to the normative ideals of femininity within a cisheteropatriarchal setting, which is dominated by the binary understanding of gender wherein any deviation from the norm is considered suspect. But, as Riddell, arguing from a transfeminist perspective, observes, transgender women are as much a product of patriarchy as cisgender women and, therefore, are as likely to be unaware of their conditioning in the latter. In such a situation, it is highly optimistic to expect transgender women to pose any direct challenge to patriarchal sexist notions about women.

Likewise, hijra motherhood also comes across as the inevitable outcome of the internalization of the dominant cisheteropatriarchal norms governing womanhood. However, despite the hijra perception of motherhood as intrinsically connected to womanhood, and the hijra acknowledgment of the role of motherhood in affirming a feminine gender identity, hijra motherhood does represent a subversion of the heteronormative and patriarchal ideologies of family and kinship. For instance, the dudh beti-dudh ma and the mother-daughter relationships found within the Hijra community clearly signify a deviation from biogenetic notions of motherhood. They defy the idea of the centrality of blood ties to the establishment of kinship relations. Additionally, by allowing an individual the possibility of calling themselves the daughter of multiple mothers, the hijra social structure accommodates the idea of polymaternalism and in the process eschews the romanticization of monomaternalism that underlies pronatalistic views on motherhood.

The hijra identity embodies multiple other contradictions as well. For instance, despite claiming nonprocreative sexual identities, hijras do tend to idealize heteronormative ideas of marriage and yearn to establish enduring relationships with their panthis or husbands (Nanda Reddy). Thus, as Reddy notes, "They do not, in any simple way, merely subvert or reinscribe gender difference, but actively and intentionally court ambiguity in this regard" (141). In doing so, they clearly pose a challenge to "hermetically sealed theorizations of sexual/gender difference by showing their embeddedness in other forms of difference" (45). In the process, hijras broaden our understanding of how individuals incorporate cultural meanings in constructing and presenting their selves in and to society, of how culture is perceived and experienced by those at the margins, and of the ways in which different individuals perceive and play similar roles.

Endnotes

1. Throughout the chapter, my spelling of the word "hijra" reflects two variations—Hijra and hijra. I have capitalized the first letter of the word to indicate the community as a whole. The second variation has been used to either refer to individual members of the community or to qualify the word that follows it (for instance, hijra social structure or hijra motherhood).

2. *Dudh betis* of the same mother; literally, milk sisters.

3. Although, at present, they are legally recognized as the third gender, the Hijras do not enjoy a respectable social status (Stief) and

can be said to constitute a subaltern form of trans-queer identities (Goel, "The Lifestyle"), who are denied dignity and respect and are neglected by the state.

Works Cited

Banerjee, Sikata. *Make Me a Man!: Masculinity, Hinduism, and Nationalism in India.* State University of New York Press, 2005.

Basu, Subho, and Sikata Banerjee. "The Quest for Manhood: Masculine Hinduism and Nation in Bengal." *Comparative Studies of South Asia, Africa and the Middle East,* vol. 26, no. 3, 2006, pp. 476-90.

Boyce, Paul. "Conceiving Kothis: Men Who Have Sex with Men in India and the Cultural Subject of HIV Prevention." *Medical Anthropology,* vol. 26, no. 2, 2007, pp. 175-203.

Butalia, Urvashi. "Mona's Story." *Granta,* May 2011, https://granta.com/monas-story/. Accessed 17 Apr. 2021.

Chandralekha. Personal interview. 17 Apr. 2018.

Chandrika. Personal interview. 3 Apr. 2018.

Chandrika. Personal interview. 8 Apr. 2018.

Collinson, David L., and Jeff Hearn. "Naming Men as Men: Implications for Work, Organization and Management." *Gender, Work and Organization,* vol. 1, no. 1, 1994, pp. 2-22.

Connell, R.W. *Masculinities.* University of California Press, 1995.

Creswell, John W. *Qualitative Inquiry and Research Design: Choosing Among Five Approaches.* Sage, 2007.

Dasgupta, Rohit K., and K. Moti Gokulsing. "Introduction: Perceptions of Masculinity and Challenges to the Indian Male." *Masculinity and Its Challenges in India: Essays on Changing Perceptions.* Edited by Rohit K. Dasgupta and K. Moti Gokulsing. Jefferson Publishers, 2013, pp. 5-26.

Dearden, Georgina Elanor Mary. *Transwomen's Memories of Parental Relationships: An Interpretative Phenomenological Analysis.* 2009. University of Hertfordshire, PhD dissertation.

Deepthi. Personal interview. 7 Feb. 2018.

Deepthi. Personal interview. 28 Feb. 2018.

Goel, Ina. "Beyond the Gender Binary." *Economic and Political Weekly*, vol. XLIX, no. 15, 2014, p. 9.

Goel, Ina. "The Lifestyle of Hijras Embodies Resistance to State, Societal Neglect." *The Wire*, April 2018, thewire.in/gender/the-lifestyle-of-hijras-embodies-resistance-to-state-societal-neglect. Accessed 17 Apr. 2021.

Goffman, Erving. *Stigma: Notes on the Management of Spoiled Identity.* Simon and Schuster, 1963.

Hossain, Adnan. "Beyond Emasculation: Being Muslim and Becoming *Hijra* in South Asia." *Asian Studies Review*, vol. 36, no. 4, 2012, pp. 495-513.

Jain, Kajri. "Muscularity and Its Ramifications: Mimetic Male Bodies in Indian Mass Culture." *Sexual Sites, Seminal Attitudes: Sexualities, Masculinities and Culture in South Asia.* Edited by Sanjay Srivastava. Sage, 2004, pp. 300-41.

Jyothika. Personal interview. 13 Apr. 2018.

Jyothika. Personal interview. 27 Apr. 2018.

Kavi, Ashok, R. "The Rise of the Third Set: LGBT Community Is By No Means Returning To the Closet." *The Hindustan Times,* May 2014, www.hindustantimes.com/india/the-rise-of-the-third-set-lgbt-community-is-by-no-means-returning-to-the-closet/story-GMMBn6b2wOu9jsMuNaQD8M.html. Accessed 17 Apr. 2021.

Koyama, Emi. "Whose Feminism Is It Anyway? The Unspoken Racism of the Trans Inclusion Debate." *The Transgender Studies Reader.* Edited by Stephen Whittle and Susan Stryker. Routledge, 2006, pp. 698-705.

Lynton, H., and Mohini Rajan. *The Days of the Beloved.* Orient Longman, 1974.

Nanda, Serena. *Neither Man nor Woman: The Hijras of India.* Wadsworth Publishing Company, 1999.

Neelima. Personal interview. 8 Mar. 2018.

Neelima. Personal interview. 12 Mar. 2018.

O'Flaherty, Wendy Doniger. *Asceticism and Eroticism in the Mythology of Siva.* Oxford University Press, 1973.

Oakley, Ann. *Sex, Gender and Society.* Sun Books, 1972.

Radhika. Personal interview. 7 Dec. 2017.

Radhika. Personal interview. 22 Dec. 2017.

Radhika. Personal interview. 3 Feb. 2018.

Rao, Bhooshana, I. "Male Homosexual Transvestism—A Social Menace." *Antiseptic,* vol. 52, no. 1955, pp. 519-24.

Reddy, Gayatri. *With Respect to Sex: Negotiating Hijra Identity in South India.* The University of Chicago Press, 2005.

Revathi, A. *A Life in Trans Activism.* Zubaan, 2016.

Riddell, Carol. "Divided Sisterhood: A Critical Review of Janice Raymond's the Transsexual empire." *The Transgender Studies Reader.* Edited by Stephen Whittle and Susan Stryker. Routledge, 2006, pp. 144-58.

Rohini. Personal interview. 6 Feb. 2018.

Rohini. Personal interview. 10 Apr. 2018.

Saurav. Personal interview. 15 Apr. 2018.

Saxena, Piyush. *Life of a Eunuch.* Shanta Publication House, 2011.

Smith, Jonathan A. *Qualitative Psychology: A Practical Guide to Research Methods.* Sage, 2003.

Sonali. Personal interview. 7 Feb. 2018.

Sonali. Personal interview. 28 Feb. 2018.

Srivastava, Sanjay. "Indian Masculinities." *International Encyclopedia of Men and Masculinities.* Edited by Bob Pease et al. Routledge, 2007, pp. 329-31.

Stief, Matthew. "The Sexual Orientation and Gender Presentation of Hijra, Kothi, and Panthi in Mumbai, India." *Archives of Sexual Behavior,* vol. 46, no. 1, 2017, pp. 73-85.

Supreme Court of India. *National Legal Services Authority Versus Union of India and Others.* Supreme Court of India, 2014.

Vanita, Ruth. *Love's Rite: Same-Sex Marriage in India and the West.* Palgrave Macmillan, 2005.

Vimala. Telephone interview. 2 Mar. 2018.

Vimala. Personal interview. 5 Mar. 2018.

Vyas, M.D. and Y. Shingala. *The Lifestyle of the Eunuchs.* Anmol Publications, 1987.

Chapter 7

Getting to Understand Guerrilla Mothering[1]

Victoria Team

Introduction

People know very little about women combatants, their numbers, and, particularly, their mothering experiences in military camps and on the battlefield (Geisler). Similar to other countries, the experiences of wartime motherhood of Ethiopian women guerrilla fighters have been insufficiently researched (Negewo). There is a lack of published materials in academic literature on this topic. By way of what I refer to as "getting to understand," I provide an autoethnographic account of how my perceptions of motherhood and motherwork changed after interacting with Tigray People's Liberation Front (TPLF) guerrilla fighters and particularly with Hagosa (a pseudonym), a mother of a two-month-old baby girl. I met Hagosa approximately two months after the fall of the Derg regime in 1991, when the TPLF division quartered at one of the hostel compounds located on the outskirts of Addis Ababa, the capital city of Ethiopia, where I worked as a general medical practitioner.[2]

Autoethnography is defined as "a qualitative research method that uses a researcher's autobiographical experiences as primary data to analyze and interpret the sociocultural meanings of such experiences" (Chang, 444). This research method allows autoethnographers to bring personal and sociocultural perspectives together (Chang). In applying this research method, I aim to critically analyze the concept of guerrilla mothering while connecting the experience of women guerrilla fighters with the literature and comparing it with my own experience of Westernized mothering. I also aim to highlight the intricate nature of the guerrilla mother's identity, which reflects women's complex roles.

I also seek to introduce the concept of "guerrilla mothering" as it emerged at the end of the Ethiopian civil war in contrast to traditionally Western, but as well as Ethiopian, normative concepts of motherhood. The distinction between mothering as experience and motherhood as a form of institutional control was first described by Adrianne Rich (13). As Andrea O'Reilly further explains: "The term 'motherhood' refers to the patriarchal institution of motherhood that is male-defined and controlled and is deeply oppressive to women, while the word 'mothering' refers to women's experiences of mothering that are female-defined and centered and potentially empowering to women" (*From Motherhood* 2).

Mothering and combat are rarely discussed together, perhaps because according to traditional patriarchal standpoints mothering and combat are considered incompatible (Stachowitsch). Women's involvement in combat is a disputable topic, even among feminist groups. Feminists interested in liberation and equality rights argue that women's involvement in combat will result in a shift in how women are represented, from their needing to be defended to being defenders themselves. Cultural and conservative feminists, in contrast, argue that women should abstain from participation in the military—the most sexist social institution (Wibben and Turpin).

The limited publications on guerrilla mothering suggest that mothering was either embraced by guerrilla fighters or perceived as a burden and a barrier to their struggle for liberation. For example, Namibian girls who joined the liberation movement against apartheid and undertook training in military camps in Tanzania and Angola in the 1960s were perceived as too young to have children (Namhila). Nevertheless, those that did have children treated them with love and care, although some lacked elementary childcare skills. While fighting for liberation, some of the guerrilla mothers left their children under the care of other women in the camps. However, these cases were rare; and all children were reclaimed by their parents after victory (Namhila). In the 1970s and 1980s, some Nicaraguan guerrilla mothers were fighting with a gun in one hand and a baby in the other (Enloe, *The Morning*

After) ; others were separated from their young children who were left at home with their grandparents (O'Connor). During this period, Zimbabwean guerrilla mothers fighting white rule in Rhodesia were concerned about the fact that although military authorities were promoting motherhood and prohibiting the use of contraceptives, they did not pay attention to or promote the family as an important entity. Pregnant women were sent to the women's camp in Osibisa in Mozambique, where they remained until delivery and the postpartum period. During this time, their partners often created new relationships with new female recruits (Lyons, "Guerrilla Girls").

Early Mothering in Westernized and Ethiopian Contexts

O'Reilly writes that the concept of motherhood and its official definition do not reflect the diversity in women's experiences of motherhood (*Mothers and Sons*). Moreover, as a result of the Westernization of the "motherhood" concept, normative motherhood is now associated with the behavior and lifestyle of the "thirty-something, white, middle-class, able-bodied, married, and heterosexual mother situated in a nuclear family, preferably as a stay-at-home or full-time mother" (Minaker 126). However, a growing interest in the experiences of mothering over the last two decades has given rise to scholarly publications that deconstruct motherhood as an umbrella term. The shortened postpartum period now common within Westernized contexts tends to include the following: a one-day stay in a hospital, first latching, breastfeeding, breastmilk expression, using pumps, hospital discharge, and arriving home to resume the usual daily activities as soon as possible. These activities also include measuring bath water temperature, baby bathing, complying with the recommmended baby sleeping positions, choosing baby care products, booking maternal and child health nurse home visits, attending parental support groups, dealing with mental health issues, and focusing on weight loss management.

Normative mothering at the beginning of the postnatal period in Ethiopia differs from normative Western expectations. In Ethiopia, most Christian women remain secluded in the house for forty days postpartum if they had a son and eighty days if they had a daughter because they are considered unclean (Hanlon et al.). They are looked after by their mother, mother-in-law, sisters, and other female relatives. They abstain from all household chores, such as gathering water and fuel, cooking food, cleaning, washing, and looking after their other children. They stay either in a separate room or in a part of the room separated by a curtain and remain inactive inside the house, often lying down in bed alongside their infant. They are not supposed to go outside until the baptism of the baby. Until this celebratory event has taken place, people believe that postpartum women and their babies are open to the influence of the evil eye, evil spirits, and witchcraft (Warren). They also believe that both mother and infant are vulnerable to the cold environment. Postpartum women usually drink plenty of warm fluids, including milk, tea, barley, and wheat drinks. To their traditional food, they add large amounts of melted butter, kebe, believing that buttery food and hot drinks will increase their milk production and strengthen their bodies, particularly their backs. Women are expected to prepare the required food products prior to giving birth. They usually look forward to this period, since it's the time they can rest with the newborn baby, be surrounded by warmth, and be cared for by the immediate family members and other close relatives (Hanlon et al.).

Describing these common postpartum practices in Ethiopia, I do not want to represent them as homogenous. Variations of these traditional postpartum care practices and women's lack of capacity to follow them are quite common. Some women do not have the resources to prepare the required food ahead of time and, therefore, cannot follow the traditional diet for postpartum women. Women who have no relatives to take care of them are required to get out of bed much earlier than either forty or eighty days (Hanlon et al.). Women who have their children out of wedlock may leave their children in a village with their distant relatives where they gave birth and return to the city immediately after birth. Street beggars who have babies as a result of rape and gang rape have no place to stay and just make do with lying down with their babies on the street (Misganaw). Servant girls are generally expelled from the family for which they worked soon after birth, since their employers do not want to provide care for both mother and child (Belete).

TPLF Womanhood

The TPLF is an ethno-nationalist movement that originated in Tigray province in 1975 to confront the Derg regime and eventually brought about its fall in 1991 (Berhe). Women comprised one third of all TPLF fighters. Many of them were combatants and contributed significantly to the victory (Veale; Negewo). They also participated in mass political and gender equality education and helped farmers at the time of harvest, carrying sickles in addition to their weapons (Connell; Berhe). The TPLF soldiers were on the move and relied on local people for housing and food. Local people willingly supported them (Connell). Nevertheless, they sometimes experienced severe hardship, hunger, and thirst to a degree that they drank either their own or someone else's urine in order to survive (Negewo-Oda and White).

The TPLF soldiers were educated in gender equality and empowerment. Although sexual contacts, marriage, and childbearing were initially restricted among the TPLF fighters, these were later approved, and some soldiers officially registered their marriages and had children (Veale; Berhe). Unlike what occurred in other African countries (Lyons, *Guns and Guerrilla Girls*), there were no cases of rape or forced sexual relationship and pregnancies as a result of unwanted relationships among TPLF guerrilla fighters (Veale). TPLF women fighters were treated as comrades by the males. TPLF feminism, in contrast to Western notions of feminism, was rooted in the idea of class struggle (Young) and was a joint struggle against oppressors, as one of Jenny Hammond's interviewees noted: "We are more concerned of course because if we don't work with men for equality, we will be separated and alienated from society and we won't achieve anything at all" (58).

TPLF women's personal stories related to their day-to-day activities, marriage, pregnancy, labour, and mothering during the warfare period seem to have been overlooked in the available literature published or translated in English. One of the TPLF women ex-combatants in a study conducted by Beza Negewo-Oda and Aaronette White said: "When we gave birth all traditional treatments that civilian women get were unthinkable, and we were still expected to return to our responsibilities shortly after giving birth" (175).

Getting to Know Guerrilla Mothering

My interaction with guerrilla fighters started approximately two months after the fall of the Derg regime, when the TPLF division was quartered at one of the hostel compounds next to the compound for overseas-trained medical doctors. Hagosa, one of the neighbouring guerrilla fighters, came first to our compound to borrow a traditional brass plated teakettle. When she heard from our neighbours that my husband and I were doctors, she approached me later that day seeking help for her health problems. She also said that she recently given birth to a baby girl. Hagosa complained that she was feeling a bit tired. She mentioned that she was able to sleep sufficiently because other soldiers, both male and female, were happy to look after her baby.

Although she was eligible for free medical treatment in the military hospital, she did not want to go there because she believed that in the early postwar period, there were a lot of people with more urgent issues. We provided her with the necessary medicines. I offered her a head scarf because she believed that her ear infection was caused by the windy and cold weather. When she put the head scarf over her Afro-style hair, my children laughed at her. Next day, she came without the scarf, saying: "I am a soldier. I am not used to wearing head scarves as civilian women do." The head scarf obviously did not match her military uniform, but, in addition, it might have represented subservience, passivity, and feminine indulgence to her.

From that time, Hagosa started coming to our part of the hostel almost every day. I was happy about this new friendship and was pleased to share kitchen and laundry utensils and to provide health advice. One day, she arrived with one of her breasts swollen and quite painful. When I suggested that she express stale milk, she said that she had never heard of this procedure, and she did not know what to do. We began expressing her breastmilk together, taking turns to squeeze her breast. When my older children saw breastmilk, they asked if she had a baby. When Hagosa said that she had a baby-girl, they asked her to bring her baby girl so that they could play with her, so Hagosa began bringing her infant daughter. She borrowed our plastic tub to bathe the baby and to use the tub as a bassinet. While giving her baby a cold-water bath, she said that her daughter would "grow strong to become a fighter like her mum." At the time, her willingness and readiness to sacrifice her child appeared patriotic to me. I came to learn otherwise when I later interacted with civilian mothers.

Three weeks later, Hagosa and her husband, who was a military commander, invited our family to their daughter's christening party. Their daughter's name included the word "peace". Hagosa's husband said that they had chosen this name because she was born soon after the victory, at the time of peace, and they hoped that the TPLF would be able to keep peace for their children's sake. In fact, it was just slightly more than two months since the end of the Ethiopian civil war.

We were late to the party, but Hagosa's room was still full of people. Dark injera (traditional sourdough pancakes) and cold shiro (pea-powder sauce) were served to our family on a large round tray with such warmth that this simple food became the best tasting food that I'd ever had. I felt honoured eating food served by guerrilla fighters. I also thought how insufficient it was for a breastfeeding woman. One of the soldiers said that foreign people might not like injera because they eat cakes in their country. Hagosa started to unpack all the cakes and biscuits that were brought to her, placing them on the tray with injera with warmth and generosity.

She asked other soldiers to buy soft drinks for us, thinking that we might not like the traditional brew. I was unable to refuse. Hagosa took the Coke bottles one at a time and skillfully opened them with her pistol. Noticing my widely opened eyes one of the other soldiers said, "You have scared this foreign lady with your tricks." Hagosa asked me: "Have I scared you? It is empty, no bullets." She pointed out her grenade belt and asked: "Do you feel scared of this? I will take it off." She took off her fully equipped belt and placed it on her bed under the pillow where her baby girl was peacefully sleeping. My daughter said, "Hagosa, you will blow your baby girl up with these weapons." Everyone laughed.

My first impression was that this was very reckless behaviour because the mother was endangering her child's life. However, Hagosa saw no risk in this because she knew than nothing would happen. For example, no Western woman would think that she was endangering her children's lives when driving them in a car. Being a woman combatant, she also treated her military equipment as typical household equipment, as part of her limited belongings, not as weapons of destruction.

Hagosa's ability to assess the situation was outstanding. One of the local service ladies had dropped a plastic bucket in the water well. She was walking around the well crying that if it was impossible for her to get this bucket out, she would have to reimburse the person who had lent her the bucket. Hagosa did not know what had happened and came to comfort the crying lady. As soon as she understood why the woman was crying, she became angry. She said: "How can you cry over the plastic bucket at a time when other mothers are crying for their children who had died on the battlefield? Go home and forget about this bucket."

Hagosa's behaviour can be understood as arising from the differences in the expectations of being a woman/mother and a combatant. She did not have the luxury of choosing one or the other. As a woman, Hagosa was compassionate and tried to comfort the crying lady. As a mother, she expressed sympathy with the grieving mothers who lost their children in war. As a combatant, was ready to sacrifice her own life. She understood that real value is in human life and not in material belongings. As Hagosa's story shows, the combined experience of mothering and fighting has the potential of changing the personalities of women.

Hagosa was so sharp and precise in assessing people that sometimes I had the impression that she was able to read people's minds. Once, I, Hagosa, and a lady from Europe were talking, and Hagosa asked me to interpret for that lady. Referring to me, she said: "So many times I was in your house, but this lady has never invited me to her house. Can you ask her, if I can come as a guest to her house?" I interpreted this question from Amharic to Russian. The lady said: "Tell her that in our culture, people can become guests when they are invited, and not when they are asking to be invited." I hesitated for a few seconds, wondering how best to interpret this so that the message would not be offensive. These few seconds of my uncertainty were sufficient for Hagosa to understand the reply. She said: "I got it. No need to interpret."

As any woman, Hagosa wanted to chat with other women over a cup of tea. The ability to understand what was said even without my translating the lady's response and Hagosa's ability to read the body language of others suggested to me that Hagosa had developed heightened skills in situational assessment, which I believe most combatants develop. There is another issue here, which Hagosa would have understood. When Europeans deal with Africans in Africa, they do not generally assume that they should alter their behaviour to suit the African context. However, when Africans are in Europe, they are expected to alter their behavior to suit the host country. This inequality in expectations was common at that time and remains so. Most of the studies on acculturation patterns have been conducted in North America and Western European countries, and a limited number of studies exist on acculturation patterns in Africa (Adams and van de Vijver).

One night, Hagosa knocked on my door and said that their division had received an order to relocate to another place. She returned the borrowed tub and said that they were leaving the hostel in the next few minutes. She agreed, however, to wait for a minute for me to bring some baby clothes for her little daughter. I wept. No tears were in her eyes. There was only a sigh, a strong hug, and a confident walk away—she was used to separations.

Complex Roles. Complex Identities

According to traditional patriarchal expectations, an Ethiopian man should possess the identity of a strong warrior, which entails the elements of superiority, power, aggression, and even violence (Levine). In contrast, the ideal woman is expected to be "virginal, chaste, modest, submissive, respectful, domesticated, serene and, of course, beautiful" (Heinonen:38). Becoming a guerrilla, a woman accepts a non-traditional role, which is usually reserved for a man (Bernal, "Equality to Die For?"; Falola and Ter Haar). Accepting this non-traditional role requires a lot of skills and sacrifices. Becoming a mother, a woman accepts a traditional women's role. As Joanne Minaker argues, a woman's identity as a mother may intersect with her other identities, and "motherhood is recognized as a blending of the two sides of each of the traditional binaries or divides through which women mother—public/private, family/work, child(ren)/mother, self/society, and personal/political" (128).

The explanation of a mother-warrior identity can be taken as a good example of the feminist thesis that life is often not an either/or proposition as generally assumed in both Western and Ethiopian patriarchal logic; rather, so much in life is both/and. A mother-warrior identity does not fit with historically routed gender expectations of mothers and warriors, which is similar to the gendered expectations of mothers and workers (McQuillan et al., 477). Moreover, the mother-warrior identity creates dialectical tension. The concept of "dialectical tension" or "contradiction" is defined as "the dynamic interplay between the unified oppositions" (Baxter and Montgomery 8). Social life is "an unfinished, ongoing dialogue in which a polyphony of dialectical voices struggle against one another to be heard" (4). The nature of dialectical perspective—which emphasizes "the interplay of oppositions" that is both/and—becomes contrasted with the nature of a dualistic perspective, which emphasizes opposites in parallel that are either/or (10).

Combining both roles, being a mother and a guerrilla fighter, requires tremendous effort and motivation rather than just simply having more masculine traits than other women have. A mother guerrilla fighter accepts responsibility for her country and for her child; moreover, she often sacrifices her motherhood, her child's and her own health and wellbeing, and sometimes their lives for the sake of the country (Parashar). Glorified images of women guerrilla fighters with a gun in one hand and a child in the other, as a sign of victory, do not represent women's day-to-day struggle towards this victory (Lyons, *Guns and Guerrilla Girls*; White).

The problems encountered by mother guerrilla fighters in a war-affected country were life endangerment, ongoing relocations, reliance on others, lack of a balanced diet, lack of stability, and unmet personal health needs and baby care requirements. These experiences were in sharp contrast to the common pregnancy and maternity care concerns of Western and Ethiopian civilian women. Instead of drawing attention to pregnancy cravings, no matter what they craved when they were pregnant, guerrilla fighters ate what was available. Regarding the problem of eating a balanced diet during the postpartum period, their food was no different from the ration given to other TPLF soldiers. Recalling my own postpartum periods and my insatiable thirst, which for me was related to breastmilk production, I cannot comprehend how Hagosa was able to deal with her thirst. However, whenever she wanted a cup of tea, she came to our compound to borrow the teakettle. She did not have the opportunity to get the traditional drinks usually prepared for postpartum women in Ethiopia.

Hagosa's baby girl was washed in well water; the water temperature was not measured. Hagosa refused to use healthcare services for her own and her daughter's health needs even though she was eligible to receive them for free. Regarding baby care products, Hagosa used traditional cloth nappies, which she handwashed in well water and dried on the nearby shrubs. Although these washing and drying methods were no different from the methods used by the Ethiopian civilian women, the main difficulties were related to the ongoing relocations and prolonged travel. I know nothing about Hagosa's pregnancy and labour, but I am confident she received all necessary informal support from her fellow women combatants. Similar to Ethiopian civilian women, TPLF women combatants are collectivist. There were no other children in their division, and fellow women combatants willingly helped Hagosa take care of her child. The timing of Hagosa's final months of pregnancy and labour coincided with the activation of the military and combat operations leading to TPLF victory. Hagosa risked her life as a soldier to make this victory happen, and she risked her life as a mother receiving little or no professional care during pregnancy and childbirth.

Sometimes, these efforts are not recognized by the family or by the country. Families and particularly mothers-in-law believed that female guerrilla fighters lacked feminine skills to perform the required traditional women's roles. In contrast, the government expected them to return to their families rather than be given high-ranking military positions because they were seen as lacking the necessary masculine skills (Negewo-Oda and White). Transfer from this nontraditional role to women's traditional roles in the postwar period was always to be problematic (Colleta, Kostner, and Wiederhofer; Bernal, "From Warriors to Wives"; Bernard et al.).

Some academic sources indicate that Ethiopia's demobilization and reintegration program was successful in meeting the objectives of reintegrating ex-combatants into civilian life, particularly in rural areas (Berhe). However, other sources suggest that in the postwar period, women ex-combatants experienced various problems with reintegrating into civilian life (Negewo-Oda and White). Only a few women managed to receive local leadership and management positions; the majority of them were textile factory workers, guards, and doorkeepers (Veale).

TPLF women combatants who were active agents of the war became victims in the postwar period because of their femininity, since the military authorities expected them to be more masculine. Simultaneously, they also become victims of their masculinity, since their husband and mother-in-law expected them to be more feminine. In general, the social reintegration of female ex-combatants has proven to be difficult. During the period of warfare, they were alienated from their families and from civilian life, and as Negowo-Oda writes, "readjusting to the patriarchal way of life in their communities created difficulties regarding their chances of employment, marriage and motherhood" (27). Women ex-combatants did not meet the traditional expectations of mothers, wives, and daughters-in-law and, therefore, were considered misfits by the civilian population. Moreover, they believed that only disobedient women who did not comply with the traditional norms imposed by the parents, husbands, elders and the local government would join the guerrilla forces.

Women's Devalued Sacrifices

Women's sacrifices were not taken as seriously as men's once the war ended and TPLF came into power (Negewo-Oda). Historically, there have always been conflicts between the notions of empowerment and sacrifice. For example, Algerian and Zimbabwean women fighters complained bitterly of their problematic reintegration after the liberation wars in their countries. The contribution of Zimbabwean women combatants to the country's liberation struggle (1962-1979) went "largely unsung" (Sadomba and Dzinesa, 51). After liberation, female combatants were awarded lower ranks and received fewer opportunities to choose a career in the military compared to male combatants. Civilian men considered them "too independent, rough, ill-educated and unfeminine to be good wives" (*The Sunday Mail* qtd. in Sadomba and Dzinesa 57). The whole community tends to see them as misfits: "Single mothers were looked down upon in the African tradition; while the communities rejoiced at the return of male ex-combatants, they despised female ex-combatants, particularly those with fatherless children" (Sadomba and Dzinesa 57).

Analyzing Algerian women fighter's accounts, Mildred Mortimer writes that after the country's independence women were left with their "memories of heroic exploits" (105), as the society failed to integrate them into political life. And women fighters who were kept in prisons or in captivity were left unaided to deal with their tortured bodies and the psychological consequences of torture, preferring to remain in silence because rape, sex, and the loss of virginity before marriage in Muslim Algeria is considered a taboo (Mortimer 110). Their sacrifices were silenced, hidden, and forgotten, contributing to an "occulted" history (Mortimer 102) of Algeria's liberation struggle (1954–1962).

Nancy Scheper-Hughes and Margaret Lock (7) define the body as "simultaneously a physical and symbolic artifact, as both naturally and culturally produced, and as securely anchored in a particular historical moment" (25). They also state that "in a time of crisis, societies regularly reproduce and socialize the kind of bodies that they need" (25). Applying this concept to postliberation women combatants, it becomes obvious that their feminine-masculine bodies, which were reproduced, socialized, and used in the struggle for liberation, became useless and were often rejected after the liberation.

Masculinity versus Femininity

Adopting some masculine behaviours and norms, however, does not necessarily limit women's femininity (Badaró; Falola and Ter Haar). Feminine and masculine models of mothering have been discussed in the literature in relation to women's employment and their financial independence as well as the sharing of household tasks and care provision (Doucet and Dunne). Accepting a masculine model of mothering and participation in paid employment (army forces, guerrilla warfare)—forms of behaviour considered to be deviant from the patriarchally assigned role for women—does not necessarily make a particular woman masculine. Besides, women in the military are frequently presented as "conventionally feminine, sexual and appealing in the eyes of their male colleagues" (Enloe, *Globalization and Militarism* 75). As a mother, Hagosa did not lack femininity. Although she did not rest with her baby for eighty days behind the curtain, she did not eat fatty foods and drink traditional warm drinks provided for postpartum women, she did, given her circumstances, provide the best possible care for her daughter. She breastfed her daughter and had intended to breastfeed her longer. She was concerned with her daughter's health and came to seek health advice. She shared her women's health concerns with me and not with my husband, who was a medical doctor and who spoke her language.

I do not want to limit Hagosa's femininity just to the few sentences that I use to briefly describe her as a mother. While talking about femininity and masculinity, the sociopolitical environment should also be considered. During the warfare period, wearing a pair of pants instead of a full-length traditional dress and having an Afro hairstyle instead of time-consuming braids were more suitable options for women guerrilla fighters. These options were more about the practicality of this outfit for direct combat, military activities, and ongoing relocations than about gender traits.

When I saw Hagosa in her new uniform, she was no doubt a soldier. When she refused to wear a head scarf, she did what men are expected to do. When she refused to book an appointment in the military hospital to give priority to the wounded guerrilla fighters who overthrew the Derg, she did what men are expected to do. Some tricks, such as opening bottles of Coke with her pistol, reflected her masculinity. Her sharpness of mind, her ability to quickly assess a person, and her lack of sentiment when she came to say goodbye too reflected her masculinity. These behaviours and actions were no doubt related to her role and her identity as a guerrilla fighter.

Jodi York argues that a mother guerrilla fighter may not feel that she is not feminine even if involved in violence because "she is doing what she needs to do to protect her children's future" (22). Negewo-Oda and White believe that the "[TPLF] female fighters were 'androgynous,' adopting certain positive masculine traits in their dress, communication style, and military abilities, which transformed their perceptions of themselves as women" (180). As these authors also point out, women who joined TPLF, following their political ideology and their motivation to overthrow the Derg, struggled for gender equality and equal recognition by fellow male fighters and adopted some masculine behaviours. Some women, however, joined the TPLF as child soldiers and were brought up in the camps, where they were socialized into the role of a female guerrilla fighter. Although civilians may consider some of their traits as masculine, these were gender specific traits typical for female guerrilla fighters. I argue that a guerrilla fighter's identity is more complex than just simply being masculine. It is therefore inappropriate,

I believe, to perceive women guerrilla fighters as masculine, as it is inappropriate to perceive civilian men as feminine.

As Yvonne Due Billing, and Mats Alvesson argue, "Masculinity is often viewed as the antithesis of femininity" (146); however, "masculine" and "feminine" concepts can be applied to both genders. Lately, more complex concepts have been developed, such as "masculine femininity" and "feminine masculinity" (Paechter). All four concepts cannot fully describe the complex identity of a mother guerrilla fighter. A woman-guerrilla fighter is suggestive of masculine femininity; she does what is generally expected of men. A guerrilla fighter, who is a nursing mother, is an example of feminine masculinity. However, I purposefully do not want to apply this concept to female TPLF combatants, who were fighting for gender equality; the concept of feminine masculinity might sound offensive to some of them. Studies on leadership in the workplace, for instance, reveal that men and women construct different leadership roles (Due Billing and Alvesson). For example, women may listen more and may mediate more between people in the room. Some men take this to be a sign of weakness, but it is a form of leadership that has its benefits. In other words, women do not have to act in identical ways to men even if they are in the same role.

I never asked Hagosa how she became a guerrilla fighter, and she never shared this story with me. Unfortunately, I cannot reflect upon Hagosa's personal perspective regarding her feminine and masculine traits or on her roles and behaviours. There is also the issue of how she might have changed over time, especially after joining the guerrilla fighters or after she became a mother. So far, I have discussed how the complex role of mother guerrilla fighters helps shape their identities. In the following section, I discuss how the guerrilla identity may influence women's mothering approach.

Guerrilla Mothering: Raising Warriors While Thinking of Peace

Recruitment, conscription, army service, and the battlefield have been frequently discussed in the literature in relation to mothering adult or almost adult sons. Mothering approaches are described as protective, sacrificing, bereaving, resisting and protesting, as well as complying.

Mothers are often encouraged and usually forced by militarized governments to adopt a sacrificing approach to motherhood. Some mothers adopt this sacrificing approach and are happy to commit their sons to the land (Farhat). Some mothers are not sure whether "being a good mother meant waving a tearful though proud goodbye to a son going off to do his military service or hiding him from the army's recruiters" (Enloe, *The Morning After* 18). Many women adopt a complying approach, believing that army service is "a duty to the homeland" and "a rite of passage to manhood where the soldiers would become 'real men' after the completion of their service" (Kaptan 253). Mothers of martyrs blame themselves for adopting the sacrificing approach and feel that they were deceived by the military authorities (Ronel and Lebel; Farhat; Loadenthal). After the death of their adult children, their sacrificing motherhood approach was replaced with grieving. Learning from the experiences of mothers of martyrs, other women have begun to adopt protective approaches to mothering (Team). They either hide their adult sons from the authorities or help them to emigrate, thus allowing their sons to escape the dangerous practices established by the patriarchal system. When mothers are against government authorities, they then adopt resisting and protesting approaches (Eichler).

Protective, resisting, and protesting approaches are similar to the feminist approach to mothering sons, which "seeks to destabilize the normative practice of masculinization" (O'Reilly, *Mothers and Sons* 4). At the same time, the feminist approach to mothering sons is also similar to the traditional African American mothering approach, which teaches sons to survive (O'Reilly, "In Black and White"). The mother "both provides protection and teaches her son how to protect himself" (O'Reilly, "In Black and White" 18).

The complex guerrilla mother's identity, as a guerrilla fighter and as a mother, has shaped her parenting approaches. Some feel that their motherhood has become split. For example, a Filipina mother of an adolescent daughter noticed that as a mother, as a traditional mother, she wanted her daughter to stay home, but as a former guerrilla fighter, she wanted her daughter to join the guerrilla movement (Cruz).

In one way, TPLF guerrilla fighters' mothering approach entailed sacrifice. They voluntarily sacrificed themselves, their womanhood, their femininity, their motherhood, and their life for the sake of liberation—their country's liberation, their people's liberation, and their children's liberation. A good mother in the Westernized understanding of this concept prioritizes children's needs, sometimes, at the expense of her own (Hays; Mauthner). However, a mother-guerrilla fighter may perceive liberation not only in terms of her own needs but also in terms of her children's needs. This was reflected in Hagosa's mothering approach, as she overcame difficulties to raise a warrior while thinking of peace. Thoughts about peace in the country, thoughts about peacetime mothering, and thoughts about the peacetime childhood of their children were another side of guerrilla motherhood. And they were fighting for peace. Although Hagosa saw her daughter as a future warrior for the country as she herself had been, she obviously dreamed about peace and that is why the word "peace" was included in her daughter's name.

In war-torn countries, the militarized government usually calls on women "to produce more sons for the military" (Wibben and Turpin: 365). However, TPLF fighters equally viewed their sons and daughters as future fighters. Petra Büskens writes: "As the mother is conceived an agent in her own right, so the daughter can claim this agency for herself. The mother can expand her daughter's horizon ... by expanding her own.... That is, by being the woman she hopes her daughter can become" (178). Daughters can achieve empowerment through their identification with their mothers (O'Reilly, "I Come from a Long Line of Uppity Irate Black Women"). Female TPLF guerrilla fighters were empowered as mothers because motherhood in African cultures is placed at the centre of womanhood (Littlefield) and were also empowered as warriors. Hagosa wanted her daughter to be empowered, which would be possible through her daughter's identification with her as a mother and as a guerrilla fighter. Hagosa's goal was to raise her daughter as a future guerrilla fighter. According to traditional paternalist views, giving birth to and raising a child is part of a woman's identity as a mother; and in having a baby, female TPLF guerrilla fighters were no different from civilian women. However, Ethiopian civilian women see the ultimate goal of motherhood as raising a child who will then support them later in life as a matter of reciprocal care (Team). In contrast to this, the TPLF mother's goal was to raise a future guerrilla fighter, which reflects their identity as a warrior.

Concluding Remarks

In this chapter, I have presented an autoethnographic account of interaction with TPLF guerrilla fighters, focusing on their mothering experience. I have discussed women's complex identity, which is related to the combination of their roles as mothers and as guerrilla fighters. I have also talked about how women's involvement in combat has influenced their mothering approach. In writing this chapter, my aim was to complement the available yet scarce literature on guerrilla motherhood. Through sharing my autoethnographic account of day-to-day interactions with TPLF guerrilla fighters, I planned to enrich the contemporary understanding of guerrilla motherhood in Ethiopia, which contests the conventional representation of motherhood and maternal roles both in Western countries and in Africa. Reflecting upon their mothering approaches, I have challenged the traditional paternalist understanding of the mother-infant dyad as needing protection by a male soldier. As soldiers, these women were capable of protecting themselves, their babies, and their country. As women, they had reached equality with male soldiers. During wars, female soldiers have temporary empowerment, which is often taken away after the war ends. I would like to conclude that gender equality is only relative to the war situation. As a result of patriarchy, women do not receive the honours given to men after fighting. Even other women gave them a hard time because women themselves have imbibed patriarchal values, as I have discussed in this chapter.

This war-time equality, in fact, did not make women masculine. Their femininity was reflected in their mothering. Their ultimate goal as mothers was to raise warriors for the country, which differed from the goal of civilian mothers. Theirs was ultimately to receive reciprocal care and support in old age. Although the traditional expectation of motherhood shaped by the patriarchal system was to raise a son as a future warrior, Hagosa was raising a daughter, whom she wanted to become a warrior if need be. I hope that motherhood scholars will further use this analysis of situational difference—but, perhaps, typical experience of guerrilla motherhood—to expand our theoretical conceptions of motherhood or develop additional empirical research on mothers in military contexts.

Given that this chapter is my autoethnographic account, I also would like to provide a brief summary of how my understanding of mothering has changed. As a young, white, upper-middle-class mother and health professional, I thought that good knowledge of how to provide the best care for children largely led to successful mothering. Working as a general practitioner, I openheartedly shared my knowledge and skills with Ethiopian women. I quickly realized that although some of these skills were helpful, others were inapplicable and useless in a country-specific situational context. I also realized that it is not only knowledge that shapes mothering.

Although I knew that mothers have multiple social roles and frequently combine studying, working, and caregiving with mothering, I never thought that it was possible to combine mothering and liberation fighting. Is it a masculine way of mothering? Yes, if this concept is applied to women combatants in comparison to civilian mothering. No, if applied to the mother guerrilla fighters themselves. This way of mothering is just typical mothering in the context of a liberation struggle.

Finally, although this chapter was written prior to the current Ethiopia-Tigray conflict, I want to make some contrasts between the situation when TPLF came to Addis Ababa and the current situation in the Tigray region. TPLF fighters who led Ethiopia to victory over the Derg and who changed the face of the country—growing its economy, improving its infrastructure, and achieving its health-related millennium development goals (Assefa et al.)—are now becoming victims of genocide and crimes against humanity (Ghebrehiwet). When TPLF fighters came to Addis Ababa in 1991, they shared their limited provisions with the impoverished neighbours—orphans, domestic workers, and property guards. Conversely, the Ethiopian government under the current leadership of unelected Prime Minister Abiy Ahmed blocks humanitarian access into the Tigray region for aid organizations (Zelalem), as civilian people die of starvation, their crops are destroyed, their livestock are slaughtered, and their houses are looted (Annys et al.).

As a mother, Hagosa was against war. However, I now also realize that she had foreseen the future, deciding to raise her daughter as a liberation fighter. However, there are deep concerns about the masculinity of the current leader of the country, who said: "The youth should not die, mothers should not cry, homes should not be destroyed, and people should not be displaced to bring politicians to power"

(Ethiopia Insight). Given the current situation, his promise has not been kept. Internationally, people are now outraged by how quickly the Nobel Peace Prize winner has turned out to be a war criminal (The Washington Post Editorial Board). And Tigrayan, Ethiopian, Eritrean, and Somali mothers are crying.

Endnotes

1. Dedicated to TPLF mothers-guerrilla fighters.
2. My outsider's perspective as a Europe-born, white, young female medical doctor will be obvious in this work. However, I do not want to present myself as a complete outsider to the Ethiopian community. I was married to an Ethiopian man, who is my husband and with whom I have five children. I witnessed and survived the fall of the Derg. I am a civilian woman. However, I undertook military train-ing in the former USSR as part of my graduate degree in medical university and had the title of reserve officer. In Ethiopia, I was serv-ing injured soldiers as part of my medical and surgical internship rotations. I was then informally helping some TPLF fighters quartered in the neighbouring compound for the period of their stay.

Works cited

Adams, Byron G., and Fons J. R. van de Vijver. "Identity and Acculturation: The Case for Africa." *Journal of Psychology in Africa*, vol. 27, no. 2, 2017, pp. 115-21.

Annys, Sofie, Tim Vanden Bempt, Emnet Negash, Lars De Sloover, and Jan Nyssen. "Tigray: Atlas of the humanitarian situation". *Journal of Maps*, preprint. 2021. https://www.researchgate.net/publication/349824181_Tigray_Atlas_of_the_humanitarian_situation

Assefa, Yibeltal, et al. "Successes and Challenges of the Millennium Development Goals in Ethiopia: Lessons for the Sustainable Development Goals." *BMJ Global Health*, no. 2, 2017, http://dx.doi.org/10.1136/bmjgh-2017-000318

Badaró, Máximo. "'One of the Guys': Military Women, Paradoxical Individuality, and the Transformations of the Argentine Army."

American Anthropologist, vol. 117, no. 1, 2015, pp. 86-99.

Baxter, Leslie A., and Barbara M. Montgomery. *Relating: Dialogues and Dialectics.* Guilford Press, 1996.

Belete, Yohannes Mersha. "Challenges and Opportunities of Female Domestic Workers in Accessing Education: A Qualitative Study from Bahir Dar City Administration, Amhara Region, Ethiopia." *International Journal of Sociology and Anthropology*, vol. 6, no. 6, 2014, pp. 192-99.

Berhe, Aregawi. *A Political History of the Tigray People's Liberation Front (1975-1991): Revolt, Ideology and Mobilisation in Ethiopia.* Vrije Universiteit, 2008.

Berhe, Mulugeta Gebrehiwot. "Transition from War to Peace: The Ethiopian Disarmament, Demobilisation and Reintegration Experience." *African Security Review*, vol. 26, no. 2, 2017, pp. 143-60.

Bernal, Victoria. "Equality to Die For?: Women Guerrilla Fighters and Eritrea's Cultural Revolution." *Political and Legal Anthropology Review*, vol. 23, no. 2, 2000, pp. 61-76.

Bernal, Victoria. "From Warriors to Wives: Contradictions of Liberation and Development in Eritrea." *Northeast African Studies*, vol. 8, no. 3, 2001, pp. 129-54.

Bernard, Belinda, et al. *Assessment of the Situation of Women and Children Combatants in the Liberian Post-Conflict Period and Recommendations for Successful Integration. Prepared for Short-Term Technical Assistance and Research under Egat/Wid Management to Support Usaid Washington and Field Mission Anti-Trafficking Activities Gew-I-00-02-00017-00 Task Order #1 (Atto). December 2003.* Development Alternatives Inc., 2003.

Berry, John W. "Immigration, Acculturation, and Adaptation." *Applied Psychology*, vol. 46, 1997, pp. 5-34.

Büskens, Petra. "A Review of Mothers and Daughters: Connection, Empowerment and Transformation." *Journal of the Association for Research on Mothering*, vol. 5, no. 2, 2003, pp. 170-80.

Chang, Heewon. "Autoethnography in health research: Growing pains?." *Qualitative Health Research*, vol. 26, no. 4, 2016, pp. 443-51.

Colleta, N., J., M. Kostner, and I. Wiederhofer. *Case Studies in War-to-*

Peace Transition: The Demobilization and Reintegration of Ex-Combatants in Ethiopia, Namibia and Uganda - Discussion Papers 331: World Bank, 1996.

Connell, Dan. *Taking on the Superpowers: Collected Articles on the Eritrean Revolution (1976-1982), Vol.1.* NJ Red Sea Press, 2003.

Doucet, Andrea, and Gillian Dunne. "Heterosexual and Lesbian Mothers Challenging 'Feminine' and 'Masculine' Concepts of Mothering." *Mothers and Daughters: Connection, Empowerment, and Transformation.* Edited by Andrea O'Reilly and Sharon Abbey. Rowman & Littlefield, 2000, pp. 103-20.

Due Billing Yvonne, and Mats Alvesson "Questioning the Notion of Feminine Leadership: A Critical Perspective on the Gender Labelling of Leadership." *Gender, Work & Organization*, vol. 7, no. 3, 2000, pp. 144-57.

Eichler, M. *Militarizing Men: Gender, Conscription, and War in Post-Soviet Russia.* Stanford University Press, 2011.

Enloe, Cynthia. *Globalization and Militarism: Feminists Make the Link.* Rowman & Littlefield Publishers, 2007.

Enloe, Cynthia. *The Morning After: Sexual Politics at the End of the Cold War.* University of California Press, 1993.

Ethiopia Insight. "Prime Minister Abiy Ahmed: "We are building a constitutional democracy." 14 May 2020." *Ethiopia Insight*, www.ethiopia-insight.com/2020/05/14/prime-minister-abiy-ahmed-we-are-building-a-constitutional-democracy/. Accessed 29 Jan. 2021.

Falola, Toyin, and Hetty Ter Haar. *Narrating War and Peace in Africa.* University of Rochester Press, 2010.

Farhat, Haq. "Militarism and Motherhood: The Women of the Lashkar I Tayyabia in Pakistan." *Signs: Journal of Women in Culture and Society*, vol. 32, no. 4, 2007, pp. 1023-46.

Ghebrehiwet, Yosief. "The War in Tigray: Abiy, Isaias, and the Amhara Elite." *The Africa Report*, 29 Jan. 2021, www.theafricareport.com/62232/the-war-in-tigray-abiy-isaias-and-the-amhara-elite/. Accessed 30 Jan. 2021.

Hammond, Jenny. "'My Revolution Is Like Honey': Women in Revolutionary Tigray." *Women: A Cultural Review*, vol. 1, no. 1, 1990, pp. 56-59.

Hanlon, Charlotte, et al. "Postnatal Mental Distress in Relation to the Sociocultural Practices of Childbirth: An Exploratory Qualitative Study from Ethiopia." *Social Science & Medicine*, vol. 69, no. 8, 2009, pp. 1211-19.

Hays, Sharon. *The Cultural Contradictions of Motherhood.* Yale University Press, 1996.

Heinonen, Paula. *Youth Gangs and Street Children: Culture, Nurture and Masculinity in Ethiopia.* Berghahn Books, 2011.

Kaptan, Senem. "Navigating the Tricky Waters of Maternal Militarization: Experiences of Being a Soldier's Mother in Turkey." *An Anthropology of Mothering.* Edited by Michelle Walks and Naomi McPherson. Demeter Press, 2011, 253-65.

Levine, Donald N. *Greater Ethiopia: The Evolution of a Multiethnic Society.* University of Chicago Press, 2014.

Littlefield, Marci Bounds. "Black Women, Mothering, and Protest in 19th Century American Society." *The Journal of Pan African Studies,* vol. 2, no. 1, 2007, pp. 53-61.

Lyons, Tanya. "Guerrilla Girls and Women in the Zimbabwean National Liberation Struggle." *Women in African Colonial Histories.* Edited by Jean Allman, Susan Geiger. and Nakanyike Musisi. Indiana University Press, 2002, 303-26.

Lyons, Tanya. *Guns and Guerrilla Girls: Women in the Zimbabwean National Liberation Struggle.* Africa World Press, 2004.

McQuillan, Julia et al. "The Importance of Motherhood among Women in the Contemporary United States." *Gender & Society*, vol. 22, no. 4, 2008, pp. 477-96.

Mauthner, N.S. *The Darkest Days of My Life: Stories of Postpartum Depression.* Harvard University Press, 2002.

Minaker, Joanne. "The Space Between: Mothering in the Context of Contradiction." *Moms Gone Mad: Motherhood and Madness, Oppression and Resistance.* Edited by Gina Wong. Demeter Press, 2012, 124-40.

Misganaw, Alemayehu C., and Yalew A. Worku. "Assessment of Sexual Violence among Street Females in Bahir-Dar Town, North West Ethiopia: A Mixed Method Study." *BMC Public Health*, vol. 13, 2013, pp. 825-25.

Mortimer, Mildred. "Tortured Bodies, Resilient Souls: Algeria's Women Combatants Depicted by Danièle Djamila Amrane-Minne, Louisette Ighilahriz, and Assia Djebar." *Research in African Literatures*, vol. 43, no. 1, 2012, pp. 101-117.

Namhila, Ellen Ndeshi. *Mukwahepo. Women Soldier Mother.* University of Namibia Press, 2013.

Negewo-Oda, Beza. *Post-War Narratives of Women Ex-Combatants of the Tigray People's Liberation Front (TPLF).* 2010. Addis-Ababa University, PhD dissertation.

Negewo-Oda, Beza. *Post-War Narratives of Women Ex-Combatants: Reflections from Tigray People's Liberation Front (TPLF).* Lambert Academic Publishing, 2012.

Negewo-Oda, Beza, and Aaronette M. White. "Identity Transformation and Reintegration among Ethiopian Women War Veterans: A Feminist Analysis." *Journal of Feminist Family Therapy*, vol. 23, no. 3-4, 2011, pp. 163-87.

O'Connor, Erin E. *Mothers Making Latin America: Gender, Households, and Politics since 1825.* Wiley-Blackwell, 2014.

O'Reilly, Andrea. "'I Come from a Long Line of Uppity Irate Black Women': African American Feminist Thought on Motherhood, the Motherline, and the Mother-Daughter Relationship." *Mothers and Daughters: Connection, Empowerment, and Transformation.* Edited by Andrea O'Reilly and Sharon Abbey, Rowman & Littlefield, 2000, pp. 143-59.

O'Reilly, Andrea. "In Black and White: Anglo-American and African-American Perspectives on Mothers and Sons." *Mothers and Sons: Feminism, Masculinity, and the Struggle to Raise Our Sons.* Edited by Andrea O'Reilly, Routledge, 2001, pp. 91-118

O'Reilly, Andrea. *From Motherhood to Mothering: The Legacy of Adrienne Rich's Of Woman Born.* SUNY Press, 2004.

O'Reilly, Andrea. *Mothers and Sons: Feminism, Masculinity, and the Struggle to Raise Our Sons.* Routledge, 2001.

Paechter, Carrie F. "Masculine Femininities/Feminine Masculinities: Power, Identities and Gender." *Gender and Education*, vol. 18, no. 3, 2006, pp. 253-63.

Ronel, Natti, and Udi Lebel. "When Parents Lay Their Children to Rest: Between Anger and Forgiveness." *Journal of Social and Personal Relationships*, vol. 23, no. 4, 2006, pp. 507-22.

Sadomba, Frederick, and Gwinyayi Albert Dzinesa. "Identity and Exclusion in the Post-War Era: Zimbabwe's Women Former Freedom Fighters." *Journal of Peacebuilding & Development*, vol. 2, no. 1, 2004, pp. 51-63.

Scheper-Hughes, Nancy, and Margaret M. Lock. "The Mindful Body: A Prolegomenon to Future Work in Medical Anthropology." *Medical Anthropology Quarterly*, vol. 1, no. 1, 1987, pp. 6-41.

Stachowitsch, Saskia. *Gender Ideologies and Military Labor Markets in the U.S.* Taylor & Francis, 2013.

Team, Victoria. "'God Gives Us Sons, but the Government Takes Them Away': Ethiopian Wars and Motherwork." *New Maternalisms: Tales of Motherwork (Dislodging the Unthinkable)*. Edited by Roksana Badruddoja, and Maki Motapanyane, Demeter Press, 2016, pp. 44-65.

The Washington Post Editorial Board. "Opinion: Ethiopia's Leader Won the Nobel Peace Prize. Now He's Accused of War Crimes." *The Washington Post*, 1 Jan. 2021, www.washingtonpost.com/opinions/global-opinions/abiy-ahmed-ethiopia-tigray-invasion/2021/01/27/b5ccd58e-5ff9-11eb-9430-e7c77b5b0297_story.html. Accessed 29 Jan. 2021.

Veale, Angela. *From Child Soldier to Ex-Fighter: Female Fighters, Demobilisation and Reintegration in Ethiopia. Monograph No. 85.* Institute for Security Studies 2003.

Warren, Charlotte. "Care of the Newborn: Community Perceptions and Health Seeking Behavior." *Ethiopian Journal of Health Development*, vol. 24, 2010, pp. 110-14.

White, Aaronette M. "All the Men Are Fighting for Freedom, All the Women Are Mourning Their Men, but Some of Us Carried Guns: A Raced Gendered Analysis of Fanon's Psychological Perspectives on War." *Signs: Journal of Women in Culture and Society*, vol. 32, no. 4, 2007, pp. 857-84.

Wibben, Annick T. R., and Jennifer Turpin. "Women and War." *Stress of War, Conflict and Disaster.* Edited by George Fink, Academic Press, 2010, pp. 358-71.

York, Jodi. "The Truth About Women and Peace." *The Women and War Reader*. Edited by Lois Ann Lorentzen, and Jennifer E. Turpin, New York University Press, 1998, pp. 19-25.

Young, John. *Peasant Revolution in Ethiopia: The Tigray People's Liberation Front, 1975-1991*. Cambridge University Press, 2006..

Zelalem, Zecharias "Starvation Crisis Looms as Aid Groups Seek Urgent Tigray Access. Humanitarians Sound Alarm for Millions of People in Need of Emergency Assistance in Ethiopia's Conflict-Hit Northern Region." 19 Jan. 2021." *Al Jazeera*, www.aljazeera.com/news/2021/1/19/ethiopia-hesitant-to-allow-aid-agencies-into-tigray. Accessed 30 Jan. 2021.

Chapter 8

Empowered through Mothering: Armenian Women's Agency in Trauma and War in Karabakh[1]

Sevan Beukian

Introduction

In a 2018 *Spiegel Magazine* article powerfully titled "A Woman's World in the Caucasus: Nagorno-Karabakh's Grand Experiment," Fiona Ehlers claims that the culture of women's empowerment is changing, particularly where younger women are taking over powerful government positions. Given that, is it possible to argue that forms of empowerment are developing among Armenian women in Karabakh, even though women are still grounded in their role as mothers? Knar Babayan published an article also in 2018 in Chai Khana[2] that covers the stories of the women attending the Kristapor Ivanyan Military College in Stepanakert, which has been recruiting women through a documentary photography project. While the director of the college does not plan to have women on the front lines of the war, women attending the college aim to do exactly that (Babayan). Babayan claims that after the April 2016 war, the college began to recruit women in its organization more actively. These articles show that more attention is being paid to women in Karabakh as well as the changing gender roles. I argue that there has been a change, but in the way that women are increasingly thinking of the totality of their roles in this traditional, conservative, and heteropatriarchal society.

Most studies on gender dynamics in the post-Soviet (and post-communist) region highlight the high level of inequality between men and women, in which the patriarchal system oppresses women, marginalizes them, and excludes them from the public sphere. The conflicts in the 1990s aggravated these inequalities further by reinforcing patriarchy through a militarization of society and politics because "war deepens already existing deep sexual divisions, emphasizing the male as perpetrator of violence, women as victim" (Cockburn, "Gender Relations" 144). The feminist literature in the past few decades has highlighted the necessity of looking at women's experiences of war and conflict from a gendered perspective of understanding war, security, and peace (Yuval-Davis; Cockburn, *From Where We Stand*; "Gender Relations"; Enloe, *Does Khaki Become You*; *Bananas, Beaches and Bases*; Rubio-Martin; Takseva and Sgoutas). The purpose of this chapter is to engage with such arguments and to show that although the context of war(s) in Karabakh did burden women with the extra care of soldiers (in most cases, their husbands, fathers, and sons)—in addition to the usual care of children—Karabakhi women argue that they are also empowered through their own mothering roles, which is demonstrated through their narratives. This chapter therefore asks the following questions. Is motherhood only a tool of patriarchal and militarized regimes? What can we learn about women's agency from mothering?

The theoretical framework of this chapter will reflect the complexities of this discussion. But one important distinction will be made between motherhood and mothering throughout, which is inspired by Adrienne Rich's seminal work, *Of Woman Born*, in which she shares both her theoretical and experience-based insights into motherhood and mothering. This work is vital to understanding the contrast between "motherhood," as the construction of the patriarchal institution, and the experience of a woman's caring of her children—basically the distinction between the tradition of motherhood and (transmitted) experience of mothering (Rich). This theoretical development shows that mothering must also be looked at as a form of empowerment and resistance by women (O'Reilly, *21st Century Motherhood* 3; *Mother Outlaws*). Therefore, although motherhood is not necessarily separated from the historical and political context of patriarchy, "maternal agency foregrounds the political-social dimension of motherwork" (O'Reilly, *21st Century Motherhood* 14).

Many Western feminists tend to be rightly critical of the conditions of patriarchy and oppression in the context of Global South and of postcommunist countries, but they tend to oversimplify these groups' experiences and perpetuate the notion that women are simply replicating patriarchal structures and mentalities—they are therefore always the victims. While there is some truth to this position, it is important to consider that despite patriarchy and oppression, women's experiences should not just be correlated with passivity or the absence of the capacity to act (Mahmood, "Feminist Theory"; *Politics of Piety*; Collins; O'Reilly, *21st Century Motherhood*; Short et al.). As Marie Porter posits, "mothers use the power that they have and, through their agency develop agentic skills over time" (192). This is the perspective I have also taken in analysing interviews from my conversations with many women in Nagorno-Karabakh (hereafter Karabakh) over the years. As such, the analysis is not about revealing any radical or necessarily visible expressions of feminism in these women's speeches, narratives, or even in their behaviours. Instead, it is important to reflect and think what empowerment could mean in a context of war, trauma, loss, and everyday constant grief (Ziemer; Shahnazarian and Ziemer)—that the context of war may help us think of why women living in these conditions may feel a sense of empowerment. For a nation struggling with war and relative isolation, the condition of women is therefore determined to a certain extent by the limitations within. As such, I invite the reader to think of these Armenian wo-men's mothering as an agency for empowerment in Karabakh through that framework. The agency that emerges from this specific context is defined through a politics of stability, which is ironically defined as a politics of change amid trauma and war, meaning that what is stable is the uncertainty and the change, and as recently witnessed and lived by Karabakhis, the impact of war and loss of home represent the traumatic constant. The situation in Karabakh after the attacks by Azerbaijan with Turkey's support in 2020 further reinforce this position, and more studies of the impact of the recent war would be important to build on this understanding.

Analyzing mothering and motherhood in the context of war and conflict means moving normative mothering (Ruddick) towards "difficult mothering," which is "attributable to the pervasiveness of conflict and/or the threat of violence permeating daily experiences" (Takseva and Sgoutas 7). I build this conception of mothering from a previous work, in which I argue that motherhood in the Armenian context is symbolically tied to femininity and to the essence of being a woman; it is also historically linked to the collective traumatic memory of the Armenian Genocide and the more recent conflict in Karabakh with Azerbaijan as well as the Soviet/post-Soviet transformation (Beukian, "Motherhood as Armenianness"; "Nationalism and Collective Trauma"). I argue that mothering, or maternal agency, for these women represents a gateway towards empowerment and ability to claim some recognition. I also conclude that mothering as a form of subjective agency for women can materialize into a conception of motherhood that (silently or subtly) counters patriarchal motherhood narratives. As Collins powerfully argues, Black women in the United States view "motherhood as a symbol of power and the activist mothering it might engender as an enduring theme that *politicizes* Black women" (194). Western feminism often fails to grasp the complexities of motherhood in Black families and communities, as it fails to recognize the ways in which mothering is an important space for women's agency and sense of empowerment.

The word "feminism" is taboo in Karabakh, and even younger women often distance themselves from the term, including in everyday conversations. However, I believe that as feminist scholars and researchers who value women's experiences, it is precisely our responsibility to listen and decipher these acts of empowerment and agency (see Beukian, "Motherhood as Armenianness"). Although most Karabakhi women do not see their role as countering the patriarchal system or advocating emancipatory politics as resistance and although the differing political context necessitates flexibility in thought, it is the way in which Collins reclaims mothering (she uses the term "motherhood") from white Western feminism that interests me most in this chapter's discussion. I turn to Saba Mahmood's ground-breaking ideas around agency that have been important in thinking of feminist agency outside of Western traditions and especially outside the predominantly liberal perspectives. Her contribution to agency comes from her deeper and critical reflection on and analysis of agency in nonliberal and non-Western traditions, which will help me understand the complexities of Karabakhi women's agency through mothering. In *Politics of Piety*, Mahmood states the following:

> The meaning of agency must be explored within the grammar of concepts within which it resides....we should keep the meaning of agency open and allow it to emerge from "within semantic and institutional networks that define and make possible particular ways of relating to people, things, and oneself" (T. Asad 2003, 78). This is why I have maintained that the concept of agency should be delinked from the goals of progressive politics, a tethering that has often led to the incarceration of the notion of agency within the trope of resistance against oppressive and dominating operations of power. (34)

The concepts Mahmood works with are embedded in the liberal theory that links realizing of self with individual will, and which therefore puts agency in opposition to emancipatory politics ("Feminist Theory" 208; *Politics of Piety* 34). Instead, inspired by Butler's Foucauldian perspective, Mahmood invites us to think of agency "as a capacity for action that specific relations of *subordination* create and enable," meaning that agency needs to be understood through culturally and historically specific contexts ("Feminist Theory" 210, 223). This conception of agency is relevant in the case of Armenian Karabakhi women's agency and mothering as "agential capacity [that] is entailed not only in those acts that result in (progressive) change but also those that aim toward continuity, stasis, and stability" (Mahmood "Feminist Theory" 212). As such, this chapter situates Karabakhi women's agency as resistance based on Mahmood's conception of "subverting the hegemonic meanings of cultural practices and re-deploying them for their own interests and agendas." (205)

Women engage and interact with the social and international/regional context in their everyday discussions and behaviours. In those nuanced ways, women are able to confront the system of patriarchy without necessarily organizing a movement against it, as this is not yet the case, but by giving subjective meaning to their actions in the Weberian sense. As such, through shedding light on the standpoint of mothering experiences from Armenian Karabakhi women's perspective, we can make feminist inquiries to more insightfully reflect their experiences.

In my research I noticed an important space where this nuanced strategy of challenging the status quo exists. The 1992–1994 war had an impact on the collective consciousness of Karabakh, and women bore a significant brunt of this, as they were fulfilling their roles not only as caretakers and protectors of their children but also as fighters, healers, and carers of the nation. As such, discussions of women's roles cannot be detached from the context of war, trauma, and collective memory (Beukian, "Motherhood as Armenianness"; Beukian and Graff-McRae; Ziemer).

Performing and Experiencing Motherhood in Karabakh

Karabakh, or Artsakh for Armenians, is a mountainous area located in the South Caucasus region between Armenia and Azerbaijan and has been a de facto independent state since 1994, after a ceasefire was signed to halt the war. Armenians have lived on the land for many centuries, and the colonial Soviet historical context is important to understand the self-determination claims of the Indigenous Armenian population (Beukian, Constructing the Post-Soviet). A renewed conflict occurred in April 2016 at the Line of Contact, and it has come to be termed the 2016 Four Day War or April War. While it lasted for a short period, the impact was palpable for many Karabakhi Armenians, especially in the villages and cities close to the Line of Contact, where the attacks were felt, heard and witnessed.

Increasingly, for the past decade or so, more women have been appointed and elected to positions of leadership in Karabakh, whether in government, political parties, or nongovernmental organizations. Out of the eleven ministers in the Karabakh cabinet in 2016, two were women. There were no women mayors (and only one deputy mayor) in 2016, but thirteen women (and 203 men) were elected as chiefs of villages in the seven regions of Karabakh,[3] which has 322 villages in total, according to the government website.[4] Some of the women I interviewed were eager to share information on their leadership skills and how they were able to serve as leaders within the villages, thus bringing change and improvement to people who live under difficult conditions, especially in the villages close to the 200-km Line of Contact. This raised several questions about women's roles and led to the fieldwork I conducted in 2016, which was part of a project that included interviews in both Armenia and Karabakh.[5] Interviewing the women in their village homes and in the capital city of Stepanakert—in addition to speaking to women in positions of power in government and nongovernmental organizations, as well as having several informal conversations with women from various cities and villages around Stepanakert over the years (since 2006)—provided me with a deeper understanding of the gender dynamics and the ways in which constructions of femininity and masculinity shape gender issues in a heteropatriarchal and militarized context.

The concept of motherhood in contemporary Armenian politics is constructed to maintain a heteropatriarchal discursive power in order to control women's bodies and expressions: women are the mothers of the nation and men are the fighters. Although men are supposed to care for their families, this is mostly expressed in terms of masculine protection of the home; men are not expected to express emotions that hint at love and gentle caring, which are considered to be too feminine. This context is further aggravated through the history of colonialism (Soviet Union) and the Genocide in 1915. Genocide in the Armenian national collective memory represents a disruption of identity, continuity of culture, and of its transmission from mother to child. Although the latter is often absent in discussions of memory, a few scholars have pointed out the views of Armenian women and feminists in the nation's history and contemporary contexts (Ekmekçioğlu; Zeitlian; Attarian; Beukian, "Motherhood as Armenianness"). In addition to disrupting the transmission of mothering experiences from mother to daughter, the Soviet colonial period attempted to modernize these mothering practices by pushing the women into the labour force and shifting much of the responsibility of mothering from women to the state and the colonial empire through state established bodies known as Zhenotdel (or Kinbazhin, see Matossian; Lapidus).

Feminists in the Western context in the 1960s and 1970s took a critical stance against the biological determinism of motherhood in order to counter what Adrienne Rich has called "the oppressive institution of motherhood." For various communities of colour, any feminism that calls for a strict distinction between a woman's rights and freedoms and her mothering role was not a useful distinction, nor does it make sense to many women in the Global South. Black feminists such as Angela Davis argue that for many African American women, "giving birth, when a woman's community is threatened with extinction by a racist government, is an act fraught with political significance.... Giving birth ... can be one of the most meaningful actions in the life of a woman who is denied most other meaningful opportunities." (Davis qtd. in Acholonu 84). Catherine Acholonu also counters some Western feminists' antimothering stances and their rhetoric that rejects the role of mother—a viewpoint that does not fit the social conditions experienced by Hispanic and Black mothers in the Western context, for example (83-85). Despite the commonalities embedded in the experience of mothering—such as pregnancy, nurturing, caring—the image of the mother is weighed down by orientalism's rhetoric, which often differentiates between white and non-white mothers across and within the global North and South (Craddock; Acholonu; Joseph; Mann; Zeitlian; Beukian, "Motherhood as Armenianness"). Karabakhi women's experiences of mothering are therefore positioned in response to orientalism, contrasting the European and/or Russian woman and mother to the Armenian (see Beukian, "Motherhood as Armenianness"). As such, the larger global and feminist discourses of mothering should also be understood through the continuation of orientalist and colonialist Western perceptions that derogate the lives of women in the Global South, who are often the first victims of such notions of saviour (Abu-Lughod).

Therefore, for the Armenian Karabakhi women who lived and survived the war of 1992–1994 and 2016, even under conditions of patriarchy and militarism, agency is an important angle through which to understand their lived experiences and avoid oversimplifying their responses via a Western feminist lens. Listening to women opens the possibilities for more clarity around women's everyday resistance through their mothering and motherwork (Badruddoja and Motapanyane; Porter; O'Reilly, *21st Century Motherhood*; Johnson). This chapter argues that Armenian mothers felt empowered through saving, nurturing, educating, and feeding their children and their families as well as soldiers in the aftermath of conflict. Women also played the role of healers and "psychologists" to their husbands who had fought or were involved in some way during the war of the 1990s and the recent one in 2016 (Beukian, "Motherhood as Armenianness"). Similar to the attentiveness of Mahmood in her work with Muslim women in Egypt and their conception of piety, I adhere to her highly reflexive research that accents women's standpoint with "a logic that inheres not in the intentionality of the actors, but in the relationships that are articulated between words, concepts, and practices that constitute a particular discursive tradition" (*Politics of Piety* 17) and that understands "women's subordination to feminine virtues, such as shyness, modesty, and humility ... [as a] necessary condition for their enhanced public role in religious and political life" (*Politics of Piety* 6). As mentioned in the introduction of this chapter, I am not insisting on the definition of agency in terms of the usually conceived politics of liberal feminism that may be prescriptive—often conceived as (individual) autonomy and freedom or emancipation from oppression. Instead, I want this to be the beginning of a project where I listen and learn from the discourses on agency that are embedded within the system of power structures that are producing the subordination, resistance and agency of women because such a conceptualization "sharply limits our ability to understand and interrogate the lives of women whose desire, affect, and will have been shaped by nonliberal traditions" (Mahmood, "Feminist Theory" 203). In this sense, upon first observation, all these factors can easily be labelled as the patriarchal submission of women in the system; however, in that social and political context, Mahmood astutely demonstrates how these same patriarchal features are also what provide women's agency.

Such a conception of agency allows a moving away from prescriptive notions of emancipation and liberation of an autonomous individual to a notion of agency that is embedded in a constant making towards a futurity, shaped by the specific historical and discursive constructions of a social and political context. Agency as a capacity to act provides a unique lens to explore the way in which Karabakhi women express their place in the national context of a patriarchal and militarized society. Karabakhi women perform their agentic mothering through their caring and nurturing as well as their actively being mothers. The women I interviewed and had conversations with did not engage with my questions on gender; instead, they claimed that men and women are the same and insisted on claiming their roles as the caretakers of not only the children but also the soldiers and by extension, the nation. Women in positions of power, including the heads of villages or government officials, understood their roles well and proudly expressed the achievements they had attained as women and as mothers of the nation of Karabakhi Armenians. At the same time, they did not claim superiority in their roles or emancipatory politics. In the face of oppression, agentic mothering for Karabakhi Armenian women can be seen as the capacity to act and claim an active role through the performance of the mothering roles of taking care of the nation—its children and its soldiers.

Motherhood in the Armenian National Imagining: Trauma and Empowerment

Victoria Rowe has looked at how Armenian literature portrays motherhood as central to Armenian women in the Armenian nation and in Karabakh: "The Armenian mother was conceptualized as the creator of the Armenian nation and defender of Armenian culture through her raising of children…. The ideological connection between the Armenian mother and the nation has a discernible genealogy in Armenian intellectual history" (Rowe 189). The genealogy is further cemented through a history of trauma, the separation of families, massacres, wars, forced exile, and destruction (Beukian, "Motherhood as Armenianness"; "Nationalism and Collective Trauma"). Memories of motherhood are disrupted in familial narratives as a consequence of the Armenian Genocide, Sovietization/modernization, and the more recent wars with Azerbaijan. Armenian women have therefore tended to favour the nation, the collective identity, over their own struggles for their own rights. But this does not mean that counternarratives are completely absent or that feminist struggles are impossible or non-existent. This dynamic also attests to the important distinction between motherhood and mothering as well as the importance of crafting an agentic mothering based on the particular history of these women.

The family is an important unit for Armenians. The mother is considered the hearth (odjakh) of the home, as she selflessly supports her husband and takes care of the home (Beukian, "Motherhood as Armenianness").[6] Sacrificing and nurturing, caring for her children, and living her maternal role are central attributes for Armenian women; the household remains traditionally heteropatriarchal in structure, as the man's role is the breadwinner and protector of the family (Matossian). Families are multigenerational, and Armenian motherhood constructions are often perceived to be a unique attribute for Armenian women, which has been part of the retraditionalization of post-socialist societies (Beukian, "Motherhood as Armenianness"; Zhurzhenko). The Armenian family structure in many ways sets up the role of the Armenian mother; the bride, who often moves to her husband's home, is expected to obey her mother-in-law and give birth as soon as possible. There is also a strong preference to have baby boys; Armenia was ranked third country in the world, after China and Azerbaijan, for the rate of selective abortions, with over 1,400 female births aborted (Moore). Sex-selective abortions and the strong preference for boys in Armenia are also problems in other areas of the South Caucasus region, which were also hit hard by the post-Soviet transition and the wars that followed. The outmigration of men in larger numbers than women has determined the value of the man in their ability to earn and sustain the family economically (Abrahamyan and Mielnikiewicz). However, this has also shifted the role of the woman within her family, making her sometimes the primary caretaker, even financially, as some men have abandoned their families and have remarried abroad without officially divorcing their wives in Armenia.

Within the Armenian nation, which is perceived often as a nation-family, the boundaries between the public sphere and the private one often blur: "The expectations of private spaces like the household extend out into larger private and public spaces—into residential buildings, neighbourhoods, yards, the city, and the country" (Shirinian 69). Being an Armenian woman is perceived through the understanding of motherhood: A woman wants to have children and that is precisely what is thought to be uniquely Armenian as reflected by some of my interviewees. Women in Karabakh often explicitly construct Armenian mothers as different from Russian or European mothers, for example, especially perhaps within the context of a historical memory of trauma (i.e., the Armenian Genocide of 1915), which has been transposed into the contemporary context of war (Beukian, "Motherhood as Armenianness"). For many women in Karabakh, becoming a mother is an important and meaningful action, which asserts her place in society and fulfils her in a heavily militarized social context.[7]

The cost of not conforming to the expectations of femininity or departing too much from state ideology and politics is high and often reflected in a woman's marginalization, even if she actively contributed to the war effort (Shahnazarian). Therefore, I want to emphasize here the necessity of reading not only the words but also the way women tell their stories, what they say or do not say. Their silences can be understood as both resistance and subjugation (Altinay and Peto). This was my approach during interviews, as I used a standpoint methodological approach to reinforce the women's own words and oral history (Attarian). My conclusion is that these women experienced a lot of silencing even as they discussed their roles and contributions; they wanted to talk about their roles without stressing gender because they felt they would be labelled a "feminist" or that they would be perceived as talking negatively about their men—the soldiers. It is precisely the way the women I interviewed spoke about their roles as active participants in the political field that stood out to me, as they did not differentiate themselves from men in that regard; in stronger terms, their ability to be mothers, have a successful career, and earn money puts their capacity as nation builders perhaps even above that of men in this context.

Armenian Mothering as Agency

In my conversations and interviews with women in Karabakh (and Armenia), they did not merely share their understanding of motherhood; they also talked with great nuance about how their mothering experiences and agency were important for their self-realization and self-understanding, despite the fact that they were not always explicitly critical of the institution of motherhood. A woman in a high political position in the government, at the time of interview, explained to me how postwar rehabilitation and adaptation became the burden of the woman, as she was helping a soldier transition to his normal civilian life and to reintegrate into society. Her words conveyed how important motherhood is to assert Armenian identity, but I also noted how much of her own and her relatives' experiences of mothering during the war and especially after were an important part of women's self-identification as mothers. She narrated the experience of her mother-in-law and many of her relatives, and through that she was able to identify with the mother who protects, struggles, and carries her family on her shoulders during and in the aftermath of the conflict. As she put it:

The men had a difficult time adjusting to peace after the war. The readaptation was difficult; their morale had changed. (Some had lost their friends at war in their arms.) Their psychological status needed to be lifted and that required a lot of effort. That effort was taken on by women, who played an important role in that. Women are the educators in schools in Armenia it seems. And that gives a specific role to women, as if the men can take a more physical and protective role, and women can do more caring, teaching the children, raising them. So the role of women in child education and rearing is extremely valuable. (Personal interview, conducted by Beukian, 2011)

Some of my interviewees, especially the younger ones, wanted to explain how their success had not impacted their desire and capacity to be good mothers. A woman in a very high position in the government clearly articulated this sentiment when she explained the following:

You know, I never prioritized my career development.... I saw your child, and I was very happy because to me as well, in life the most important thing I believe, for every woman the most significant mission [arakelutiun] is to be a mother ... and the child to be valuable [liarjek] in the family. And in all circumstances the woman is given the grace [shnorh] to become a mother, so she should become one. So I cannot say that I sought after having a good career, but it just happened that it was so. (Personal interview, conducted by Beukian, 2016)

This politician was in her early forties, and she already had a successful career in government, being appointed as a minister in Karabakh prior to her position at the time of interview. Her words could be read through a patriarchal lens as the words of a woman who has accepted the image of the patriarchal mother and who emphasizes her role and achievements as a mother first. And although I agree with this interpretation to a certain extent, I want to propose that this same situation could also be read through a woman feeling agentic by reiterating her powerful role as a mother that does not distract from her position as a successful woman. She did not shy away from stating her achievements and accomplishments, which was similar to many of the women I spoke to. There is a deeper and more complex meaning to be understood from her words than a narrative of patriarchy that identifies a woman's actions and words as merely submissive. As such, it is important to also understand some of the ways women speak about their roles and place in society, and embracing femininity especially in the role of mothering can be the important precondition for accessing those public roles. (Mahmood, *Politics of Piety* 6).

Similarly building on the context, and in line with Nadera Shalhoub -Kevorkian's analysis of Palestinian women, Karabakhi women's self-perception should not be analysed without a strong consideration of the intersection between the militaristic state and the trauma inflicted due to the length of the war, the uncertainty of the ceasefire, and the culture of social patriarchy, as presented in the previous section. The conditions of oppression, colonialism, and war present challenges but also shape women's discourses because "the machinery of oppression turns women's bodies, their sexuality and minds, into symbols of heroism, victimization, helplessness, and identity, and ultimately creates them as boundary markers" (Shalhoub-Kevorkian 2). Although the context of settler colonialism affects Palestinian women differently, Armenian women face both a global context of marginalization and local militarization that requires their conformity to fight both global orientalism and regional militarism.

Unlike Shalhoub-Kevorkian's interviews in which women were honest about their positions at home, their suffering in the patriarchal system, and their constant struggle against the oppression and violence they face from the state of Israel, women in Karabakh did not always express their frustration and discontent with me, and in some cases, they did not see their position as unequal to that of men. Although there are some exceptions, for example one of my interviewees—who had lost her brothers and father to the war and who had herself used weapons to kill the enemy and avenge her relatives' deaths—became more open after several conversations about the domestic abuse she faced in her household and the way the state treated her. She was also critical of the way some Armenian men treat their wives and told me how great it was that my husband was taking care of our son while I was away on this trip with my baby daughter. Some of the interviewees also openly pointed out—in response to how the war might have impacted women's status in the home, especially in relation to domestic violence—that women were perhaps doing better during the war, given the fact that men were away fighting and women's situation would later become more problematic after the war for various reasons. As the head of a woman's organization in Karabakh told me, women in most cases do not reflect on their problems as more important than the overall tense situation in Karabakh (Personal interview, conducted by Beukian, 2016). However, in some cases, women did share about their experiences with their husband's domestic violence that was inflicted on them and this had been present before the war and became worse after. As such, it is clear that "in the post-conflict society, the role of women had focused not just on caring for their families, putting food on the table, and educating their children, but also on the role of psychologists who were to help their husbands' transition from the war to their lives as fathers and husbands" (Beukian, "Motherhood as Armenianness" 258).

My understanding from the fieldwork and time spent in Karabakh is that women usually do not openly express their dissatisfaction with patriarchal oppression, although many "kitchen talks" over coffee revealed a lot more about the unequal gender dynamics within the household and those related to childcare responsibilities. At the same time, women felt strength in their role as the caretaker of these soldiers (i.e., war veterans), and talked about their role with a sense of pride as evidenced in the interviews: In these instances, women felt empowered in their role and their ability to hold the family together, yet these conversations also reveal the ways in which masculinity can impose on womens great emotional labour, which is often unrecognized. Such notions of masculinity also inhibit women's ability to express their subjection to domestic violence. It seems that focusing on their powerful roles within their families gives them a sense of empower-ment, and it is difficult to take that away from them. But it is also through such narratives of caring and loving that women feel empow-ered through their agentic mothering.

In most cases when I asked women about their roles as women, they preferred to talk about their achievement as political leaders, village chiefs, and their positions at work. They talked about their achieve-ments with pride and enthusiasm, which is reflective of how much they focused on their actions—their subjective agency and mothering agency.

An active woman in the area of Martakert in Karabakh was outspoken about how much women continue to contribute to the nation and how she, as a medical doctor, had been actively engaged during the war in the 1990s and again in 2016, especially since Martakert was strongly affected during the shelling, as it was located less than three kilometres away from the Line of Contact with Azerbaijan. This woman shared her experiences from the 2016 war with me:

As a doctor, I can say that from the very first day, I took part in all operations, in the first war of Karabakh [1992–1994] and the Four Day war. In the last war, I did not go home. I was at the hospital day and night. All the images you witnessed in the news about the war [she mentioned Kayram Sloyan].[8] When the corpses of the dead were brought, I was the one who first witnessed the bodies. The principal doctors on site were busy with other business, and I asked them to expose the bodies in order to register the deaths, and I realized they were decapitated. In the first war, I saw many bodies and corpses; actually I was one of the first to see them, our men who sacrificed [mer dgherke]. In 1992, I participated actively in the war; then I was in emergency assistance, then on the first front, Noratagh, Alashan, Shenteradz, Stepanakert. (Personal interview, conducted by Beukian, 2016)

It is in line with this type of thinking that many women expressed their own success and their duty to participate as caretakers through agentic mothering. Two women who were part of a nongovernmental organization in a region of Karabakh explained the following in our interview (they spoke simultaneously, while inserting personal narratives, and I kept their response together):

We were very active in civil society. We are Karabakhis. We are not like any other nation. The situation calls for this, with all equality with the men we do what is needed. Women's participation is necessary. It is an issue of consciousness..... We always visit the soldiers on the Line of Contact ... we take gifts with us. We take students for a visit.... I go during their lunch. I know when their lunch time is. They call me Auntie and [the soldiers] know I am there." (Personal interview, conducted by Beukian, 2016)

Through these acts of mothering—caring for the soldiers with food and attention—these women feel they have made a strong contribution to the nation and just in the sense of the pride and accomplishment these roles give them. They also repeatedly stressed that there was no difference between women's and men's participation. Women, they insisted, must act out of necessity and duty under the conditions of war. Beyond their caring roles, they also felt pride when they took over men's work. For example, one of the women I spoke to highlighted how much she had done to reconstruct the school and fix windows and fences after the war, which had destroyed the school in the Martakert region due to its proximity to the Line of Contact with Azerbaijan. She powerfully stated that she had rebuilt the walls and windows of the school herself with the help of some men (Personal interview, conducted by Beukian, 2016). These women stressed their equality with men rather than emphasising the burdens they felt as women. How these women constructed themselves as having agency should not be dismissed out of hand, as would be the case if we only viewed their narratives through the Western feminist lenses of emancipation and resistance against oppression. By taking the women's constructions seriously, we avoid defining agency only through the narrow lenses of fighting against oppression. The women saw their own situation as more complex than Western feminists' perspectives would allow.

Most of the women I interviewed emphasized the specific context of a postconflict society, in which women had to inevitably become part of public life and were recruited in various positions, including more senior positions, such as ministers, after the ceasefire. But in their explanation of their duty to the nation, some women talked about their mothering and their caring of children as roles that afford them a sense of pride and feelings of empowerment. A woman I interviewed described how she had played an important role in getting children out of Karabakh during the war in the 1990s; she kept them in a facility, where she fed and housed them, with some help from other Karabakhis and Armenians, until the situation was calmer and their parents could come and retrieve their children. In some cases, women fully understood and recognized the sacrifice and role they played, as one of my interviewees who ran a childcare facility at the time of interview explained:

The majority of women became widows during the war, and they had to take over the responsibility of the whole family. They played the roles of the father and mother. And this also strengthened the woman. But there is also another side to the story. In my view, I do not think the woman is the weaker side of society. The woman is a very strong being, a solid being [bind, amur]. And she is more trustworthy. In 1988, when the OMON[9] was standing against us, the collective Armenian struggle was saying, "women first." This has several interpretations/reasons. Perhaps the OMON would not shoot because they would see the women approaching. Or perhaps because women are stronger beings, I do not know, but it has always been like that. Well, this also played a role to empower women, to make women believe that they are strong and capable. (Personal interview, conducted by Beukian, 2016)

Indeed, the OMON was used as a mechanism of repression, As Erica Marat explains: "the mere sight of OMON forces arriving at a protest is sufficient to discourage protestors from taking more aggressive action. At various times in Ukraine, Azerbaijan, Armenia, Russia, OMON have been at the forefront of containing protests" (57-58).

Conclusion

Mothering is a powerful self-identification tool for women because it is through caring roles and fulfilling their femininity that women become the sacralized keepers of the hearth and guardians of memories. Their experiences and memories of war, fighting, caring for the children, feeding the children and soldiers, even healing their men after the end of the war, provided these women feelings of empowerment through their ability to tell their stories and share them with others. Women expressed a certain sense of pride— not masculine arrogance—as they told the stories about their election in the villages, their participation in the frontline and their defence of their own villages and towns, as well as their successful careers and high positions. The realities of societies in transitioning contexts, or in wars, include differences that need to be investigated outside the tight boundaries of liberal feminism in order to understand the much more local and authentic expressions of feminism that exist in those contexts.

The chapter contributes to the literature on feminist mothering as well as agency and empowerment in a specific context. Its main focus has been the experience of Armenian women the way they explained how they felt, what they did, and how they position their own roles in society. These women emphasized their own contributions to the nation and their communities. The context, therefore, is important in order to evaluate more carefully women's agency in discussing their roles as mothers or caretakers in society. These women cared for their own children, the children as well as the soldiers on the frontline, who were often very young. Their caretaking roles were not limited to cooking and caring for the wounded, as their caretaking could also be seen in their work as doctors and fighters on the frontline.

As such, I conclude this chapter with the words of Andrea O'Reilly and Marie Porter on motherhood and power: "The mothers recognise oppression and the constraints upon them, but have responded with an agency that is based on resistance, strength and endurance, and the value they place on their need to nurture their children as well as possible" (16). I add here that it was not just nurturing children but also caring for younger soldiers that became part of the Armenian women's extended mothering practices. Women in Karabakh consciously and perhaps sometimes silently recognise their oppression and the constraints that restrict their freedom as women in a patriarchal society at war. However, they see these specifically through the construction of Armenianness within the context of trauma, war, as well as economic and political uncertainty (especially in a unrecognized state), where war and military aggression by Azerbaijan (and Turkey) are daily threats, especially after 2020. Despite these social and political realities, or perhaps because of them, talking about women's rights and adopting an inclusive approach to women in the discussion of peace and political reconstruction is especially vital for a transformative politics within the nation and the region.

Endnotes

1. On September 27, 2020, Azerbaijan attacked Nagorno-Karabakh, with Turkey's support and the mobilization of Syrian mercenaries (Berberian; Cookman). This chapter was written and finalized in the summer of 2020 before this devastating war. It is dedicated to all victims of this conflict who lost their lives in this war and those

who had to leave all their belongings and homes behind after the Russian-brokered ceasefire was put into effect on November 10, 2020. I also dedicate this chapter to all the women in Karabakh and Armenia who have given so much of themselves to their communities and to the nation. Nationalist discourses in times of war reinforce patriarchy and militarism and overshadow possibilities for critical discussions about nationalism and in this case about the Armenian nation and its diaspora. I continue to write about these topics in hope that we can be critical towards ourselves and our beliefs. I write to also support feminist antiwar calls that focus on human lives and peaceful living in a multiethnic region (see the statement by Sev Bibar). I am very grateful to Tólá Olú Pearce and Andrea Moraes for their valuable work on this manuscript. I want to especially thank Tolá for her thoughtful input in the editing process to sharpen my argument. All Armenian to English translations are my own.

2. *Chai Khana*, or tea house as it literally translates to, is an online platform led by women, and aims to "give voice to the underrepresented across the region, amplifying their voices though the dynamic human-focused storytelling, while providing mentorship to young journalists." It publishes articles on various topics about the Caucasus region. See their website: chai-khana.org/en/about.

3. In addition, there was only one female deputy mayor (out of four) and just two female council members among twenty-three in 2016. In the Hadrout province, there were four women village chiefs, three in Martakert, two in Shahumyan, one in Shushi, and three in Qashatagh, for more information see Artsakh Republic National Statistical Services.

4. On the presidential website of the Artsakh Republic, which officially changed its name from Nagorno-Karabakh Republic in 2017, officials state that there are 322 villages in the seven regions, www.president.nkr.am/en/nkr/statePower/. Accessed on April 1, 2019.

5. This project began in 2011, when I went to Karabakh to interview several politicians, academics, and journalists for a different research project, including the question of women in power and their recollection of the war. Interviews were conducted in Eastern Armenian, and I translated them to English in the transcription process. In 2016, I went to Karabakh after the April 2016 Four Day

or April War to understand the impact the conflict had on women. This project was a collaboration with my colleague Nona Shahnazarian, an associate researcher at the National Academy of Sciences of Armenia in Yerevan. We conducted most of the interviews together, and we also did some independently during the same trip and on different occasions. This project received funding from the University of Southern California, Dornsife Institute for Armenian Studies in 2016. The situation has changed radically for the people of Karabakh since the writing of this chapter. Many of my friends and their families and relatives have now lost their homes or have been displaced from their lands due to the attacks by Azerbaijan and with Turkey's support of Armenia that began in September 2020 and ended with a Russian-brokered ceasefire effective November 10, 2020.

6. My own experience of carrying my child in the Karabakhi fieldwork context provided me access to various homes and discussions (often not recorded) that would otherwise perhaps not have occurred. My womanhood and Armeniannness were practiced at their peak—a career-oriented woman, who carries her baby with her and, thus, performs her duty of Armenian femininity through motherhood. This also shielded me from being perceived as a single woman without a male guardian in taxi cabs and public marshrutkas for eight-hour journeys with often a majority of (or only) male passengers. (This was especially my experience with taxi rides from Stepanakert to Yerevan.) The 2016 experience of travelling to do fieldwork with my baby was significantly different from my previous one travelling alone as a woman in Karabakh, with no male guardian accompanying me. The complexities of the interviews and the travels are also contextualized with my diasporan identity navigating between my Lebanese and Canadian nationalities.

7. There are generational differences among women, as the younger generation has challenged some of the patriarchal mothering practices or values. These will be important to follow in order to contrast with the previous generation's mothering practices and beliefs.

8. For more reference on the violence that was committed against the Armenian soldiers, see the following: www.azatutyun.am/a/276657 37.html and www.evnreport.com/spotlight-karabakh/war-crimes-

in-spring. In addition, see the news coverage of some of the events of the 2016 war between Karabakh and Azerbaijan as presented by the BBC: www.bbc.com/news/world-europe-35953916.

9. OMON stands for Otryad Militsii Osobogo Naznacheniya in Russian, which was the special police detachment troops that were often used to repress protests.

Works Cited

Abrahamyan, Gayane and Justyna Mielnikiewicz. "Armenia: A Woman's World in One Mountain Village," *Eurasianet*, 7 May 2011, eurasianet.org/armenia-a-womans-world-in-one-mountain-village. Accessed 6 June 2017.

Abu-Lughod, Lila. *Do Muslim Women Need Saving?* Harvard University Press, 2013.

Acholonu, Catherine Obianuju. *Motherism: The Afrocentric Alternative to Feminism*. Women in Environmental Development Series and Nigerian Institute of International Affairs, Vol. 3, 1995.

Altınay, Ayşe Gül, and Andrea Pető. "Introduction: Uncomfortable Connections: Gender, Memory, War." *Gendered Wars, Gendered Memories: Feminist Conversations on War, Genocide and Political Violence*. Edited by Ayşe Gül Altınay and Andrea Pető, Routledge, 2016, pp. 1-22.

Artsakh Republic National Statistical Services, "Women and Men in Artsakh: Statistical Booklet 2017," *Artsakh Republic*, stat-nkr.am/hy/2010-11-24-11-24-22/793--2017. Accessed on 1 June 2018.

Attarian, Hourig. "Narrating Women's Bodies: Storying Silences and Secrets in the Aftermath of Genocide." *Gendered Wars, Gendered Memories: Feminist Conversations on War, Genocide and Political Violence*. Edited by Ayşe Gül Altınay and Andrea Pető, Routledge, 2016, pp. 257-69.

Babayan, Knar. "Nagorno Karabakh, Women, and Seasonal Work," *Chai Khana*, 25 Dec. 2018, chai-khana.org/en/nagorno-karabakh-women-and-seasonal-work. Accessed 6 June 2017.

Badruddoja, Roksana and Maki Motapanyane, editors. *New Maternalisms: Tales of Motherwork (Dislodging the Unthinkable)*. Demeter Press, 2016.

Berberian, Vicken. "Captive of the Caucasus: The Long War Over Nagorno-Karabakh: How a Little Understood War between Azerbaijan and Armenia Threatens Democracy." *The Nation*, 8 Dec. 2020, www.thenation.com/article/world/armenia-war-nagorno-karabakh/. Accessed 8 Dec. 2020.

Beukian, Sevan. "Motherhood as Armenianness: Expressions of Femininity in the Making of Armenian National Identity." *Studies in Ethnicity and Nationalism*, vol. 14, no. 2, 2014, pp. 247-69.

Beukian, Sevan. *Constructing the Post-Soviet Armenian National Habitus: The Armenian Genocide and Contested Imaginations of Armenianness.* 2015. University of Alberta, PhD Dissertation.

Beukian, Sevan. "Nationalism and Collective Trauma." *State of Nationalism Project.* Edited by Robert Schertzer and Eric Woods, 2018, stateofnationalism.eu/article/nationalism-and-collective-trauma/. Accessed 6 June 2019.

Beukian, Sevan, and Rebecca Graff-McRae. "Trauma Stories as Resilience in Armenian and Irish National Identity," *Studi irlandesi: A Journal of Irish Studies,* Special issue: *Daredevils of History? Resilience in Armenia and Ireland,* no. 8, 2018, pp. 157-88.

Cockburn, Cynthia. *From Where We Stand: War, Women's Activism and Feminist Analysis.* Zed Books, 2007.

Cockburn, Cynthia. "Gender Relations as Causal in Militarization and War." *International Feminist Journal of Politics*, vol. 12, no. 2, 2010, pp. 139-57.

Collins, Patricia Hill. *Black Feminist Thought: Knowledge, Consciousness and the Politics of Empowerment.* Routledge, 1990.

Cookman, Liz, "Syrians Make Up Turkey's Proxy Army in Nagorno-Karabakh." *Foreign Policy,* 5 Oct. 2020, foreignpolicy.com/2020/10/05/nagorno-karabakh-syrians-turkey-armenia-azerbaijan/. Accessed 5 Oct. 2020.

Craddock, Karen T., editor. *Black Motherhood(s): Contours, Contexts and Considerations.* Demeter Press, 2015.

Ehlers, Fiona. "A Woman's World in the Caucasus: Nagorno-Karabakh's Grand Experiment." *Spiegel International*, 10 Apr. 2018, www.spiegel.de/international/world/women-take-charge-in-nagorno-karabakh-a-1201390.html. Accessed 20 Apr. 2021.

Ekmekçioğlu, Lerna. "The Biopolitics of "Rescue": Women and the Politics of Inclusion after the Armenian Genocide." *Genocide and Gender in the Twentieth Century: A Comparative Survey.* Edited by Amy E. Randall, Bloomsbury Publishing, 2015, pp. 215-37.

Enloe, Cynthia. *Does Khaki Become You: The Militarization of Women's Lives.* Pandora Press, 1990.

Enloe, Cynthia. *Bananas, Beaches and Bases: Making Feminist Sense of International Politics.* University of California Press, 2000.

EVN Report. "War Ends, What Follows? Live Updates." *EVN Report,* 10 Nov. 2020, www.evnreport.com/spotlight-karabakh/war-ends-what-next-live-updates. Accessed 27 Mar. 2021.

Johnson, Miriam M. *Strong Mothers, Weak Wives: The Search for Gender Equality.* University of California Press, 1988.

Joseph, Suad. "The Public/Private: The Imagined Boundary in the Imagined Nation/State/Community: The Lebanese Case." *Feminist Review,* no. 57, 1997, pp. 73-92.

Lapidus, Gail W. *Women in Soviet Society: Equality, Development, and Social Change.* University of California Press, 1978.

Mahmood, Saba. *Politics of Piety: The Islamic Revival and the Feminist Subject.* Princeton University Press, 2005.

Mahmood, Saba. "Feminist Theory, Embodiment, and the Docile Agent: Some Reflections on the Egyptian Islamic Revival." *Cultural Anthropology,* vol. 16, no. 2, 2001, pp. 202-36.

Mann, Barbara A. *Iroquois Women: The Gantowisas.* Peter Lang Publishers, 2000.

Matossian, Mary K. *The Impact of Soviet Policies in Armenia.* E. J. Brill, 1962.

Marat, Erica. *The Politics of Police Reform: Society Against the State in Post-Soviet Countries.* Oxford University Press, 2018.

Moore, Suzanne. "'We Lose 1,400 Girls a Year. Who Will Our Boys Marry?': Armenia's Quandary." *The Guardian,* 22 Feb. 2018, www.theguardian.com/global-development/2018/feb/22/sex-selection-armenia-quandary. Accessed 10 Jan. 2021.

O'Reilly, Andrea. "Introduction" *21st Century Motherhood: Experience, Identity, Policy, Agency.* Edited by Andrea O'Reilly, Columbia University Press, 2010, pp. 1-20.

O'Reilly, Andrea. *Mother Outlaws: Theories and Practices of Empowered Mothering.* Women's Press, 2004.

O'Reilly, Andrea, and Marie Porter. "Introduction" *Motherhood: Power and Oppression.* Edited by Andrea O'Reilly et al. Women's Press, 2005, pp. 1-22.

Porter, Marie. "Mothering or Motherwork?" *Theorising and Representing Maternal Realities.* Edited by Marie Porter and Julie Kelso, Cambridge Scholars Publishing, 2009, pp. 184-200.

Rich, Adrienne. *Of Woman Born: Motherhood as Experience and Institution.* W.W. Norton & Company, 1976.

Rowe, Victoria. *A History of Armenian Women's Writing: 1880-1922.* Cambridge Scholars Press Ltd., 2003.

Rubio-Martin, Ruth, editor. *What Happened to the Women? Gender and Reparations for Human Rights Violations.* Social Science Research Council, 2006.

Ruddick, Sara. "Maternal Thinking." *Feminist Studies,* vol. 6, 1980, pp. 342-67.

Sev Bibar. "Against War in Qarabağ: Decolonial, Antifascist and Ecofeminist Statement from Armenia", 12 Oct. 2020, telegra.ph/Against-War-in-Qarabag. Accessed 12 Oct. 2020.

Shahnazarian, Nona. "A Return to Tradition? Aspects of Postwar Political Culture in Nagorno-Karabakh". *PONARS Eurasia Policy Memo No. 133,* 2010.

Shahnazarian Nona, and Ulrike Ziemer. "Emotions, Loss and Change: Armenian Women and Post-Socialist Transformations in Nagorny Karabakh." *Caucasus Survey,* vol. 2, no. 1-2, 2014, pp. 27-40.

Shalhoub-Kevorkian, Nadera. *Militarization and Violence Against Women in Conflict Zones in the Middle East: A Palestinian Case-Study.* Cambridge University Press, 2009.

Shirinian, Tamar. "The Nation-Family: Intimate Encounters and Genealogical Perversion in Armenia." *American Ethnologist,* vol. 45, no. 1, 2018, pp. 48-59.

Short, Patricia, et al. *Motherhood: Power and Oppression.* Women's Press, 2005.

Takseva, Tatjana, and Arlene Sgoutas. *Mothers Under Fire: Mothering in Conflict Areas.* Demeter Press, 2015.

Yuval-Davis, Nira. *Gender and Nation*. Sage, 1997.

Zeitlian, Sona. *Hay Knoj Dere Hay Heghapokhagan Sharzhman Mej (The Role of the Armenian Woman in the Armenian Revolutionary Movement)*. Hraztan Sarkis Zeitlian Publications, 1992.

Ziemer, Ulrike. "'The Waiting and Not Knowing Can Be Agonizing': Tracing the Power of Emotions in a Prolonged Conflict in the South Caucasus." *International Feminist Journal of Politics*, vol. 20, no. 3, 2018, pp. 331-49.

Zhurzhenko, Tatiana. "Strong Women, Weak State: Family Politics and Nation Building in Post-Soviet Ukraine." *Post-Soviet Women Encountering Transition: Nation Building, Economic Survival, and Civic Activism*. Edited by Kuehnast, Kathleen and Carol Nechemias, The Johns Hopkins University Press and Woodrow Wilson Center Press, 2014, pp. 23-43.

PART III
POSTCOLONIAL
DEVELOPMENTS

Chapter 9

Kokum-Gikendaasowin[1]: Grandmother Knowledge, Epistemology, and (Re)Generation of Anishinaabeg Malehoods

Renée E. Mazinegiizhigoo-kwe Bédard

The Grandmother's Gifts to Her Grandsons

> This story is in the words of a grandmother's gift to her grandsons.
> It's here, in Naanabozho, who was sent to teach Anishinaabeg about
> life. It's about fathers, sons, and everyone in between. Like many
> journeys, it also begins with an ending. In a place not far from here,
> there lived an old woman, Nookomis.
>
> —James Niigaanwewidam Sinclair 145.

The above quote highlights the beginning of the classic Anishinaabeg[2] tale of Grandmother Nookomis and her grandson Naanabozho, and also offers a compelling story of the subtle linkages between femalehoods and malehoods in Anishinaabeg families, communities, and society.[3] The relationship between grand-mothers and grandsons frequently appears in many Anishinaabeg stories. These relationships are so prevalent in Anishinaabeg narratives that they invite us to explore their constant presence further (McNally 126). In his book, *Honoring Elders*, Michael D. McNally suggests that "at the beginning of many stories, it appears almost as a stock phrase, 'long ago there lived a boy with his grandmother' or an 'old man and old woman lived alone with their child'"(McNally 126). Although these opening scenarios are not necessarily aspiring to be representative of Anishinaabeg social order, they do offer insights into the maternal-centred configurations that position Nookomisag[4] (grandmothers) as significant parental figures, educators, disciplinarians, and mentors to Indigenous malehoods and LGBTQQ2SA+ identities.

This chapter seeks to explore the relevance of the grandmother/grandson narratives as a perspective into Anishinaabeg understandings about the linkages between the two identities as well as the connections between femalehoods informing malehoods (inclusive of LGBTQQ2SA+ individuals) for reasons of holism, health, and wellness. Using the story of Nookomis and Naanabozho, this chapter offers insight into the nature of kokum-gikendaasowin, which translates to "traditional knowledge and epistemological intelligence of the grandmothers."

As an Anishinaabe-kwe (Anishinaabe woman) and an Indigenous feminist, I am particularly interested in the ways grandmother/grandson stories emphasize the role of grandmothers in shaping the lives of Anishinaabeg males as well as LGBTQQ2SA+ people. I focus on the grandmother-grandson relationship present in Anishinaabeg narratives because it highlights an area of research that is under-represented and virtually nonexistent in current scholarship (McNally; Maracle; Buffalohead). There is substantial research on the role of grandmothers in educating female children, youth, and women, but there is limited literary discussion on the nature of grandmothers' roles in educating male as well as LGBTQQ2SA+ children (Simpson; Anderson; Lavell-Harvard and Anderson; Lavell-Harvard and Corbiere; Child; Buffalohead). Fortunately, there is literature written on Anishinaabeg oral narratives related to the grandson-grandmother relationship, which provides evidence of these relational traditions (Johnston; Benton-Banai; Sinclair; Barnouw). The written tales of Naanabozho's upbringing and early childhood antics offer insight into the specific characteristics of these relational traditions used by his grandmother and the overall cultural basis of these female-male relationships in shaping Indigenous malehoods.

Over the past couple of decades, Indigenous maternal scholarship has become a popular area of research. Currently, there is an explosion in Anishinaabe women scholars researching various topics related to femininity, womanhood, maternal culture, birth, midwifery, and maternal intellectual traditions. Furthermore, in the last ten years, the topic of Indigenous malehoods has also seen a surge in scholarship (Anderson et al.; McKegney; Alfred; Lee). However, missing from this discussion are those linkages between these two identities. I seek to draw attention to those points of connection between Indigenous malehoods and femalehoods using the teachings of the kokum-gikendaasowin (epistemology and ontology of the grandmothers) embedded in the story of Nookomis and Naanabozho, which directly reveals the role of grandmothers in shaping Anishinaabe malehoods for the purpose of establishing harmony and accord with femalehoods, thus ensuring a holistic society.

Kwe, Nini, and Niizh-Manidoowag: Anishinaabe Conceptions of Genderhoods

For me, understanding the Anishinaabeg conceptualization of genderhoods begins with our Creation stories because these stories set the theoretical foundation that provides us with the ontological and epistemological contexts (gikenjigaadewin) that enable us to understand and interpret all other dibaajaamowin (teachings, personal stories, histories) and aadizookaanag (sacred stories) that come to us, which are then retold to us in our communities throughout our life. Leanne Simpson states that "we all have a relationship with Creation" (*As We Have Always Done* 121). The Creation stories provide the ontological framework that allows us to situate ourselves within the web and fabric of life on Aki (earth). Furthermore, these sacred stories are the Anishinaabeg-specific contexts necessary to create our ways of being, thinking, relating, and behaving as human beings: malehoods, femalehoods, as well as LGBTQQ2SA+ people. Simpson writes the following: "Our Elders tell us that everything we need to know is encoded in the structure, content and context of these stories and the relationships, ethics, and responsibilities required to *be* our own Creation Story" (Simpson, *Dancing on Our Turtle's Back* 33). To this, Anishinaabe scholar Darren Courchene further adds:

When trying to understand who we are, it is important to review how we came to be known as the *Anishinaabe-Ojibweg*. The term Anishinaabe is a contraction of a string of words—*ani niisayi'iinaabe owe akiing* (a human was lowered onto the earth). This identity term harkens back to our creation story when *Giizhigookwe* (SkyWoman) was lowered onto the earth to bring new life 26).

Courchene explains that each of us embodies the original human being who was lowered onto the earth; this person survived a great flood, created and recreated life, travelled through the four stages of life, and came to understand time, space, and relationships as interrelated aspects of Anishinaabe mino-bimaadiziwin (to live the correct/good way as a human being). Furthermore, as Anishinaabeg who are "lowered onto the earth" we become, "a child of the great Mother [Aki, the earth]. It is in that and with great kindness and humility, with the utmost gentleness, that Anishinaabe touched and met his Mother" (Simpson, *Dancing on Our Turtle's Back* 39).

As gwiiwizensag (young men and boys) and LGBTQQ2SA+ that identify as male or with maleness, the Creation story is important to learn and know because they can situate their identity within the character Ani niisayi'iinaabe (Original Man). Ani, means "from whence"; niisayi'ina translates to "lowered"; and lastly, there is "abe," which refers to "the male of the species" (Benton-Banai, *The Mishomis Book* 3). Anishinaabe Elder Edward Bawdwaywidun Banaise Benton-Banai-ba[5] describes him as follows: "[He was] created in the image of Gitche Manito. He was a natural man. He was part of Mother Earth. He lived in brotherhood with all that was around him.... All tribes came from this Original Man" (Benton-Banai, *The Mishomis Book* 4). Women have a role model in Aki as the first kwe (woman), but men are taught to look to Ani niisayi'iinaabe as a gikinoo'amaaged (teacher or mentor) to understand their place, responsibilities, and gendered identity. The most critical part of the description of his name and nature is the "lowering onto the earth," which Anishinaabe Elder Edna Asinykwe Manitowabi relates as follows:

Original Man was the last to be created. Gzhwe Mnidoo wanted one who would reflect her/his thoughts, and so from the first woman [Aki] s/he took four parts of her body— soil, air, water and fire and molded a being, a vessel. Gzhwe Mnidoo blew his/ her own spirit breath into the being and gave him her/his own thoughts, and these thoughts were so vast that they spilled out of his head into his entire body. Gzhwe Mnidoo touched Original Man's breast causing his heart to beat in harmony with the rhythm of the universe and with Gzhwe Mnidoo. *Gzhwe Mnidoo then lowered him down the Earth so that he might also be a child of the great Mother.* (Simpson, *Dancing on Our Turtle's Back* 39, my emphasis)

Noticeable in the Creation story is the acceptance of gender variances and complexity.

Anishinaabeg males, females, as well as LGBTQQ2SA+ people are all taught to insert themselves into the Creation story (Benton-Banai, "Anishinaabe Creation Story" 30; Simpson, *Dancing on Our Turtle's Back* 41) and thus learn that our genders, all genders, and gender variances are sacred in the eyes of *Gizhew-Manidoo* (the Kind Spirit, the Creator). In this way, each Anishinaabe learns to theorize their own gender identity and affiliation(s) according to their personal preference, gifts, talents, and abilities.

Therefore, the Creation story is strategically used to introduce gender to gwiiwizensag because it "re-affirms that they are good, and beautiful and perfect the way they are.... For just a moment, they are complete in the absence of want" (Simpson, *Dancing on Our Turtle's Back* 41). Whatever malehoods a gwiiwizens identifies as or affiliates with, in that moment of hearing the Creation story, they are whole beings who are unconditionally loved and accepted by their mother the earth. Thus, the Creation story offers specific ontological and epistemological contexts that provide unlimited gender acceptance through the land as mother (or provider and sustainer of gakina-bimaadiziwin [all life]) (Johnston, *Ojibwe Heritage* 23-26; Benton-Banai, *The Mishomis Book* 2-34; Simpson, *Dancing on Our Turtle's Back* 35-44). This sense of unconditional and unrestricted gendered-based relationality with the land also offers freedom from judgment, restrictions, binaries, or limitations, as is the case of the oppressive gendered binaries of colonialism.

The Anishinaabeg process of theorizing malehoods through a model of self-in-context with Creation is the pedagogical framework offered by the nookomisag (grandmothers), whose cultural vocation it is to gikinoo'amaw (educate) the gwiiwizens of his place within Anishinaabe society and in relation to the rest of Creation. The pedagogy of grand-mothers is also rooted in the spiritual concept of Anishinaabe mino-miikana-bimaadiziwin (the philosophy of following the teachings or the path of living well as a human being as well as living the good life and living in a good way), which is also known as mino-bimaadiziwin (the good life). The practice of mino-bimaadiziwin provides Anishinaabeg with a sense of obligation to the community and helps to cement the idea that each person must give back to family, community, and society for benefits received. Anishinaabe linguist and scholar Basil Johnston-ba says, "that which made men and women Anishinaubae was considered to be owed to the entire heritage of the community and nation, and each person was bound to return something to his or her heritage and so add to its worth" (Johnston, *The Manitous* xix). Johnston states that it was important to have healthy, strong individuals within Anishinaabeg society, and he relays how Anishinaabeg were educated to consider their contribution and obligation to the welfare of their overall society (Johnston, *The Manitous* xix-xx).

When a grandmother relates the Creation story to their male or LGBTQQ2SA+ grandchild, there is an expectation that they not only insert themselves into the story metaphorically as Ani niisayi'iinaabe, but literally learn to embody or live the ethical teachings encoded in the story. Elder Benton-Banai teaches that as human beings, we can only begin to understand our place within family, community, society, and Creation when we truly understand our Creation story and only then can we truly be good Anishinaabe citizens. He says the following:

> Anishinaabe can see that if he knows his creation story, if she knows her creation story, they know also how all of life moves. They can know how life comes to be. All of life is a creative process that began in this original way and continues in the same way in all aspects of our life. In all places and all facets of creation, and creative activity, these seven stages are reflected. (Benton-Banai, "Anishinaabe Creation Story" 30)

In this way, the *kokum-gikendaasowin* and the *Anishinaabe kokum aanike-gikinoo'amaadiwin* (traditional grandmother education, teachings, or pedagogy) requires a presence and commitment from the learner, which means understanding that to "learn is to live and demonstrate those teachings through a personal embodiment" (Simpson, *Dancing on Our Turtle's Back* 41-42) of the ethics of Anishinaabe mino-bimaadiz -win. Furthermore, Elder Manitowabi states this requires that each Anishinaabe learner, "must *remember* these teachings, *wear* them, and *pass them on*" (qtd. in Simpson, *Dancing on Our Turtle's Back* 36, my emphasis). Wearing the teachings for gwiiwizensag means learning how to embodying the gifts, talents, and teachings bestowed on Ani niisayi'iinaabe (Original Man) in the Creation story. This means internalizing holistically (mind, body, spirit, and emotions) the concept of gaagii-izhi-minigowiziyang (we are gifted by the Creator), which is a self-love (zaagi'iwewin, the love that we feel in our heart) that Ani niisayi'iinaabe embodied naturally.

Gikinoo'amaagewikwe (She Who Teaches): The Vocation of Grandmotherhood

Johnston asserts that among the Anishinaabeg, old age was seen as a gift (Johnston, *Ojibwe Heritage* 118). Furthermore, old age marked a stage of life with its own work to complete in benefit of family and community. Anishinaabeg were taught that it was a "cherished" stage of life (Johnston, *Ojibwe Heritage* 118). Those of old age were respected for attaining long life and "living out the visions" and coming to "know something of human nature and living and life" (Johnston, *Ojibwe Heritage* 118). He explains that their value lies in not just long life but also "what they have *come to know* and *abide by* is wisdom" (Johnston, *Ojibwe Heritage* 118, my emphasis). He continues: "This is what they must pass on to those still to traverse the path of life and scale the mighty hills. Only when they finally vanish into the mists is the *work* over" (Johnston, *Ojibwe Heritage* 118, my emphasis).

Johnston asserts that grandmothers have a vocation rooted in offering children the benefit of an educational framework that is circulatory and intergenerational. Nookomisag aanike-gikinoo' amaadiwin is an intergenerational exchange of knowledge, customs, and ethical protocols for conduct among humans and nonhuman relations both living or spirit being. Anishinaabe educator and historian Thomas Peacock explains that the purpose of aanike-gikinoo' amaadiwin was to "serve the practical needs of the people (to learn life skills) and to enhance the soul" (Peacock and Wisuri 68).

Having this traditional knowledge is critical, but having good *gikinoo'amaagejig* who can guide a learner to contextualize and personalize the information or experience is also a necessary element to the learning process. Supporting this concept, McNally says that the Anishinaabe-Ojibwe worldview of grandparents was focused on "teaching proper knowledge of relationality and modeling the proper exercise of right relations among human and nonhuman 'persons' of the land and spiritual worlds" (McNally 133). Both McNally and Anishinaabe scholar Priscilla Buffalohead note that the grandmothers were the ones put in charge of educating the children, as is the matriarchal right and duty of the grandmothers (McNally 126-33; Buffalohead 241; Borrows). Grandmothers as educators of the young were also called the mindimooyenh (the old woman of authority or the ones who hold the family and community together) out of respect (Borrows 842; Vukelich, "Ojibwe Word of the Day Mindimooyenh ᕑᑎᒍᐨ"; Johnston, *Anishinaubae Thesaurus* 21; McNally 24-25). The mindimooyenh is the familial and clan matriarch, leader, and educator of the young members of the family. She, above all others, is responsible and duty bound to keep the old stories and culture of the family alive by educating the children in those ways of knowing, being, and living (Vukelich, "Ojibwe Word of the Day Mindimooyenh ᕑᑎᒍᐨ"). Furthermore, in the role of *mindimooyenh*, the Anishinaabe grandmothers became leaders as "society builders" (Child, xxvi), as they ensure that each child learns all the required traditional knowledge and customs, along with learning how to apply it so as to contribute to the welfare, functioning, and cultural growth of the community. As society builders, grandmothers used traditional learning methods, such as storytelling, as world building exercises to generate and regenerate Anishinaabeg ontological and epistemological beliefs and connections to those traditional customs that sustain cultural integrity, such as hunting, ceremonies, governance, birth, medicine, and so on.

In his book *Masculindians*, scholar Sam McKegney interviews Basil Johnston on his thoughts about the nature of Anishinaabe malehoods, and Johnston talks about the particular significance of the educational role of grandmothers in shaping malehoods (41-47). He shares with McKegney that it was the grandmothers who were the "keepers of the wisdom" and the "principal teachers" to the young men and boys (45). Interestingly, he notes the following: "It was the women ... [who] were assigned this duty by the community because the males were out and it was the grandmothers who kept the villages together. And they had the primary responsibility of training the youth" (qtd. in McKegney, *Masculindians* 45). He advocates that the Anishinaabeg need to remember this matriarchal system of education and "go back to that system, to have grandmothers taking part in schools, teaching language, teaching the literature of the people" (qtd. in McKegney, *Masculindians* 45).

Perhaps the most significant characters in Ojibwe narratives, Naanabozho, the trickster, was raised and educated by his grandmother. McNally asserts that Nookomis embody the "archetypal grandmother," who mothers and fathers the child in the absence of both parents (McNally 126). The presence of the grandmother as an educator is organized around a traditional pedagogical model of how to live well. A *Nookomis* is the archetypal grandmother because she represents "moral attainment" and represents "the possibility of becoming more and more human, more and more Anishinaabe" (McNally 25), which means she is getting closer to the original role of women embodied by Aki—the mother, the one who nurturers, and the one who teaches human beings how to live on the land in a good way. Johnston explains that "by living through all stages and living out visions, men and women know something of human nature and living and live" (*Ojibway Heritage* 112). Those who lived a good life achieved a higher level of authority within the community as a reward and acknowledgement of their achievement. Today, we often call these moral authority figures "Elders," but in the past, these were the mindimooyenyag (old women, grandmother) and akiwenzhiiyag (long dwellers of the earth, old men, grandfathers).

The vocational credentials for grandmothers are embedded in age, mastery of knowledge, customs, and Anishinaabe moralities. As in the story of Nookomis and Naanabozho, Nookomis has reached old age and a *"mastery of relatedness"* (McNally 51-52, my emphasis) or embodying the concept of mino-bimaadiziwin (good life), along with having fulfilled all the responsibilities associated with the earlier stages of life. In her book *Life Stages of Native Women*, Cree/Métis scholar Kim Anderson writes, "Once an elder had become a master of these relations, he or she had responsibilities to cycle this power back into the younger generations, to keep the life force and spirit moving" (126).

Using mino-bimaadiziwin as a pedagogy framework, grandmothers model by example, through reproof, and most importantly, through stories and storytelling practices as a means of passing on their lived wisdom (McNally 124; 133-45). Here, one can see the convergence of the grandmother/grandson lifelines in the basic circularity, from which it draws and to which it contributes motion. What is established is the completion of the circle from child to grandparent, which is reflective of the ancient and eternal rhythms of bimaadiziwin and the Path of Life teachings (Johnston, *Ojibwe Heritage* 117-118).

Nookomis Gikinoo'amaagowin Naanabozho (Nookomis Teaches Naanabozho)

The story of *Nookomis* and *Naanabozho* teaches us how Anishinaabeg grandmothers educate grandchildren, particularly regarding gwiiwizens and niizh-manidoowag. Through this story, Anishinaabeg learn the respected role of the grandmother as teacher and caregiver, but we are also witness Naanabozho's growth and what learning wisdom entails. The land, Aki, is both the classroom and teacher. The process of learning is rigorous, gendered, learner led, and also rooted in honouring the spirit of the gwiiwizens. Nookomis pursues a pedagogy prioritizing "respectful individualism," which is based on the principle of not forcing one's thinking on anybody else (Weatherford 121). Instead, the learner is given information and the necessary time and space to process the meanings. Gikendaasowin is a synthesis of personal teachings, insights, and understandings, which is then utilized and applied within the context of the learner's own lived experience as a cyclical practice of regenerating Anishinaabeg intelligence. Johnston explains it this way:

> Stories about humans, acted out by humans, tell about life, about what we should do and what we should not do....And as grandparents tell stories, children learn language, enrich their imaginations and rouse their curiosities about the herebefore and the hereafter. Stories don't need special occasions or times to be told. The tellers do not say, "Now I'm going to tell you a children's story," as if there were different intellectual levels of stories. It was children who had to uplift, improve, upgrade their understandings. (*Walking in Balance* 8)

This version of the Naanabozho and Nookomis story is inspired by the stories offered by Johnston and Anishinaabe scholar James Niigaanwewidam Sinclair. I have decided to write about *Naanabozho* as a LGBTQQ2SA+ *gwiiwizens* because in his stories he represents gender fluidity and nonconformity, which demonstrates that within the traditions of Anishinaabeg intelligence, there is a spectrum of maleness and malehoods. Furthermore, I wanted to show how grandmothers in Anishinaabeg culture respond to, educate, and shape these malehoods. Ahaaw, ninga-anishinaabe-aadizooke (Now, I will tell a traditional story).

Boozhoo, indinawemaaganag! Greetings, all my relatives!

Let me share with you a story about a kokum (granny) and her oozhishenyan (her grandchild), Naanaboozho!

A very long time ago, there lived an old woman named Nookomis, who dwelled all alone in her lodge, till one day Gizhew-Manidoo (the Creator) took pity on her and sent to her a young woman named Wiininwaa, to be her daughter.

Then, one windy day while out picking miinan (blueberries), Wiininwaa became lost in the forest. She fell asleep under a giizhikaatig (cedar tree) and had a bawaajigan (dream). In the dream, a wind swirled around her and went inside her, impregnating the kwezens (young woman). Upon waking, she was found by Nookomis and brought home. Nine months later, she gave birth to a baby, who was named Naanabozho.

The women quickly realized the child was unusual when all of a sudden, he changed into various animals, a rain cloud, then to a baby girl, and then back to a baby boy. The child was Niizh-Manidoowag or Two-Spirit, meaning he embodied both male and female human spirits, along with having additional vast supernatural powers.

Not long after the birth, the women were out in a meadow picking miskominag (raspberries) when a great storm came in from the west. Lightning struck a tree and started a fire. Unable to escape quickly enough, the fire consumed both Wiininwaa and the new baby. Strangely enough, the winds stopped, and the storm retreated. Crying could be heard from the western direction. As Nookomis sobbed in despair, she heard a baby's cry from under the debris. She dug and found the unharmed baby. In that moment, Nookomis promised herself and Naanabozho that she would care for and raise him to know his gifts and talents as a Two-Spirit being.

Nookomis spent Naanabozho's childhood teaching him skills of survival that Anishinaabe-nini (male) were required to learn, but she focused his education on learning men's traditions, female traditions, and Two-Spirit traditions in order to nurture his Gizhew-manidoo-omiigiwewinan (gifts from the Creator). She taught him to work hard, how to provide for himself, and how to think through situations. He learned to go out on the land by himself to hunt and bring back food for his family and community while also attending as an oshkaabewis (helper) for his grandmother when she went to perform her role of doodisiim (midwife, or the one who cuts the cord), conduct ceremonies, and care for the young children. Nookomis taught Naanabozho that his Two-Spirit nature was a great honour and responsibility.

Throughout his childhood, while picking medicines or cleaning the lodge, Nookomis would share her songs, prayers, teachings, histories, and stories of Wiininwaa with her grandson. She poured everything she knew into the boy. Yet when Naanabozho asked for stories of his father, she would tell him, "Later, when you are ready." He did not push the issue further, respecting her judgment on the matter. They spent many days of his childhood and youth this way, just talking, sharing, and spending time together. This is the way the old ones teach the young ones.

So when he reached maturity and had gone through all the rites of passage to become a nini (man), he asked his grandmother for the story of his parents, particularly, the one about his father. Nookomis told him what had befallen his mother and her suspicions that it was Epingishmog (the Spirit of the West) who had killed her. Pained and angry, Naanabozho decided to leave his grandmother to find and kill his father in revenge. Though wary to interfere with the lifepath of her grandson or his decisions, Nookomis told Naanabozho of the vast powers of Epingishmog.

Naanabozho travelled far west and finally found his father. Epingishmog appeared as a great tornado dancing across the prairies. He was beautiful, vast, and powerful. Naanabozho steeled himself and yelled a challenge at his father to fight. Agreeing mischievously, Epingishmog launched a war on his son. The two battled for a long time. Naanabozho almost lost several times but managed to outthink, trick, and then wound his father. The great giant crashed to the ground. Naanabozho felt remorse and fear. He cried out to Gizhew-Manidoo (the Creator) to not take his father. He knew now *that he had been wrong to fight his father, so he apologized and asked for peace between them.*

Epingishmog transformed into an akiwenzii (old man) and began to converse with his son. After realizing the depth of kindness in his son, Epingishmog presented him with a pipe of peace and showed him the appropriate ceremonies to perform with it. As his last gift, Epingishmog apologized for accidentally killing Wiininwaa.

After this exchange, Naanabozho returned to his grandmother but always looked west and petitioned the Spirit of the West to watch over his family and people. He taught the Anishinaabe the pipe ceremony. The pipe induced temperance in speech and wisdom in decision making. Furthermore, it also acted as a reminder to everyone of the importance of the role of women in men's lives. The ceremony demonstrated the Anishinaabe veneration of the primacy of womanhood and our dependency on women, mothers, and grandmothers as creators, sustainers, and nurturers of life. In the years that followed, Naanaboozho became a great teacher, hero, transformer of culture, and father figure to the Anishinaabe of how to live a good life as a human being. Mii sa iw. Miigwech (That is all. Thank you).

The story of Nookomis and her grandson is particularly significant because it not only identifies the pedagogy of grandmothers but also offers teachings on malehoods and fatherhoods that are necessary for gwiiwizens to fully embody his adult maleness. Harkening back to the beginning of this chapter where I discussed the role of the Creation story in laying down the foundations of Anishinaabe malehoods, Nookomis embodies the mothering nature of Aki (earth), who is the original archetype of mothering and femalehoods in the Creation story, whereas Naanabozho embodies Ani niisayi'iinaabe as the archetype of the child, natural maleness, and malehoods. In some ways, Epingishmog represents the antithesis of proper male and fatherly behaviours (such as nurturing, protecting, and providing for his child). The reverse of this is Nookomis as the caretaker: both mother and father. She enfolds Naanabozho in a gentle motherly embrace of love, nurturing, and caretaking as well as providing supportive education to allow his malehoods and LGBTQQ2SA+ identity to flourish, so that he might learn to live in a good way (mino-bimaadiziwin) as a human being. Elder Manitowabi says that grandmothers do this kind of work so that the grandchildren will be guided by our Mother's wisdom and so they will model themselves after this Earth [and] so they might grow up to be good and kind compassionate [Anishinaabe]" (qtd. in Simpson, *Dancing on Our Turtle's Back* 37). The Elder continues: "So they [the grandchildren] might know how to look after their children and their grandchildren. So that together, we might be a strong nation again. That is my dream. That is why I keep working. We do this work because we love our children. This is my purpose in life as a Grandmother and a Great Grandmother. This is my purpose in life as a *Kobaade* [Great Grandmother]" (qtd. in Simpson, *Dancing on Our Turtle's Back* 37, my emphasis).

Nookomisag Mino-Inanokiiwin (The Grandmothers Work in a Good Way)

Gikinoo'amaagoowin abinoojiinyag translates to those learning methods used by grandmothers to teach their grandchildren. Here, I seek to use the learning methods within the story of Nookomis and Naanabozho as a way to contextualize the traditional grandmother pedagogy used to shape Anishinaabeg malehoods. As educators of the children, grandmothers teach their grandsons and granddaughters to become proficient "practitioners of Nishnaabeg intelligence" (Simpson, "Land as Pedagogy 13). In "Adults Informal Learning: Definitions, Findings, Gaps and Future Research," David Livingston identifies "several basic types of learning [which] may be identified in terms of the organization of the body of knowledge to be learned and the primacy of teachers" (2). These methods of learning include formal, nonformal/further, informal, and self-directed education (Livingston 2).

The first method of learning involves formal education, which requires learning a required body of knowledge (Livingston 2). Nookomis ensured that Naanabozho learned the necessary knowledge and skills that would enable him not only to survive on his own once he reached adulthood but also to contribute to his family, community, and society. For this, Nookomis specifically taught him traditional knowledge related to responsibilities required by malehoods, such as hunting, collecting medicines, and men's ceremonies (as both a man and LGBTQQ2SA+ person). But he was also exposed to traditional female knowledge related to such things as women's ceremonies, midwifery, and childcare.

The second learning method includes what Livingston refers to as nonformal or further education (Livingston 2), which consists of undergoing advanced or additional training in certain skills or knowledge. As an example of how Nookomis employed this learning method, we see that Naanabozho undergoes training as a hunter within his community. She would have provided some of that training but would have also found him the necessary male teachers in the community to teach him advanced skills in traditions Anishinaabeg women are not privy to. To be trained in those male duties and traditions would have necessitated that Naanabozho formally accept that responsibility and promise to uphold those teachings. For instance, he would have been trained in how to survive entirely alone on the land for long stretches of time; identify different types of large and small game; make appropriate offerings, prayers of gratitude, and ceremonies of the hunter; clean an animal and prepare the meat for cooking; dispose of the carcass properly; preserve the meat; and clean the cooking utensils and pots. Therefore, once these teachings are learned, the community expects the learner to use these teachings and traditions to provide for their family and community. Hunters are supposed bring meat on a regular basis to the community Elders or to those with disabilities who are unable to go out and obtain food. These practices are still performed today by the men of Anishinaabeg communities and by young men and women who go on their first hunts to honour the vocation of hunters as providers.

Next, Nanabozho was taught to use informal learning methods, such as storytelling during the collection of medicines. While occupied by a single activity, Naanabozho would have been more receptive to learning through listening, intuiting, and internalizing. Kim Anderson says, "This time with the old ladies provided the foundation for a traditional and lifelong education" (Anderson, *Life Stages and Native Women* 144). Elder Musqua refers to the time he spent with the grandmothers of his community as going to the kokum's classes (Anderson, *Life Stages and Native Women* 145). In the story, Naanabozho never forces Nookomis into telling him her stories of his father, and in this way, we are witness to the honour, respect, and love he has for her as both his grandmother and as his Elder and mentor. Although these less formalized learning times were more casual, they were still struc-tured to ensure learning could best be fruitful.

Lastly, the final method includes self-directed learning, in which the learner learns independently without directly relying on either a teacher or an externally organized body of knowledge (Livingston 2). Indigenous based self-directed learning is one of the oldest modes of education, and it directly relates to the ethic of noninterference (Ross; Wax and Thomas; Brant; Prowse; Gross). Cathy Prowse notes that the central rule of Indigenous noninterference:

> To interfere in the interactions of others is actually to attempt to exert dominance over that other individual. The ethic finds expression in the freedom of people to act as they please—so long as group welfare is not compromised—with the corollary that to correct behaviour would amount to interference in an individual's inherent right to autonomy in determining their own actions and decision-making process. And, as long as your own behaviour does not compromise the well-being of others, individuals should be left to determine their own actions. (251)

In the story, Nookomis steps back from the teacher role, and instead, she allows Naanabozho to go off on his quest to find his father. Using his prior education, survival skills, and Nookomis's teachings, Naanabozho navigates challenges rationally and uses his judgment to slow down, pull back, and redirect his energies to reconcile with his father rather than seeking revenge. In this way, he comes to know his place in the world as a nini (adult male). During and after his confrontation with his father, Naanabozho learns some key teachings about his malehood. First, he learned he had been rash to leave and should have better interpreted the information Nookomis shared about the dangers of his father's nature. Second, he learned that good parenting and grandparenting, as Nookomis performed it, requires educating, providing, nurturing, and protecting children; all of which were absent from his relationship with his father. Third, he came to understand that human beings, particularly men, should endeavour to follow the teachings of the sacred pipe and seek the path of peace, which includes teachings on temperance, goodwill, and respect for femalehoods. From that brief exchange he experienced with his father, *Naanabozho* came to learn how to live *mino-bimaadiziwin* (the good life) as an Anishinaabe: "A life of peace, a life of balance, and a life without conflict or contradiction" (Vukelich, "Gizhewaadiziwin").

Lastly, by meeting and interacting with his father, Naanabozho understands Nookomis's teachings of gizhewaadiziwin, meaning "kindness, loving kindness, unconditional love" (the Ojibwe People's Dictionary). Throughout the duration of his life, she exudes kindness and unconditional love. These teachings harken back to the Creation story, in which man was lowered onto the earth and the earth accepted man with unconditional love—gizhewaadiziwin. Gizhe refers to kindness." Anishinaabe/Cree Elder Peter O'Chiese-ba taught that the greatest lesson an Anishinaabe man can come to know and understand is the original gift to man, which is kindness ("Interview with Peter O'Chiese"). When a man can embody this gift, he is then living as the "natural male" (Benton-Banai, *The Mishomis Book* 4), which means living within the malehoods that have been individually crafted and then gifted to each male spirit at the time of their conception in their mother's womb.

In these ways and using these educational learning methods, grandmothers facilitate male as well as LGBTQQ2SA+ grandchildren to learn what it means to embody malehoods regarding the duties to be performed for the benefit of their family and community as well as Anishinaabeg society.

Closing Thoughts

Anishinaabeg grandmothers employ strategies of survival to lift up the next "rising generation" (McNally 133) of women, men, and LGBTQQ2SA+ leaders of today and tomorrow. The pedagogies, teachings, and stories of the grandmothers need to be used by our Anishinaabe families and communities as "radical wisdom" (Alfred, *Wasáse* 197), which can allow us to "break out from under the weight of colonial oppression," since "the old understandings have served our people well as shields and, indeed, have allowed us to survive" (Alfred, *Wasáse* 197). In modern contexts, we can use the radical wisdom of the grandmothers as tools for not only survival but also for the recreation, regeneration, reclamation, and resurgence of our traditional lifeways (Alfred, *Wasáse*; Simpson, "Land as Pedagogy"). We often speak of how colonization has fragmented much of our culture and language, but there is still a vast storehouse of knowledge that we must continue to utilize in new ways in order to ensure the process of strengthening and regenerating our cultures outside the colonizer's reality. Furthermore, we must find ways to incorporate those ways of knowing that do not compromise our cultures but enhance and enable our cultures to evolve. This chapter is about preserving as well as creating new indigenized spaces for an Anishinaabe reality open to a spectrum of understandings on Indigenous malehoods and its subtle linkages with Indigenous femalehoods and LGBTQQ2SA+ people through the caretaking of grandmothers whose radical wisdom shapes the nature and function of malehoods to prioritize holism within the family, community, and society.

I have chosen to end this chapter with a poem by Anishinaabe Elder Art Solomon, who offers some further insight into the linkages and connections of the masculine and feminine within Anishinaabe reality. He writes:

Everything in the Creation is created

Male and Female.

Everything is based on that

Sacred principle, and from it flows All life, to accomplish its destiny

As the Creator intended. (Solomon, *Songs of the People* 42)

Endnotes

1. Kokum is the shortened version of the term Nookomis, which means grandmother.

2. Anishinaabeg is an umbrella term for those nations that are rooted in the same root linguistic dialect, cultural teachings, and intellectual traditions. Those who use the term to describe themselves as Anishinaabe (meaning "human being") are comprised of the following "nations": Anishiniwag (Oji-Cree), Ojibweg, Odaawaag, Bodéwadmik, Odishkwaamagiig (Nipissing), Misizaagiwininiwag (Mississaugas), Omàmiwininiwak (Algonquin), and Leni Lenape (Delaware). The Anishinaabeg peoples inhabit the upper Great Lakes region.

3. Malehoods encompasss any individual who identifies as male on the spectrum of maleness, or who identifies with maleness, which can include anyone who identifies as LGBTQQ2SA+/*ikwekaazo* (men who choose to function as, or be like, a woman) or *ininiikaazo* (women who choose to function as, or be like, a man). Femalehoods describe the spectrum of feminine genders, affiliations, or those who identify with the feminine from within the LGBTQQ2SA+ community.

4. Grandmothers may also be either biologically female or Two-Spirit. Further, grandmothers can be biological or adoptive. Those who are biologically related or an adoptive grandmother, can assume the role of parent and take up the responsibilities of both mothers and fathers.

5. In Anishinaabemowin, "-ba" or "-ban" is a preterite suffix that is added to a noun stem to indicate a past state or absence. For example,"-ba" is added to a noun that refers to a person who is now deceased.

Works Cited

Alfred, Taiaiake. *Heeding the Voices of Our Ancestors: Kahnawake Mohawk Politics and the Rise of Native Nationalism*. Oxford University Press, 1995.

Alfred, Taiaiake. *Peace, Power, Righteousness: An Indigenous Manifesto*. Oxford University Press, 2009.

Alfred, Taiaiake. *Wasáse: Indigenous Pathways of Action and Freedom*. University of Toronto Press, 2005.

Anderson, Kim. *Life Stages and Native Women: Memory, Teachings, and Story Medicine*. University of Manitoba Press, 2011.

Anderson, Kim. *Recognition of Being: Reconstructing Native Womanhood*. Sumach Press, 2000.

Anderson, Kim, et al. "Indigenous Masculinities: Carrying the Bones of the Ancestors." *Canadian Men and Masculinities: Historical and Contemporary Perspectives*. Edited by C. J. Grieg and W. J. Marino, Canadian Scholars Press, 2012, pp. 206-84.

Anderson, Kim, et al. *Indigenous Men and Masculinities: Legacies, Identities, and Regeneration*, University of Manitoba Press, 2015.

Anderson, Kim, et al. "'To Arrive Speaking': Voices from Bidwewidam, Indigenous Masculinities Project." *Indigenous Men and Masculinities: Legacies, Identities, and Regeneration.* Edited by Kim Anderson and Robert Alexander Innes, University of Manitoba Press, 2015, pp. 283-308.

Ball, Jessica. "Fathering in the Shadows: Indigenous fathers and Canada's colonial legacies." *The ANNALS of the American Academy of Political and Social Sciences,* vol. 624, no. 1, 2009, pp. 29-48.

Ball, Jessica. "Indigenous Fathers' Involvement in Reconstituting 'Circles of Care.'" *American Journal of Community Psychology,* vol. 45, no. 1-2, 2010, pp. 124-138.

Barnouw, Victor. *Wisconsin Chippewa Myths and Tales.* Madison: University of Wisconsin Press, 1977.

Benton-Banai, Edward. "Anishinaabe Creation Story." *Ways of Knowing Guide. Ways of Knowing Partnership Turtle Island Conservation,* 2010, www.torontozoo.com/pdfs/tic/Stewardship_Guide.pdf. Accessed 10 July 2018.

Benton-Banai, Edward. *The Mishomis Book: The Voice of the Ojibway.* Indian Country Communications Inc., 1988.

Borrows, John. "Heroes, Tricksters, Monsters, and Caretakers: Indigenous Law and Legal Education." *McGill Law Journal,* vol. 61, no. 4, 2016, pp. 795-846.

Brant, Clare. "Native Ethics and Rules of Behaviour." *Canadian Journal of Psychiatry,* vol. 35, no. 6, 1990, pp. 534-39.

Buffalohead, Priscilla K. "Farmers, Warriors, Traders: A Fresh Look at Ojibway Women." *The American Indian: Past and Present.* Edited by Roger L. Nichols, Knopf, 1986, pp. 236-44.

Child, Brenda J. *Holding Our World Together: Ojibwe Women and the Survival of Community.* Penguin, 2012.

Courchene, Darren. "Language as the Root of Ojibwe Knowledge." *Geez Magazine.* Fall 2015, pp. 26-27. www.academia.edu/30414319/ Language_as_the_root_of_Ojibwe_knowledge. Accessed 29 May 2018.

Gross, Lawrence W. *Anishinaabe Ways of Knowing and Being.* Routledge, Taylor & Francis Group, 2014.

Lavell-Harvard, Dawn Memee, and Kim Anderson, editors. *Mothers of the Nations: Indigenous Mothering as Global Resistance, Reclaiming, and Recovery.* Demeter Press, 2014.

Lavell-Harvard, and Jeannette Corbiere Lavell, editors. *"Until Our Hearts Are on the Ground" Aboriginal Mothering, Oppression, Resistance, and Rebirth.* Demeter Press, 2006.

Lee, Lloyd L. "Diné Masculinities, Relationships, Colonization, and Regenerating an Egalitarian Way of Life." *Indigenous Men and Masculinities: Legacies, Identities, and Regeneration.* Edited by A. Innes and Kim Anderson, University of Manitoba Press, 2015, pp. 214-28.

Lee, Lloyd L. *Diné Masculinities: Conceptualizations and Reflections.* Createspace Independent Publishing Platform, 2013.

Livingston, David W. "Adults Informal Learning: Definitions, Findings, Gaps and Future Research." *SSHRC Research Network, New Approaches to Lifelong Learning Papers.* Centre for the Study of Education and Work, OISE/University of Toronto, 2001, tspace. library.utoronto.ca/retrieve/4484/21adultsinformallearning.pdf. Accessed 1 June 2018.

"Interview with Peter O'Chiese." *Office of Specific Claims and Research,* 1 Mar. 1976, ourspace.uregina.ca/bitstream/handle/10294/2193/ IH-198.pdf?sequence=1&isAllowed=y. Accessed 27 May 2018.

Johnston, Basil. *Anishinaubae Thesaurus.* East Lansing: Michigan State University Press, 2007.

Johnston, Basil. *Ojibway Heritage.* McClelland Stewart, 1976.

Johnston, Basil. *The Manitous: The Spiritual World of the Ojibway.* Key Porter Books, 1995.

Johnston, Basil. *Walking in Balance, Meeyau-Ossaewin.* Kegedonce Press, 2013.

McKegney, Sam. *Masculindians: Conversations about Indigenous Manhood.* University of Manitoba Press, 2014.

McKegney, Sam. "'Pain, Pleasure, Shame. Shame': Masculine Embodiment, Kinship, and Indigenous Reterritorialization." *Canadian Literature,* vol. 216, 2013, pp. 12-33.

McKegney, Sam. "Warriors, Healers, Lovers, and Leaders: Colonial Impositions on Indigenous Male Roles and Responsibilities." *Canadian Perspectives on Men and Masculinities: An Interdisciplinary*

Reader. Edited by J. A. Laker, Oxford University Press, 2012, pp. 241-68.

McNally, Michael D. *Honoring Elders: Aging, Authority, and Ojibwe Religion.* University Press, 2009

Peacock, Thomas, and Marlene Wisuri. *The Four Hills of Life: Ojibwe Wisdom.* Minnesota Historical Society Press, 2006.

Prowse, Cathy. "Native Ethics and Rules of Behaviour" in the Criminal Justice Domain: An Abstract Career in Retrospect." *International Journal of Humanities and Social Sciences,* vol. 1, no. 5, 2011, pp. 251-57.

Ross, Rupert. *Dancing With a Ghost: Exploring Aboriginal Reality.* Penguin Canada, 1992.

Simpson, Leanne. *As We Have Always Done: Indigenous Freedom through Radical Resistance.* University of Minnesota Press, 2017.

Simpson, Leanne. "Birthing an Indigenous Resurgence: Decolonizing Our Pregnancy and Birthing Ceremonies." *"Until Our Hearts Are on the Ground" Aboriginal Mothering, Oppression, Resistance and Rebirth.* Edited by D. Memee Lavell-Harvard and Jeannette Corbiere Lavell, Demeter Press, 2006, pp. 25-33.

Simpson, Leanne. *Dancing on Our Turtle's Back: Stories of Nishnaabeg Re-Creation, Resurgence and a New Emergence.* ARP Books, 2011.

Simpson, Leanne. "Land as Pedagogy: Nishnaabeg Intelligence and Rebellious Transformation." *Decolonization: Indigeneity, Education & Society,* vol. 3, no. 3, 2014, pp. 1-25.

Simpson, Leanne. *The Gift is in the Making: Anishinaabeg Stories.* Highwater Press, 2013.

Sinclair, James Niigaanwewidam. "Oshki Ishkode, New Fire." *Indigenous Men and Masculinities: Legacies, Identities, Regeneration.* Edited by Robert Innes and Kim Anderson, University of Manitoba Press, 2015, pp. 145-64.

Solomon, Art. *Songs for the People: Teachings on the Natural Way.* NC Press Limited, 1990.

The Ojibwe People's Dictionary. "Gizhewaadiziwin." *Ojibwe,* ojibwe. lib.umn.edu/main-entry/gizhewaadiziwin-ni. Accessed 1 June 2018.

Vukelich, James. "Gizhewaadiziwin." *Vimeo*, vimeo.com/241224266. Accessed 10 July 2018.

Vukelich, James. "Ojibwe Word of the Day: Mindimooyenh, 'an Old Woman, an Old Lady.'" *YouTube*, 6 Jul. 2017, www.youtube.com/watch?v=TbOudyaLNwk. Accessed 16 May 2018.

Wax, Rosalie, and Robert K. Thomas. "American Indians and White People." *Native Americans Today: Sociological Perspectives.* Edited by Howard M. Bahr, et al. Harper and Row, 1972, pp. 305-317.

Weatherford, Jack. *Indian Givers: How the Indians of the Americas Transformed the World.* New York: Fawcett Columbine, 1988.

Chapter 10

Masculinity and Motherhood: Engendering Indian Nationalism

Zairunisha

O Thou, Mother of the Universe, vouchsafe manliness unto me!
O Thou, Mother of Strength, take away my weakness,
Take away my unmanliness and make me a Man!
—Swami Vivekananda, Complete Works, 67.

Mother and Motherland— where ends the one and where
begins the other. Before which does a man stand with
folded hands, when he bows his head still lower,
And says with a new awe: My salutation to thee mother!
—Sister Nivedita 326

Introduction

At the time of India's struggle against British rule, many nationalists addressed India as the sacred motherland. Most Indian males envisage and revere their nation as the mother goddess. As her valorous sons, they consider it their responsibility to guard and protect the honour of Mother India from any possible foreign danger. However, Indian nationalism is predominantly patriarchal, and its socially constructed gendered vision of the nation is rooted in a hegemonic framework and stereotypical images of masculinity and femininity. In India, Hinduism is an influential religion in which a mother is perceived as the embodiment of a goddess, but it seems such deification of the mother in colonial India (1757 to 1947) was constructed as part of an ideology whose aim was to confine women exclusively to maternal work. In India, motherhood is regarded as the "ultimate identity" of a woman (Bagchi 66). Women are to have no status and value except as reproducers and nurturers of heroic sons, who are destined to defend Mother India. The lived experiences of Indian mothers are grounded in and regulated by this masculinist patriarchal compass.

This chapter will explore the relationship between the two social identity markers—that is, masculinity and motherhood—and how they implicitly and explicitly work in the making of India as a Hindu nation under the lens of gender difference. I will attempt to trace the sources of contemporary masculinist Hinduism—from the very beginning of the anticolonial struggle against British rule to current ideas about Hindu nationalism dominating contemporary political discourses. In doing so, I will critically analyse the historical, political, and cultural emergence of masculine Hinduism in relation to motherhood and its effects on women's lives as mothers today. I will also draw illustrations from Hindu mythological texts to explore the ways in which Hindu ideology dominates, controls, and shapes men's and mothers' sensibilities in contemporary social life in India.

Emergence of Masculinity in India

India, or "Bharat," is a land of unity in diversity, which is reflected in its diverse physical features, ethnic and cultural patterns, and religious beliefs and practices. The Indian territory is metaphorically seen as sacred. As an ancient civilization, it has existed for twenty-five thousand years and is framed by the Himalayas, the Indus River, and an ocean; it has also been mentioned in various scriptures (Varshney 234). Having the world's second largest population (more than one billion people), India is the most populous democracy in the world. Culturally, Indians believe in pluralism, syncretism, and tolerance. The country is comprised of people with a set of distinct bodily features, colour, caste, creed, custom, language, race, and so on. Not only is the Indian subcontinent the birthplace of many religions (i.e., Hinduism,

Buddhism, Jainism, Sikhism), but it has also received, accommodated, and assimilated several "arrived" religious beliefs, such as Judaism, Christianity, Islam, and Zoroastrianism. Nevertheless, according to the 2011 census report, Hinduism is the most common and dominant religion, accounting for 79.8 per cent of the population. The second most popular religion is Islam, with 14.23 per cent of the population, and the remaining 6 per cent includes Christianity (2.30 per cent), Sikhism (1.72 per cent), Buddhism (0.70 per cent), Jainism (0.36 per cent), and others. India is a sovereign, socialist, secular state, as well as a democratic republic, in the sense that its national identity is an amalgamation of various ethnic and religious groups, whose fundamental human rights are constitutionally protected and whose cultural beliefs are given equal respect. However, in colonial India, Hinduism emerged as a martial religion and became the representation of a national identity by Hindu nationalists, which was then transformed into the ruling Hindu masculinity. To understand this, we need to investigate the way three main religious ideologies as markers of masculinity—Hinduism, Islam, and Christianity—intersect in making India.

Masculinity, as one of the expressions of identity, is historically, culturally, socially, and politically constructed and contrary to femininity, it is also hegemonic. Such hegemonic masculinity had a multifaceted existence within the British Raj.[1] Historically, the idea of Hindu masculinity formerly appeared as a mode of political resistance to some Hindu rulers and the Muslim empire (who were the ruling class) in precolonial India. Nevertheless, it strongly and extensively evolved as a religious-political reaction to the construction of Hindu effeminacy by the colonial rulers. The masculine British colonisers conceived of an unbridgeable gulf between Indian and European men. The British viewed Hindus as feminine, weak, passive, irrational, nonviolent, compassionate, and nonmartial. The British, in contrast, saw themselves as rational, strong, aggressive, decisive, warriors, and martial—masculine. For example, Lieutenant General Sir George MacMunn wrote the following about Indians: "We do not speak of the martial races of Britain as distinct from the non-martial, nor of Germany, nor of France. But in India we speak of martial races as a thing apart and because the mass of the people has neither martial aptitude nor physical courage" (2). Such an ideal of masculine superiority was culturally associated with and derived from Christian religious and gender practices.

In her article "Gender and Nationalism," Sikta Banerjee notes that the ideal of the muscular English man was influenced by the notion of Christian manliness, which first appeared in the book titled *Christian Manliness: A Book of Examples and Principles for Young Men* (1866). The book extensively and exclusively explored the various features of muscular Christianity and Christian manliness in order to draw a picture of an "ideal Christian man," who is faithful, courageous, energetic, strong, gentle, loyal, prudent, competent, and so forth (170). This notion of masculinity was later used by the British as a tool in their ability to conquer India and Indian men. British colonizers compared themselves to Indians and other Europeans. They defined Europeans as similar to themselves, but saw Indians as feminine men in need of correction and instruction about the physical and moral dimensions of manliness. Lord Macaulay, a British-appointed Indian colonial administrator, describes the feminine character of Bengali Indian men as follows:

> The physical organization of the Bengalee is feeble even to effeminacy. He lives in a constant vapour bath. His pursuits are sedentary, his limbs delicate, his movements languid. During many ages he has been trampled upon by men of bolder and more hardy breeds. Courage, independence, veracity are qualities to which his constitution and his situation are equally unfavourable ... [He] would see his country overrun, his house laid in ashes, his children murdered or dishonoured, without having the spirit to strike one blow. (386)

This picture given by Macaulay was projected onto all Indian men, who were consequently portrayed as unmanly. They were also seen as uncivilized, barbaric, and lacking rational thought. All this made them inferior to the British. Indu Chowdhury talks about the fixed rigid boundaries drawn by the British: "'Civilized' and the 'barbaric,' 'the rational adult' and the 'illogical child,' and the 'manly Englishman' and the 'effeminate Bengali.' The last became a comic stereotype, which, by virtue of being rooted in notion of colonial masculinity, came to be used as a justification of colonial rule in India" (2). These lines express the stereotypical mindset of British rulers regarding Indian masculinity and above all these men's inability to protect their families and nation. British colonisers saw India as "the white man's burden" and projected themselves as the superior race who had the qualifications to educate Indians and to rule these uncivilized creatures they met in India. By emphasizing British masculinity and Indian femininity, the imperialists attempted to construct sociopolitical reasons for their success in colonizing India as well as the invasion of Muslims and other aggressors in the past.

However, it is important to note that at the same time, a few high-caste Hindu communities as well as Muslims and Sikhs were praised by British military officers as being manly and exemplary soldiers, whose martial attributes were part of their ethnic prowess. These were seen as martial races because of their moral attitude (loyalty towards British rule) and physical hardiness. As a result, the British recruited native soldiers exclusively from such ethno-religious communities as the Maratha and Rajput Hindus, Muslim Pathans, Punjabi Sikhs, and Nepalese "Gurkhas" into the Indian army for the preservation and extension of their colonial masculine authority (Gavin and Wanger 234). However, after the 1857 Indian sepoy mutiny, the British Raj reversed this policy and ceased recruiting Muslims and Hindus into the army.

In response to this colonial threat against Indian masculinity, Muslims and Hindus have collectively constructed a powerful Indian hegemonic masculinity along two different lines. First, through remembering past glories, they reclaimed the manliness of historical warriors who were rejected by the British as unmanly and started agitating for self-rule. In this process, the union of Hindu and Muslim communities was the first step to dislodging British colonialism. Nationalist leaders—including Abdul Ghaffar Khan, Abul-Kalam-Azad, Ali brothers, Ashfak-Ullah Khan, Gandhi, Nehru, Patel, and many others—began fighting for the Vatan or Bharatdesh: a nation in the secular sense. Sir Sayyid Ahem Khan asserted that "Hindu and Mussalmans are words of religious significance otherwise Hindu, Mussalmans and Christens who live in this country constitute one nation" (qtd. in Jalal 5). Similarly, the father of the nation, Mahatma Gandhi, believed in the spirit of Islamic brotherhood and the integration of all religious faiths. He supported three national slogans: "Hindu-Mussalman Ki Jai" (Victory of Hindu and Muslims), 'Allahhu-Akbar' (God is greatest), and 'Bande Mataram' (I bow to thee, motherland). Simultaneously, there were groups of Muslim and Hindu nationalists who took their icons from ancient traditions to primarily construct manhood from India's history of fights and martial heroes. Muslim nationalists overwhelmingly chose King Zainul-Abedin, Akbar, and Aurangzeb, whereas Hindu nationalists accepted Lord Rama (incarnation of god Vishnu), Shivaji, Rajputs, and Marathas as their valiant icons (Banerjee 170).

Gradually, these different but ideologically secular iconographies of the nation were turned into a religious communal form of masculinity by a group of radical Hindus, whom I will discuss later. Second, in opposition to the occidental image of the country as a fatherland, some Hindus represented themselves as valorous sons of their motherland. Hindu nationalists envisaged India as the "mother" or a "feminine body," who had been exploited and dishonoured many times by foreign invaders. Now, however, it was her sons' great responsibility to protect her from any foreign yoke at the cost of their own lives, if need be. As Spike Peterson states, "Motherland is a woman's body and as such is ever in danger of violation—by 'foreign' males. To defend her frontiers and her honor requires relentless vigilance and the sacrifice of countless citizen warriors" (174). Many Hindu nationalists came forward to save their motherland from British rulers and to prove their Hindu manliness. To this end, Swami Vivekananda took the lead as a young Bengali Hindu nationalist in pointing the direction that a spiritual, materialistic, and masculine national movement must take. He expressed strong patriotism to his countrymen in order to arouse the Indian dormant spiritual manliness:

> I will go into thousand hells cheerfully if I can rouse my countrymen, immersed in tamas [darkness], to stand on their own feet and be men inspired with the spirit of Karmayoga [righteous actions]. Or: ... the older I grow, the more everything seems to me to lie in manliness. This is my new gospel. Do even evil like a man! Be wicked, if you must, on a grand scale, or: No more weeping, but stand on your feet and be men. It is a man-making religion that we want. It is man-making theories that we want. (qtd. in Kakar 205)

Vivekananda appealed to Indian men to conquer their passivity, weaknesses, compassion, and nonviolent nature that were said to make them feminine. These qualities were seen as barriers to becoming strong men who would have the power to save their family and motherland from foreigners. He called out to the men of India:

> What we want is muscles of iron and nerves of steel, inside which dwells a mind of the same material as that of which the thunder-bolt is made. Strength, manhood, Kshatra-Virya [warrior courage] ....we have wept long enough. No more weeping, but stand on your feet and be men. It is man-making religion we want...take away my weakness, take away unmanliness, and make me a man (qtd. in Jyotirmayananda 29).

In order to remind people of the virility of Indian men, Vivekananda had no difficulty mentioning male invaders, such as the British, Muslims. and other Europeans. He said that "he wanted to build an India with a Muslim body and a *Vedantist* brain, and maintained that no race understood as the British did 'what should be the glory of a man'"(qtd. in Kakar 205). Vivekananda's description of masculinity was not just based on physical prowess but had a spiritual dimension that provided a foundation for disciplining and expanding physical strength and power, through which Indians could claim Hindus' spiritual superiority over the British colonisers (Roy and Hammers 552). Thus, Vivekananda encouraged and helped Indian youth realize their latent masculine power, which he felt was needed. Apart from him, there were many other nationalists who, at the time of the struggle for independence, were trying to persuade Indian men to express manliness in the face of British aggression. I will discuss these people later.

Nonetheless, the nationalist obsession with masculinity was not only confined to men. It also had a great influence on women's lives in that it helped to construct Indian femininity. The developing nationalist discourse looked at woman's sexuality through the lens of a type of hegemonic femininity. The focus was on motherhood, and "mother" embodied the nation's honour and represented the pure female body, devoid of all desires, filled with maternal love and sacrifice. The anthropomorphism of India into a mother became a glorified feminine image of women; India became a "mother goddess," which was closely linked to the independence struggle. Hindu nationalists projected women onto the national stage but only as a maternal icon and as passive participants, not as independent feminine subjects.

Nationalist Representations of Motherhood

During the independence struggle against British rule, the ideology of motherhood was given the highest value in representing Hindu nationalist aspirations. In Hinduism, a woman is idealized as two contradictory images of the mother—a gentle social reproducer of cultural heritage and the divine mother goddess. The domesticated gentle matronly ideal of a mother is expected to absorb all types of suffering. In this image, she is conceived as compassionate, selfless, harmless, kind, and the reliever of other people's pain who produces valorous sons. She is a loving and supportive mother who provides comfort to her troubled sons and always tries to strengthen their hidden power and elevate their low spirit. Vivekananda described this mother as a "marvellous, unselfish, all-suffering, ever-forgiving mother" (qtd. by Bagchi 66). The Hindu woman is also regarded as the personification of the divine mother goddess Shakti. This goddess reveals herself in both creative and destructive imageries. Thus, we have two constructions: the gentle, creative, and benevolent goddess Parvati, and the goddess, Lakshmi, who represents the tranquil side. In contrast, the goddess Kali and the goddess Durga represent the aggressive, dark, ferocious, destructive, and malevolent side. These goddesses have inherent feminine power to create and preserve as well as to destroy the cosmos for new creation. They are able to incarnate into destructive forms to demolish evil forces in order to protect their devotees and the universe. In this manner, the malevolent goddesses are primarily associated with masculine traits, such as flesh and blood, destruction, violence, anger, dread, militarism, and terror. Vivekananda in his poem "Kali the Mother" described the destructive mother goddess in these words:

> Dancing made with joy, Come, Mother come,
> For terror is thy name, Death is in thy breasts
> Thou 'time' the All-Destroyer! Come, O Mother, come!
> Who dares misery love and hug the form of Death
> Dance in Destructions dance, To him the mother comes.
> (qtd. in Roychowdhary 435)

Thus, nationalists took these two maternal images of a woman from Hindu tradition and used them in the national movement as a strong political and martial feminine ideal to confront masculine British colonizers. Primarily, the process began during the renaissance period in colonial Bengal, when the domestic mother was transformed into the exalted mother goddess.

Along with Vivekananda, other Indian nationalists from Bengal—such as Bankimchandra Chattopadhyay, Rabindra Nath Tagore, and others—worked hard to combine the contradictory images of a mother and the mother goddess Shakti; they shaped them into an omnipotent mother goddess, who is not only ferocious towards her enemies but also loving towards her sons. As Tagore said, "Sword in your right hand you remove fear with your left! Two eyes smile with affection, the third emits fire" (qtd. in Bagchi, 66). The Hindu Bengali mother in her association with goddess Shakti not only became the symbol of ideal womanhood but also acted as a bridge between the social, political, and religious realms of India. As Jasodhara Bagchi points out: "The mother image that was projected by the anti-colonialist uprising was a combination of the affective warmth of a quintessentially Bengali mother and the mother goddess Shakti, known under various names as Durga, Chandi or Kali, who occupies a very important position in mainstream religious practice" (66).

This patriarchal idea of the motherland, symbolizing as ever nurturing—with an unconditional loving, self-sacrificing, and prosperous nature to be eulogized, protected, and served—was extremely influential and was immediately accepted as an integral part of the entire Indian national movement. A set of Bengali Muslims and Hindu nationalists from all over the country symbolically started representing India as Bharatmata. or "motherland Bharat." Nonetheless, this metaphor of Bharatmata was explained and projected differently by different Indian scholars. For instance, Tanika Sarkar explained the imagery of Bharatmata painted by Abanindranath as an "archetypical, hapless, female victim" (Sarkar 2021) with tears in her eyes? Contrarily, for Sugata Bose, the same imagery looks radiant, calm, and reassuring. The most popular imagery of Bharatmata—that is, Srinkhalita Bharatmata, the mother bound with chains that depicts the vulnerable condition of the motherland—was used everywhere as a powerful emotive medium in nationalist posters for Indian mass gatherings and to spread and boost the message of a glorious past but a painful colonial present (Bose 7). Following this, for the first time, it was Bankimchandra Chattopadhyay who politicized the image of the mother goddess by presenting her as the motherland of India. In his novel *Anandamatha*, he writes the first emblem of the country as a mother through the song "Vande Mataram," meaning the veneration of Mother India. It gradually became the powerful political anthem for Hindu nationalists. In this manner, the mother-son relationship turned into a strong iconography in Hindu nationalist psyche, which had no space for any other understanding of womanhood, including issues related to woman's sexuality and her emancipation. Her role as a good wife, lover, sister, friend, and daughter remained secondary or was neglected. Swami Vivekananda highlights the peculiarity of the mother image within the Indian mindset through these lines: "Now the ideal woman in India is the mother, the mother first and the mother last. The word woman calls up to the mind of the Hindu, Motherland; and god is called mother. In the west, the woman is wife. The idea of womanhood is concentrated there as the wife. To the ordinary man in India the whole force of womanhood is concentrated on motherhood" (Vivekananda 57).

The whole image of Indian nationalism, it seems, revolved around the image of motherhood as the motherland, which contrasts with the Western idea of motherhood; it focused on something that nationalists could call their own. In this regard, Sister Nivedita has explained how these two ideologies of motherhood are distinct yet complementary to each other. According to her, the Western cult of mother worship in the form of Virgin Mary, who is a caring and loving mother, achieved its completeness in the Indian spiritual icon of the mother goddess Shakti, who is motherly as well as destructive by nature. She describes the image of Shakti as follows: "In the east, the accepted symbol is of a woman nude, with flowing hair, so dark a blue that it seems in colour to be black; four handed—two hands in the act of blessing and two holding a knife and bleeding head respectively garlanded with skull and dancing, with protruding tongue, on the prostrate figure of a man all white with ashes" (20). For nationalists, the mother goddess in both her forms—affectionate and terrifying—was a caring mother for her own sons and family. This way, they not only domesticated the image of Shakti but also attempted to create another political metaphor—an ideal national Hindu family in which only a mother and her sons were allowed to reside together. Sister Nivedita writes about this national imagination of one family: "For the mother of the universe shines forth in the life of humanity, as a woman, as family life, as country" (324). Such domestication of the divine mother goddess affected women's lives to a great extent. Women are glorified as the mother goddess but are also circumscribed in the domains of motherhood, marriage, and family.

Women are expected to perform their maternal work in two ways—procreative and cultural. They are seen as social procreative machines for producing more and more sons, even at the cost of their own lives. At the same time, as cultural carriers, women have a great responsibility to train their sons as future warriors for the protection of the nation by passing on and teaching them traditional norms, culture, myths, rituals, and so forth from one generation to another. As Bagchi aptly points out: "The ideology of motherhood strengthened the social practice of [the] hidden exploitation of women. It made a negative contribution to the lives of women ... mothers upheld the hierarchy of patriarchal control within the family. No wonder she was mythologized as a symbol of order" (71). In this way, she is identified solely with motherhood; her work is childbearing. Caring and transferring skills became the key purpose of her life.

It is important to note that Indian women of all castes and communities were encouraged to participate in the national movement to free Mother India from the clutches of alien rulers—but only under the masculine framework through the domain of motherhood and marriage. Thus, a masculine ideology still dominated their lives. They were perceived as the gentle image of mother goddess Parvati and Lakshmi—who are the creator and preserver of life—but not as the powerful image of goddess Kali and Durga who also possess masculine trades and have the power to destroy. Additionally, Hindu women are taught to emulate Sita (the incarnation of the goddess Lakshmi) and Savitri as icons of the ideal mother and wife by remaining pure, chaste, and loyal towards their husbands. During the freedom struggle, women were expected to carry out their traditional roles and duties as chaste, devoted, and caring mothers of male sons. As the Indian nationalist and religious reformer Keshaw Chundern Sen asserts, "People will celebrate her entrails implying that her son has glorified her womb" (qtd. in Bagchi 65).

Gandhi was the first Congress leader to utilize the potential strength and emotional power of such mythological icons for mobilizing modern women to participate in the freedom struggle. Although Gandhi was aware of woman's sexuality and accepted it as a natural urge of human beings, he expected women to be more disciplined and virtuous. He lauded traditional Hindu values and promoted the iconic Sita as a national role model for Indian women by glorifying their chastity, devotion, and domestic virtues: "If you want Swaraj [self-rule], or Ramarajya [rule of King Rama] you have to become as pure as Sita ... only a woman who keeps her body and mind pure is worthy of our reverence[;] therefore, sisters wear Khadi ply Charkha and become pure" (538). Despite their active participation in the freedom movement, it was expected that women should place their primary value in their traditional roles as wives and mothers to produce valorous sons for India's freedom. By recasting the mythical ideals of Sita and Savitri, nationalists attempted to control and represent the view of gendered identity within Hindu nationalism that highlights women's chastity. Their femininity was envisaged under influential Hindu traditional ideology that accepts female sexual identity as mothers of heroic sons who predominantly serve the nation. In other words, nationalism imagined men and women in a gendered way: heroic, brave men and self-sacrificing, chaste women.

Markedly, British rulers played a significant role in improving women's condition by legally prohibiting horrendous practices, such as widow burning (sati), child marriage, female feticide, which was rampant in Indian society, and permitting widow remarriage. In this scenario, extreme Hindu forces or reformists (later known as Hindutva forces)—who saw themselves as self-appointed guardians of Hindu tradition—emerged as a strong reaction to Christian missionary work and the spread of Western values; they also began perpetuating communal aggression against the Muslim community. They started claiming to be the sole source of Indian national identity and construed India as a Hindu nation. The terms "Hindu" and "India" became synonymous for them; there was no space for Muslims and Christians (Varshney 241). The primary question for them was to define who is Hindu, and the father of Hindu nationalist ideology, V. D. Savarkar, answered it: "A Hindu is a person who regards this land ... from the

Indus to Seas as his fatherland (Pitrabhumi) as well as his holyland (Punybhumi) " (Savarkar, 110-13). With this definition, Savarkar made it clear that India predominantly belongs to those people who have their holy places here. According to such criteria, only Hindus are the real Indians, whereas Muslims and Christians are seen as foreigners and not accepted wholly in India as it is not their holy land (Varshney 231). Hindutva nationalists started insisting that Muslims had to accept the superiority of Hindu culture and tradition in order to live in India. There were two motifs of Hindutva. The first was to construct a united nation by Hinduizing the polity and a nation into which Muslims would be assimilated if they accepted the political and cultural centrality of Hinduism. And if minority groups did not agree to assimilation, Hindu nationalism would simply become exclusionary, both in principle and practice (Vershney 232).

In this manner, Hindutva nationalists attempted to force their version of masculinity on Muslims and other minority groups. After achieving independence, the new democratic government was established with the stated vision of providing justice, equality, freedom, and autonomy of thought as well as freedom of expression, faith, and worship to its citizens in an attempt to stop the idea of rigid gender roles and the hierarchical social order it supported. However, the protection of citizens' rights remains a challenge to the Indian government, since the forces of Hindutva continue to pursue the goal of preserving the Hindu masculine tradition for the nation.

Masculinity and Mothers in Contemporary Nation Building

Modernization has had a strong and significant impact on the personal and social lives of many Indians. Women are becoming aware of their social status and rights. They are consciously participating in outside activities and interacting with the external world. Moreover, they have started questioning the traditional role attributed to them and the patriarchal gendered ideology. Despite the progressive spirit of modernity in Indian culture and society, there are serious critiques of modernity by extremist groups as well. For instance, they think modernity and Western thought negatively affect Indian traditional culture and values that require urgent protection. In this scenario,

Hindutva activists have come forward to affirm and insist on their right to be the masculine protectors of Hindu tradition. Beyond affirming their ideas on Hindu masculinity, they believe it must be protected from all that modernity would impose on Hindu traditions. Sangh Parivar is a conglomeration of four major Shakha (organizations/branches)—RSS, VHP, Shiv Sena, and BJP—that share some common ideas with minor differences: They believe that India is a Hindu nation in which Christians and Muslims are outsiders. With the departure of the British, Christianity lost its political edge, and Muslims became the principal rivals not only because they are the second largest group in India, but also because of their religious link to Pakistan—a Muslim nation established by the partition of India in 1947.

Muslims in India were thus seen as the threatening "other" against whom Hindu masculinity had to be built. They constructed Muslim masculinity as something negative; Muslims were lustful and sexually charged. In order to do this, they referred back to the extraordinary events of abduction and conversion outlined in medieval stereotypes. Historically, the picture painted was of licentious Muslim rulers and the debauchery of the Prophet. These descriptions were then extended to the general population, and Muslim men were depicted as violent, virile, and focused on their sexual appetites. Theirs was nothing but a life of luxury and religious fanaticism (Gupta 8). As part of these developments, the Hindu woman was portrayed as vulnerable to Muslim aggression and sexuality, who must be safeguarded. In this way, the primary purpose of Hindutva was to save the superiority of Hindu masculinity and to rehabilitate gender roles. They saw it as their duty to protect their women from foreign males and demanded that Hindu women continue to serve in their traditional role as mothers (Gautam 56). They insisted that all Hindus must recognize Ram and Shivaji as their male icons (Banerjee 172). Shiv Sena described such a sentiment as the following: "We are Hindustanis [Indians] and therefore, Hindu is the belief of our party. We love Hindustan more than we love ourselves" (www.shivsena.org). The various branches of Hindutva use only Hindu male icons, myths, songs, and scriptures as their medium to reinforce masculine Hindu ideology over contemporary India. Similarly, they employ the ideas of Vivekananda, V. D. Sawarkar, and Tilak to attract younger generations to their program. Today, however, there are a few Muslim and non-Muslim organizations who have begun to counter, in a limited way, this Hindutva masculine ideology. These include liberal and secular Hindus and Muslims, leftists, communists, Ambedakaraists, Bhim Army, Indian feminists, constitutionalists, AIMIM, Asaduddin Owaisi and Akbaruddin Owaisi. However, due to their independent thinking, secular ideology, and sometimes extremist style, they are less popular and unable to get the support of many in the Muslim and other communities, and Hindutva remains effective in perpetuating hatred against Muslims.

Moreover, using masculinist strategies, Hindutva organizations convinced some Hindu women to participate in their Hindu masculine mission. They try to control women's autonomy and their visibility in the public sphere. The women's wing of Sangh Parivar is known as RSS (Rashtria Sevika Samiti) and was exclusively established to protect women and mothers from corrupt modern thoughts and values and to teach them their traditional roles as mothers and chaste wives. For this reason, Sangh Parivar uses two strategies against women: They promote the ideology of motherhood for national discourse, and they preach masculine supremacy over women by emphasizing the institution of patriarchy. As Thomas Blom Hansen states:

> Being a mother and looking after the family lies at the core of national life, and of the reproduction of cultural values in Hindu culture. Women's performance in the public sphere should not be an impediment to motherhood. Education and work must be encouraged but should, simultaneously, be adapted and subordinated to the supreme goal of motherhood whose rationale is derived from the nationalist discourse: raising children as patriotic citizens in the nation states as defined by Hindu culture. (89)

For Sevika Samiti, the ideology of motherhood can work for nationhood in three ways: 1) A woman is a mother; nurturing her family, raising the children, and serving the husband are her supreme duties; 2) A mother is a cultural carrier; she can transfer traditions from one generation to another; and 3) Women should not get an education or have careers that make them individualistic and diminish the development of their family skills (Hansen 87). Hindutva forces envisage the nation as a beautiful woman who is a mother and who is to be celebrated as Matri Shakti—maternal power. Hindu men have the responsibility of protecting the honour of mothers from any outside danger. Additionally, women must accept Rani Lakshmi bai and, Jijabai who were female warriors and mothers, as their female ideals. Women are allowed to participate as female warriors so long as they follow certain masculine traits that are part of the accepted gender script in order to protect the traditional role of motherhood and nationhood.

Today, women politicians—such as Sadhvi Ritambara, Uma Bharati, Vijayraja Scindia, and Pragya Sadhvi—are prominent female proponents of Sevika Samiti who not only motivate woman to maintain their patriarchal-inspired roles but also work to affirm Hindu men's masculinity against Muslim males. To that end, it can be said that despite their advances in every field of Indian society and culture, women are supposed to remain subordinate to patriarchal traditional gender domination. Joane Nagel points out that "traditions, real or invented, are often patriarchal and point out the tenacious and entrenched nature of masculine privilege and the tight connection between masculinity and nationalism" (254). It is noteworthy that Hindutva forces cannot challenge the constitutional rights of women directly, yet they strongly and aggressively condemn women's demands for equality and freedom in every aspect of life.

In this way, Hindu nationalist gendered ideology has a strong impact on both men and women. It is evident that the Hindu nation is a masculine construct; it is portrayed as a family in which both men and women have their assigned roles to play. The men are expected to show their commitment to patriotism, nationalism, and militarism. They are the defenders of women's and the nation's honour regardless of how they feel. As Nagel writes: "Women's shame is a family shame [and] the nation's shame is a man's shame" (254). Women's role as reproducers and transmitters of traditional boundaries of the nation are important in nationalist struggles. As a result of these gender roles, one can argue that both men and women are constrained and expected to be passive recipients of these Hindu nationalist ideals. Women in particular are repressed. Their roles have been constructed for them by men within the framework of Hindu patriarchy. Sometimes female nationalists become reluctant participants in these masculine organizations.

Although they often participate directly in various national movements, struggles, conflicts and even the military, their contributions are questionable and blurry, since they must work under masculine rule and organizations, which undermines their level of autonomy, equality, and freedom. Nonetheless, there has been no backlash or resistance against the nationalist construction of women's roles and sexuality from the colonial era to today. Women quietly served as satyagrahins (women freedom fighters) and then returned to their households and continued their lives as if nothing had happened. As Nagel says, "A nationalist movement that encourages women's participation in the name of national liberation often balks at feminist demands for gender equality" (253). Similarly, men also face the same kind of constraints and suppression to maintain their assigned gender roles. War is defined as an integral part of a man's patriotic duty and honour. Those who resist this calling are framed as cowards and a dishonour to the nation. Any sign of being passive or compassionate is perceived as too feminine and as an insult to his manliness. Men are perceived as being without emotions and hard, but neither are true. They are also expected to treat women in line with the patriarchal ideals outlined by the tradition. As Nagel says:

> Giving this difference in men's and women's connection and conception of the nation and the state, it is not surprising that there is a 'gender gap' dividing men and women on so many political issues. Thus, the intimate link between masculinity and nationalism, like all hegemonic structures, shapes not only the feelings and thinking of men, it has left its stamp on the hearts and minds of women as well. (261)

Thus, in a gendered nation, both men and women are victims of their traditional roles and actions. It seems that they are just passive receptors of their situated destiny, which is sometimes beyond their control.

Conclusion: Searching for a Gender-Neutral Nation

This chapter has highlighted the way gendered ideas about masculinity and motherhood have shaped Indian nationhood. Nationalists perceive women's procreative capacity as the main ingredient that justifies their national identity. Motherhood is constructed as a strong political and social resource to be used for building the nation, but for women, it has become just another hegemonic masculine dimension of control. The woman's body has become a battlefield for developing ideologies. Thus, the idealization of the empowered woman, constructed as mother goddess, actually led to her enslavement. As Bagchi points out: "Socially and ideologically the glorified Indian mother belongs to the world of myths ... [motherhood] strengthened the social practice of hidden exploitation of women" (71). Women are oppressed in the garb of divinity and encouraged to embrace it as their path to emancipation.

Although globalization, modernization, and advances in science and technology have played significant roles in eroding traditional forms of patriarchy in India, which no doubt provide physical and social space for women's emancipation, women are still pressured to carry forwards an ever-evolving Hindu tradition. They are expected to work within this communal and masculinized landscape, which is reinforced by Hindutva forces. Hindu nationalists expect their women to be pure, chaste, caring, and dedicated mothers and wives, regardless of any progressive attitude towards education or careers that women may have. The forces of Hindutva have systematically organized masculine social structures in large parts of India by claiming to be revivalists of the Hindu traditional family, the Indian nation, and its women.

It is important to note that these traditions are being promoted to suit the image of a modern India that is envisioned by the Hindu narrative. However, the problem with these constructs is that they are rooted in and emphasize just one aspect of India: that is, its glorious past! The Extremist interpreters of Hinduism puts immense stress on and exalts the Indian historical past, so that they sometimes ignore other religious ideologies and the military strength of India. Hindutva nationalists are not ready to accept any models of femininity or masculinity in the modern era that are different from their own constructions. In this scenario, women have to struggle for their rights, freedom, autonomy and dignity which can only be possible through a gender-neutral conceptualization of India. There is always hope that patriarchy can be transcended. We have to construct the right way for it to happen. I finish with the words of the renowned Indian feminist Arundhati Roy: "Another world is not only possible. She is on her way. On a quiet day, I can hear her breathing."

Endnotes

1. Many historians believe that British rule in India began after the Battle of Plassey (1757), in which the British East India Company defeated the King of Bengal NawabSiraj-ud-Daulah and started expanding their empire in various parts of Bengal.

2. In the term "British Raj," the word "Raj" is a Hindi word, which means "rule." So "British Raj" means British rule in India.

3. Sister Nivedita, or Margaret Noble, was an Irish woman and Vivekananda's disciple, who became an Indian nationalist. She came to India in the 19th century and decided to make Kolkata her home.

4. Mahatma Gandhi emphasized wearing self-made or homemade cloths made of indigenous material called Khadhi, and Charkha is a hand-run spinning wheel for making Khadhi.

Works Cited

Bagchi, Jasodhra. "Representing Nationalism: Ideology of Motherhood in Colonial Bengal." *Economic and Political Weekly*, vol. 25, no. 42-43, 1990, pp. WS65-WS71.

Banerjee, Sikata. "Gender and Nationalism: The Masculinization of Hinduism and Female Political Participation in India." *Women's Studies International Forum*, vol. 26, no. 2, pp. 167-79.

Bose, Sugata. *The Nation as Mother and Other Visions of Nationhood.* Penguin Random House India, 2017.

Gandhi, M.K. *Collected Works.* Navajivan Press, 1969.

Gavin, Rand, and Kim A. Wagner. "Recruiting the Martial Races: Identities and Military Service in Colonial India." *Patterns of Prejudice*, vol. 46, no. 3-4, 2012, pp. 232-54.

Gupta, Charu. "Anxious Hindu Masculinities in Colonial North India: 'Shuddhi' and 'Sangathan' Movements." CrossCurrents, vol. 61, no. 4, pp. 441-54.

Hansen, Thomas Blom. "Controlled Emancipation: Women and Hindu Nationalism." *The European Journal of Development Research*, vol. 6, no. 2, pp. 82-94.

Jyotirmayananda. *Vivekananda: His gospel of Manmaking with a Garland of Tributes and a Chronicle of His Life and Times with Picture.* All India Press, 1992.

Kakar, Sudhir. *The Inner World: A Psychoanalytic Study of Childhood and Society in India*. Oxford University Press, 2015.

Macaulay, T. B. *Macaulay: Prose and Poetry*. Harvard University Press, 1967.

Nagel, Joane. "Masculinity and Nationalism: Gender and Sexuality in the Making of Nations." *Ethnic and Racial Studies*, vol. 21, no. 2, 1998, pp. 242-69.

Nivedita, Sister. *Kali the Mother*. Advaita Ashram, 1900.

Peterson, V. Spike. *The Woman and the War Reader*. Edited by Lois Ann Lorntzen, and Jennifer Turpin, New York University Press, 1998, pp. 41-49.

Roy, Arundhati. "Another World." *Spirituality Health*, www.spiritualityhealth.com/quotes/another-world-not-only-possible-she-her-way-quiet. Accessed 27 Apr. 2021.

Roychowdhary, Satyam. *Vivekananda for You: Selected Lectures, Writings, Letters and Coversations of Swami Vivekananda*. Deep Prakashan, 2012.

Roy, Abhik, and Michele L. Hammers. "Swami Vivekananda's Rhetoric of Spiritual Masculinity." *Western Journal of Communication*, vol. 78, no. 4, 2014, pp. 545-62.

Sarakar, Tanika. "Nationalist Iconography: Image of Women in 19th Century Bengali Literature." *Economic and Political Weekly*, vol.21, no 47, p.2021.

Savarkar, V.D. *Hindutva*. Veer SavarkarPrakashan, 1989.

Jalal, Ayesha. "Communalism Exploding The Politics of Muslim Identity in South Asia." *Nationalism, Democracy and Development: State and Polities in India*. Edited by Sugata Bose and Ayesha Jalal. Oxford University Press, 1997, p.5.

MacMunn George. *The Martial Races of India*. Sampson Low, Marston and Co. 1933.

Varshney, Ashutosh. "Contested Meaning: India's National Identity, Hindu Nationalism and Politics of Anxiety." *Reconstructing Nations and States*, vol. 122, no. 3, 1993, pp. 227-61.

Vivekananda, Swami. *The Message of Vivekananda*. Advaita Ashram, 2016.

Vivekananda, Swami. *Complete Works*, 10th edition, Vol. 8. Advaita Ashram, 1978.

Chapter 11

"A Husband Is the Firstborn Child": Networks, Masculinities, and Motherhood in Tanzania

Rasel Madaha

Introduction

Discussions on motherhood are not new within feminist discourse, and there are at least two scholarly lines of thought. The first line focuses on motherhood as a pathway to attain a socially assigned identity as a mature woman. Women feel obliged to fulfil the role as mothers in their societies. In addition, they may sacrifice their personal goals to fulfil such motherhood roles. As such, the socially assigned role, as claimed by some feminists (West and Zimmerman; McMahon), subjects women to patriarchal control. The second line of thought focuses on the role of motherhood in helping women attain a cultural space that serves as a privilege for mothers only. Women derive some happiness after gaining membership in such spaces, as it provides cultural privileges associated with being a mother (Nelson).

Within the mentioned milieu, this chapter discusses the importance of modern forms of women's social networks, as well as how they can support the role of women as mothers and wives and positively affect gender relations. This chapter argues that most social capital theories have overlooked the transformative character of women's networks. They have instead focused on the bridging, bonding, and linking functions of networks (Woolcock and Narayan; Narayan). The bottom line is that social capital theories assume a gender-neutral position. For that reason, they have ignored the role of gender in theorizing about such networks (O'Neill and Gidengill). They overlook structural inequalities and gender oppression in community development.

The empowerment of rural communities through networks and networking are part of the Tanzanian government's commitment towards the creation of a pro-poor development environment, which is meant to enable rural communities to achieve sustainable livelihoods. Within this context, the objective of this chapter is to high-light the roles of one of the social networks—Transformative Village Community Networks (TVCONEs)—in shaping and redefining gender relations in favour of motherhood. The transformation of gender relations, in turn, leads to community development. It also underscores that although TVCONEs offer some microfinance services, they are mainly social networks providing social services to members. Microfinance is simply an add-on to the motherhood role of the TVCONEs. In other words, this chapter focuses on the social aspects of TVCONEs and not the microfinance aspect. The empirical data in support of the analysis were gathered in the Mkalama district of Central Tanzania.

Theoretical Framework

The chapter draws some insights from socialist feminism and social network theories for their ability to analyze context-specific challenges within a neoliberal context. This framework assumes that neoliberalism and associated market economic reforms lead to the disproportionate exploitation of women (Calkin) and that women need to capitalize on their collective power to deal with such exploitation (Mohanty). One of the key arguments of socialist feminists is that no single universal socialist feminism exists for the whole world. Johanna Brenner highlights the fact that socialist feminism acknowledges all feminisms that synthesize women's oppression by capitalism and patriarchy within particular identities, such as race, sexuality, ethnicity, gender, and nationality. It calls for inclusive feminist movements among women who collaborate with interested men to transform power relations for a just society. Socialist feminists, states Diana Kendall, view women's oppression as a result of their dual roles as paid and unpaid workers in a capitalist market economy. In the workplace, women are exploited by capitalism. At home, women are exploited by patriarchy.

Several African scholars are of the opinion that there are several African feminisms (Aina; Nkealah) that attempt to deal with neo-liberalism and patriarchy. These are strands of socialist feminism. Although it is not common for one to relate African women's struggles with socialist feminism, Gender and Development (GAD)—one of the socialist feminist approaches as might be argued by Brenner—has become a buzz phrase on the continent, including Tanzania. Gender mainstreaming is the main tool to achieve GAD through addressing Practical Gender Needs (PGN) in the short term and Strategic Gender Needs (SGN) in the long term (UNESCO; Connelly et al; Joekes; Mitter; Park).

Social Network Theory

Social network theory synthesizes the way people network to deal with their day-to-day challenges. Networking people and communities are stronger than isolated people and communities. According to Patricia Cook-Craig (314) networking involves two major assumptions: homophily and propinquity. Homophily refers to the phenomenon in which individuals and entities are likely to connect to others with whom they share similar characteristics, whereas propinquity refers to the phenomenon in which individuals and entities connect with those that are geographically close to them.

Networking provides organizational structure based on the pattern of flow of information, membership composition, and the activities involved (Haverkort et al; Farrington and Nelson). In modern times, social media tools increasingly provide outstanding ways for online networking. Social network theory also states that men and women are not isolated individuals in their communities because they always network (Wellman; Cook-Craig) to cope with crises of different kinds. Networking among men and women does not take place in isolation but tends to involve both sexes. Network theorists view a community as composed of essentially related individuals in groups, which can be identified through observation (LeCompte and Schensul 52). People do not act in isolation; instead, they are influenced by the cobweb of networks to which they belong.

Literature Review

Since the mid-1980s, women in Tanzania have been relying on networks to cope with difficulties associated with the market economic context and in particular the government's withdrawal of free social services. Similar challenges and associated strategies have been reported elsewhere (Alders, Haverkort, and van Veldhuizen; Parpart, Connelly, and Barriteau; Jackson; Archambault; Cook-Craig; Eisenstein). Village Community Banks (VICOBAs) are among the most recent form of women's networking in Tanzania. The term "VICOBA" was coined in Tanzania around 2002 and has successfully been mainstreamed into the Tanzanian urban and rural culture. VICOBA involves the provision of rotating savings and credit to marginalized people without access to formal financial institutions. They are registered as community-based organizations (CBO) at the local government level.

More recently, through my own research, I came across the existence of TVCONEs and their relationship to VICOBA. TVCONEs are the evolution of VICOBA into women's social networks. TVONEs are led and dominated by women for the common collective good of each member, which is important to know because Tanzanian women form collectives for the sole purpose of addressing their motherhood role and dealing with patriarchal exploitation. Specifically, the shortcoming of VICOBA in addressing motherhood roles is what led to the emergence of TVCONEs, which are voluntarily self-selected groups whose key role is to enable women to perform their reproductive and community managing roles. They are more sustainable than VICOBA because the drive for the formation of such social networks originates from the members themselves. They also provide a platform for saving money through purchasing shares to create a cumulative loan fund for the provision of social welfare soft loans—that is, the provision of microfinance services is meant to help the members better perform their motherhood roles. Details on the social roles and motherhood roles of TVCONEs in particular will be presented in the findings section of this chapter.

In the same vein, TVCONEs play a significant role in enabling marginalized communities to develop capacities to deal with their challenges. Several studies show how networking can lead to community development. Some studies focus on how networking can lead to positive change (Rice and Yoshioka-Maxwell; Lee). Others focus on how networking can be used as a survival mechanism among the poor (Oracion; Wallace; Kasper and Mulder). Some scholars use network analysis to examine decision making, social capital development, and community development (Rainie and Wellman). Specific to Tanzania, feminist elite formal networks defend the rights of vulnerable populations, including poor men and women (Madaha, "Organized and Gendered Media Advocacy"). Feminist elites are scholars, entrepreneurs, and activists who reside in urban areas. However, the urban feminist networks are dependent on donor assistance and are not sustainable in the absence of such assistance. Networks do not exist in a vacuum because they exist in a context, and this has ramifications. Communities are not idling or just waiting for external intervention; local forms of organizing existed prior to any external assistance. Brian Dill further argues that new forms of networking do not readily fit into the Tanzanian indigenous context. This calls for some compromise between the desired forms of networking and local social norms.

Although the aforementioned studies present useful information on networking and networks, they have not adequately explained the role of self-created feminist networks in improving motherhood and the attainment of community development within the neoliberal context in Tanzania. The existing literature on self-created networks (Oracion; Wallace; Kasper and Mulder; Rice and Yoshioka-Maxwell; Lee) has taken a gender-neutral position that ignores the role of motherhood. In other words, networking, if poorly managed, may lead to further marginalization of poor women and other marginalized people because it may create social structures that reinforce oppression.

The History of Masculinity and Women's Networking in Tanzania

Colonization by the British and the Germans introduced a cash economy that created a context in which Tanzanian men were integrated into the economy. Women were left to develop traditional ways to fit into that context to supplement and complement men's efforts. The introduction of a cash economy and greed for material wealth over and above communal needs signified further reinforced patriarchy in Tanzania as we know it today (Mbilinyi, "The 'New Woman' and Traditional Norms in Tanzania"; Madaha, "Organized and Gendered Media Advocacy").

Women relied on informal ways of solving their problems and on Upatu schemes in particular. At that time, these schemes served as platforms for grassroots women's organizing for addressing social and economic needs. More precisely, participants of Upatu would put some money in a kitty each day, and then after a specified and agreed upon time, a designated participant would claim the entire kitty. The time for depositing money in the kitty varies from one group to another and from one location to another (Jellicoe; Tripp, "Gender, Political Participation"; Tripp, *Changing the Rules*). Upatu enabled women to participate in the informal sector through the creation of informal income-generating activities. The Upatu schemes continue to operate to date, although their numbers have diminished. Some use Upatu schemes as well as VICOBA or TVCONE schemes. However, Upatu was one of the key informal savings and rotating schemes serving as a platform for grassroots feminist struggles until the mid-1980s and the onset of neoliberalism in the country (Tripp, "Gender, Political Participation"; Cranenburgh; Mbilinyi, "The State of Women in Tanzania"; Msongazila; Madaha, "Organized and Gendered Media Advocacy").

In addition, there was also women's political networking during the independence struggles, which played a key political supporting role from 1955 to 1961—the year the country became independent. The women's movement helped the nationalist political male leaders to seize power from the British colonialists (Geiger, "Tanganyikan Nationalism"; Geiger, *TANU Women: Gender and Culture*). Following independence, male leaders deliberately reduced the influence of women's formal networking and organizing as part of the plan for socialist national building (Madaha, "Organized and Gendered Media Advocacy"). The reforms further intensified patriarchal exploitation, as women were assigned the role of reproducing children and taking care of household matters. Men remained the owners of women, children, and other household material wealth (Meena, *Gender in Southern Africa*; "The Impact of Structural Adjustment"). Following the failure of government socialist initiatives in the mid-1980s and coupled with the liberalization of the economy, all Tanzanians were permitted to formally organize outside party lines. This led to a rapid increase of new forms of autonomous networking. Some women, especially those in urban areas, formed women advocacy NGOs. Women in rural areas who had been excluded from the cash economy were brought on board through joining savings and credit associations (ROSCAs) that were donor funded. It is worth noting that the aim of such associations was integrating women into a neoliberal capitalist economy under Women In Development (WID) projects (Jellicoe; Meena, *Gender in Southern Africa*; The Impact of Structural Adjustment"; URT, *Cooperative Development Policy*; Tripp et al.).

Although the networks continue to exist to date, other new forms of networking have emerged. For instance, VICOBAs—which are also referred to as Village Savings and Loans Associations (VSLA) in Uganda, have become the most famous donor funded microfinance scheme across rural and urban areas of Tanzania since the early 2000s. They are an offshoot of the Grameen microfinance model from Bangladesh and developed to address the challenges associated with the failure of WID ROSCAs schemes. The overemphasis of VICOBA on microfinance at the expense of other social roles, such as motherhood, led to the emergence of TVCONEs. In other words, TVCONEs allow women to pay more attention to their motherhood roles. The motherhood role of TVCONEs is undocumented, and for that reason, it is the focus of this chapter.

Methodology and Findings[1]

The empirical data were collected using a longitudinal ethnography, which began in 2006. Additional instrumental data were also gathered during the author's PhD research from April 2015 to November 2015 at Mkalama district, Singida region, which is located in Central

Tanzania. The study employed an exploratory research design using an embedded multiple-case study research method. The data analysis was done through content analysis and descriptive statistics.

This section presents the findings on the role of TVCONEs in improving motherhood and gender relations (see Table 1). I argue that the networks enable women to perform their role as mothers who have to take care of their households. Furthermore, the networks, among other things, also help to increase respect for network members in their households, reduce domestic violence, improve intimacy relationships, and grant women more freedom to do things that interest them. Overall, the findings suggest improvements in gender relations in favour of better performance in women's role as mothers and increased collaboration between women and men, since neoliberalism has reduced sources of income that in the past enabled men to take pride in their masculinity. Women have been able to step up to the plate and contribute more to the care of husbands and children in what can be termed as an extension of their motherhood responsibilities. As such, men have been brought into the loop of motherly care. Before that, men engaged in farming and petty business. The private sphere has become a refuge for desperate men negatively affected by neoliberal economic policies, as the free market economy does not necessarily favour marginalized men. Men with adequate capital are the ones with a better chance of surviving in a neoliberal context. In other words, I believe that following this crisis of masculinity, gender relations are being transformed to the benefit of women.

Table 1. Role of TVCONEs
(N=178 where TVCONE members are 100 and 78 are spouses)

Role of TVCONE	Ward	Members of TVCONEs		Spouses	
		Freq.	Perc. (%)	Freq.	Perc. (%)
Increase respect for women	Ig.	25	100	19	95
	Kiny.	25	100	21	100
	Kikh.	25	100	16	84
	Ms	25	100	15	83
Reduce domestic violence	Ig.	25	100	20	100
	Kiny.	25	100	21	100
	Kikh.	25	100	19	100
	Ms	25	100	18	100
Improve intimate relationships	Ig.	24	96	20	100
	Kiny.	22	88	20	95
	Kikh.	19	76	17	89
	Ms	20	80	18	100
Grant women more freedom	Ig.	25	100	18	90
	Kiny.	25	100	21	100
	Kikh.	25	100	17	90
	Ms	25	100	17	94

Key: Freq=frequency, Ig.= Iguguno, Kiny.=Kinyangiri, Kikh=Kikhonda, Ms.= Misingi

Source: Survey Data (2015) in Madaha, *Networking by the Rural Poor*

In general, patriarchal gender relations lead to gender inequality because they affect perspectives of people's needs. Gender relations determine whether women have control over their lives and can realize their rights as mothers. This also holds true for men. Neoliberalism and globalization have transformed gender relations resulting in, among other things, unequal burdens for unpaid work in the household for women, resulting in poor health and insufficient rest for women and girls. Women have increasingly become breadwinners. Although men provide some support with household chores, women's burdens have increased outside the home. The breadwinning role traditionally belonged to men. National policies, however, have been changed to go hand in hand with the neoliberal market economy, which has led to a reduction of funds for health and education, with a disproportionately negative impact on girls' and women's access. With the reduction of funds, women were expected to fill the gaps. Within this context, the role of women as mothers is seriously hindered. Even more, global-ization has led to a rise in violence in general linked to the changing political economy of nation-states in the international order (Sen and Östlin). Nonetheless, Table 1 presents the new social dynamics brought about by TVCONEs, which are as explained in the following sub-sections.

Women's Social Status

The findings of this study reveal that TVCONE members have relatively higher household income than nonmembers, which means they are in a better position to perform their motherhood roles than nonmembers. Neoliberalism has opened new room for motherhood. Those women who are members of TVCONEs are perceived as better mothers because they rely less on men, who increasingly have diminishing resources. As such, women with higher incomes gain increased respect from their spouses. All respondents (TVCONEs) of the questionnaire claim to have gained respect from their spouses. Over 80 per cent of male spouses from across all four wards support the view (see Table 1). The view was also shared by one of the key informants:

> My husband values TVCONEs because [they] have been not only instrumental to the lives of our children but also for my husband. For example, using the funds accrued from my TVCONE, I managed to support his studies at an agricultural college. He graduated successfully with a diploma in agricultural sciences. The support I gave him increased the respect and value I gained as woman in our household. Similarly to the additional respect I gained in my household, my community has benefitted immensely from the agricultural expertise acquired by my husband. My husband currently serves as an agricultural

extension officer working for the local government at the district main office. But perhaps more importantly, the entire district benefits from his expertise. In short, a woman with membership in TVCONEs has access to more opportunities, which can boost the respect given at home and in the community much more than that obtained by a nonmember working at home. Women without businesses are being labelled "goal keepers" waiting for free handouts from their husbands. (Secretary of TVCONE, Iguguno ward, 11 May 2015)

The income gained through membership in TVCONEs, as revealed in the above quotation, is used to meet traditional male responsibilities, such as feeding the household. The income gained by women enabled them to perform their motherhood roles.

Focus Group Discussions (FGDs) also revealed that women's contributions to household expenses increase their social status. Despite their traditional role as caretakers and men's dependants, women are seen as key players in the welfare of the entire household. Men in Mkalama district have accepted the power gained by women in exchange for household support. And this is because men's resources have increasingly diminished, making it harder for them to provide the required household support. The opportunities that were available to men are fast diminishing. Men spent less on household expenses in the past. However, following government and welfare NGO withdrawal from providing free and subsidized social services, men needed more financial resources to support their households. Subsequently, women who did not take bold steps to be less dependent on their spouses are often subjected to domestic violence. In other words, requesting support from men who have no means to provide it is seen as an insult to them. From the women's (traditional) perspective, the husband is a firstborn child. As such, women do not find it difficult to support the needs of their husbands and those of their children. This is an important development towards improved gender relations in the Tanzanian context.

In addition to the loss of conventional avenues for obtaining revenue, men are increasingly affected by the new neoliberal policies which allow the patriarchal elites to purchase huge tracts of land, leaving a significant number of impoverished men without land. Given all these developments, gender roles assigned to men and women have been redefined because women now engage in new productive roles to meet household financial needs. The findings support those of some other feminist scholars (Staudt; Tripp et al).

Overall, there is ample evidence that there is a crisis with respect to the workings of patriarchy in places that have adopted neoliberalism, as in the Mkalama district and the rest of Tanzania (Chant, "Men in Crisis"; Kabeer; Mannon, "Love in the Time of Neo-Liberalism"; Mannon, "Pampered Sons, (Wo)manly Men"; World Bank). Nevertheless, the crisis has brought mixed results across a variety of countries. Although some men in Mkalama district expect their wives to join TVCONE to support their households, men in the northwest of Costa Rica, for example, perceive increased participation of women in the labour market as giving too much power to women (Mannon, "Love in the Time of Neo-Liberalism"; Mannon, "Pampered Sons, (Wo)manly Men"). The situation also holds true in other developing countries (Chant, *Researching Gender*).

Domestic Violence

Another important role of TVCONEs in improving gender relations is the reduction of domestic violence. TVCONEs have enabled women to become breadwinners in their households; they no longer need to rely on men. However, most have decided to collaborate with their spouses in the business. Although women in the study area often tolerate violence in the name of performing their roles as mothers, domestic violence seriously interferes with their motherhood role. There are few avenues from which to escape from gender-based violence (GBV). All of the TVCONE members and their spouses who responded to the semistructured questionnaire agree with the statement. Similar responses were also seen in other qualitative methods, including observations, FGDs, in-depth interviews, and transect walks specifically conducted to further probe this issue. Based on the findings, it seems that intimate relationships among TVCONE members and their husbands have improved significantly. TVCONE members whose incomes have increased do not bother their husbands with frequent requests for money to purchase food items. Such items include but are not limited to salt, tomatoes, onions, cooking oils and spices. Moreover, wives now assist with the payment of important social services, such as school fees for their children. Their contributions have led to a reduction in domestic violence. Most notably, the key source of domestic violence in the study area is the demand for cash from husbands, whose sources of income have shrunk. Rising household expenses coupled with the new cost sharing policies for services formerly provided by the government have reduced men's ability to support their households.

The findings of this study support a phenomenon discussed by Anne Maria Möller-Leimkuhler known as "maladaptive coping strategies"[1]. Following a study of men living in advanced industrialized and transitional economies, Möller-Leimkuhler's study highlights men's vulnerability regarding traditional masculinity, whereby men assume desperate and at times violent coping strategies, such as emotional withdrawal, reluctance to seek help, and even alcohol abuse. Similarly, a man who fails to provide for his household in Mkalama district using traditionally male income-generating activities is subjected to similar severe stress which results in domestic violence. Moreover, an even worse problem associated with patriarchy is husbands running away from their families.

A similar problem can be found among women who have patriarchal values and believe that men who fail to adequately provide for the household are worthless. Wives leaving their husbands has been widely reported among women living within the study area. I would argue that women with these traditional values need to change. Unfortunately, many people believe that once a woman has economic power, there may be negative and not merely positive consequences for the household. Although this study's findings reveal that spousal bonds tend to be stronger in families with membership in the TVCONEs, there are a few cases in which women, following the rise in their income levels, have left their marital homes. Consequently, there is now a call for public education on good marital relationships.

Nonetheless, even though women have taken on breadwinning roles, most of them in Mkalama district have successfully managed to handle the transformation through compromise with their husbands. Community members generally believe that TVCONE members should try and establish family cohesion, keep their husbands from running away, and improve their businesses. This is a tall order, but they appreciate that the new context enables them to better perform their roles as mothers.

The findings of this study do not support the popular belief that poor husbands refuse to give their wives permission to engage in productive activities because they need to maintain their authority over women. Naila Kabeer argues that power within marital relations in widely differing contexts, such as Latin America, sub-Saharan Africa and Asia, rests on female dependence on men (17-18). Men maintain their power by, among other things, refusing to give their wives permission to work outside the household, despite household poverty or their own unemployment. An older study by Sender and Smith suggests that Tanzanian husbands do not like to give their wives permission to enter the labour market because they want to keep women dependent on men and retain maximum control over the household economy. Thus, generally, those free to join the labour market tend to be female household heads.

Some of the problems associated with women's new employment do exist in the Mkalama district, but married women need to be creative in arriving at a compromise that enables them to secure the needed permission to join TVCONEs and engage in other entrepreneurial ventures. The tendency of arriving at a compromise with husbands—at times when there is a shift in gender role—is not a new phenomenon. Kabeer argues that wives need to overcome their husbands' opposition through "strategic use of local discourses of domesticity as well as their own intimate knowledge of their husbands to reassure their anxieties" (18). In this respect, women in Mkalama have attained this through collaborating with their husbands in their businesses.

Status of Marital Relationships

Over 75 per cent of TVCONE members and over 80 per cent of male spouses of TVCONE members are of the opinion that they have managed to improve their spousal relationships (see Table 1 for details and disaggregated data for each ward). A strong relationship develops in a household when men do not have to worry about being belittled for failing to meet the expenses necessary for running their households. They appreciate the idea of being involved in their spouses' businesses. A longstanding problem that has existed in Mkalama district is that women have been expected to take care of husbands with little income of their own. Women have been expected to somehow extend their motherhood role to caring for husbands. There is a common saying in the community and elsewhere in Tanzania that "a husband is the firstborn child of a woman." Within the abovementioned context in the district, male spouses of TVCONE members collaborate with their wives by engaging in a variety of activities. While it is one thing to stand at a stall in a market, men feel that it is quite another to purchase merchandise from suppliers for their wives' businesses. This brings the respect they expect as men. But in reality, they have created a family business in which women have greater decision-making powers than the men. Members of TVCONEs who involve their husbands in their businesses have managed to mask the declining role of men as breadwinners by involving men in traditional patriarchal tasks, such as travelling to market towns to purchase merchandise as well as transporting agricultural produce from the farm to the market. This has improved collaboration among TVCONE members and their spouses.

The reward for increased collaboration between TVCONE members and their husbands is improved relationships. Stated in a different way, because of deeply rooted patriarchy in the Mkalama district, men do not necessarily enjoy the increased power women have acquired. However, the benefits associated with women's participation in TVCONEs are worth it. This view is also supported by in-depth interviews that probed further into the issue as paraphrased here:

> Successful businesses owned by TVCONE members are those which accommodate participation of male spouses. Women continue to perform many of the household chores. Therefore, it is difficult for them to engage in some labour-intensive activities. For example, transporting grain from farms to market towns requires one to use an oxen cart. The task is difficult for women. Accordingly, a significant number of women entrepreneurs collaborate with their husbands to gather grain from farms during harvest time and during sale of the same at price pick time. (Leader of a Local NGO, Kinyangiri ward, 26 June 2015)

The above quotation indicates that gender roles are being redefined in the Mkalama district. Although the changes favour women, it is still important for both men and women to collaborate to attain maximum gains as previously explained. Men should also be willing to do more household chores to assist women.

Freedom for Women

TVCONEs have also increased the freedom of their members. The view is supported by 100 TVCONE members (100 per cent) and 70 (90 per cent) of their respective male spouses (see Table 1). Nearly all women are engaged in productive activities, such as agriculture and small businesses, and this gives them more freedom to do things of interest to them, including motherhood roles. FGD findings show that TVCONEs have transformed lives of their members, enabling women to travel to different places to purchase merchandise for their businesses. They usually travel to market towns where they can buy items cheaply. The freedom allows them to network with other female entrepreneurs and increase their knowledge about many things. As such, they have managed to develop more entrepreneurial skills to engage in profitable businesses. The profits gained have enabled the households to meet social expenses, including sending both girl and boy children to school. In the past, Mkalama women used to send their daughters, who generally only had a primary education, to urban areas such as Arusha and Dar es Salaam to work as housemaids. This denied the girls the right to further their education. These girls were expected to send remittances home regularly. Nowadays, with increased profits from TVCONEs, the Mkalama district is no longer seen as a hub of house girls for urban areas because the women's ability to send girls to secondary schools has increased.

The findings further indicate the following: First, women now have the freedom to participate in multiple networks. On average, members of women's networks have membership in two to four TVCONEs, which allows women to access the membership benefits of more than one network. For any woman bound to the household, life becomes more difficult because she has to depend on a man with diminishing resources. As a result, not only does this lead to violence in the home, as noted earlier, but it also affects the quality of mothering. Mothers with little or no personal income cannot assist their own children.

Second, women have more freedom to collaborate with other women in businesses. For instance, women who belong to the same network often exchange business information on potential customers. They also share information on places to get merchandise and support one another in times of emergencies. Here, women watch over one another's businesses if someone has to attend to other duties, such as taking children to the hospital. They also share business premises. For example, members of a TVCONE in Kinyangiri ward take turns to operate a small cafeteria.

Third, women now have the opportunity to travel away from their homes and to pursue various opportunities. TVCONE members in Mkalama district travel to Singida municipality and Igunga town to purchase merchandise for their businesses. This happens during the dry season after the harvest. The dry season starts in June each year. Fourth, women have a greater ability to send their children, regardless of sex, to school. One of women's key interests rests in the welfare of their sons and daughters. This is not necessarily the case for some men, especially those who abandon their households. Simply put, women spend a significant amount of their income taking care of the needs of their children, male or female. Overall, the new economic developments enable women to perform their motherhood roles more effectively.

The findings of this study contradict those of Mayra Buvinic, who analyzed several case studies conducted in countries of the Global South, including Tanzania. She argues that women's networks, and the saving and credits (microcredit) associations in particular, maintain a focus on traditional welfare, which maintains the status quo. Specifically, Buvinic notes that developmental interventions targeting women are usually transformed into welfare projects by the beneficiaries to extend women's reproductive gender roles. For that reason, they continue to perpetuate deep rooted patriarchy and fail to economically empower women. The findings of my study reveal that the transformation of microfinance networks into welfare projects—as has been the case with TVCONEs—which extend women's reproductive gender roles is not necessarily a bad thing. In fact, it has changed the status quo by improving gender relations in favour of women. I have argued here that TVCONEs do empower women economically and have successfully transformed gender relations in favour of women. For instance, mothers have gained more respect from their communities, husbands, and children when they help fund children's education.

Conclusion

Contrary to the popular view on the role of women's networks, this chapter has revealed that TVCONEs play an important role in improving gender relations among network members and their spouses. In so doing, they have enabled women to improve the performance of their motherhood roles, which has led to significant changes in response to neoliberal policies that had caused so many problems for women as mothers and as wives. The domestic sphere is no longer a location for the exploitation of women by men operating under strong patriarchal values. Instead, the home front has become a refuge for marginalized men who have been victimized by neoliberalism. Motherhood has gone beyond taking care of children to include assisting husbands. Before that, men were ashamed to receive any support from women. Women, with the help of TVCONEs, have shielded their men from neoliberalism. Within that milieu, TVCONEs have increased the respect of network members in their households, reduced domestic violence, improved marital relationships, and granted women more freedom to do things that interest them. Members of TVCONEs can protect their husbands from the present crisis of masculinity and, in turn, gain support for their businesses. This creates a more peaceful environment, which helps improve the lives of women as well as other members of the household. This milestone achieved by TVCONEs networks serves as a blueprint for increased gender equality in Tanzania. Overall, I have argued in this study that Tanzanian communities are witnessing positive changes in gender roles, and our communities are becoming more sensitive to gender issues. Thus, there is a gradual move away from modern patriarchy with its colonial roots to a more collaborative culture, which existed before colonialism, although it too was not egalitarian.

This study has added to the discourses on social capital, feminist theories, and socialist feminism in particular. Socialist feminists emphasize that there is a strong connection between neoliberalism and changing forms of patriarchy. Patriarchy helps neoliberalism to exploit women and vice versa. Women experience double exploitation in the home as wives and outside in the public sphere as cheap labour. However, this study has pointed to the fact that global neoliberalism created a context that disproportionately disempowered men in their role as household breadwinners. For that reason, a vacuum has been created, which enabled women to leave the domestic sphere and engage in small-scale entrepreneurship in public places. Following this, men took refuge in the home, away from neoliberal oppression. TVCONEs played an instrumental role in mitigating the crisis of masculinity by improving gender relations between women entrepreneurs and their spouses. Women, among other things, were able to bring their spouses on board by working closely with them in joint businesses, allowing some men to recover from the economic problems that had undermined their former sense of masculinity. Within this milieu, the difficulties emanating from neoliberalism created many challenges, which prompted the development of new community organizations and a redefinition of gender roles. It is important to state that TVCONEs are increasingly regarded as feminine organizations due to the perception, now widespread in the district, that they play a caretaking role for households and the community at large. As a result, men who are still conscious of the gender power rooted in patriarchy do not seek membership in such networks. However, men encourage women to participate in these networks so that they can help support their households. Besides, women enjoy spending their incomes to improve their motherhood role in a context where husbands are seen as firstborn children. Whenever Tanzanian women form collectives, they do so partly to improve their motherhood roles. In this regard, conventional microfinance networks fail to sustain themselves because they do not help women better perform their motherhood roles.

Endnotes

1. I wish to acknowledge the organizations that funded this long-itudinal study: the Fulbright Programme of the U.S. Government, the American Political Science Association (APSA), the Tanzania Gender Network Programme (TGNP), and the Sokoine University of Agriculture.

Works Cited

Aina, Olabisi. "African Women at the Grassroots: The Silent Partners of the Women's Movement." *Sisterhood, Feminisms and Power: From Africa to the Diaspora*. Edited by Obioma Nnaemeka, Africa World Press Inc, 1998, pp 65-88.

Alders, Carine, Bertus Haverkort, and Laurens van Veldhuizen. *Linking with Farmers Networking for Low External Input and Sustainable Agriculture.* Intermediate Technology Publications, 1993.

Archambault, Caroline S. "Women Left Behind? Migration, Spousal Separation, and the Autonomy of Rural Women in Ugweno, Tanzania." *Signs,* vol. 35, no. 4, 2010, pp. 919-42.

Brenner, Johanna. "21st Century Socialist Feminism." *Social Studies,* vol. 10, no.1, 2014, pp. 31-49.

Buvinic, Mayra. "Projects for Women in the Third World: Explaining their Misbehaviour." *World Development,* vol. 14, no. 5, 1986, 653-64.

Chant, Sylvia, "Men in Crisis? Reflections on Masculinities, Work and Family in Northwest Costa Rica." *European Journal of Development Research,* vol. 12, no. 2, 2000, pp. 199-218.

Chant, Sylvia. "Researching Gender, Families and Households in Latin America: From the 20th to the 21st Century." *Bulletin of Latin American Research,* vol. 21, no. 4, 2002, pp. 545-75.

Calkin, Sydney. "'Tapping' Women for Post-Crisis Capitalism: Evidence from the 2012 World Development Report." *International Feminist Journal of Politics,* vol. 17, no. 4, 2015, pp. 611-29.

Cook-Craig, Patricia G. "Using Social Network Theory to Influence the Development of State and Local Primary Prevention Capacity-Building Teams." *Journal of Family Social Work,* vol. 13, no. 4, 2010, pp. 313-25.

Connelly, Patricia, et al. "Feminism and Development: Theoretical Perspectives." *Theoretical Perspectives on Gender and Development.* Edited by Jane L. Parpart, Patricia Connelly, and Eudine Barriteau. International Development Research Centre, 2000, pp. 51-159.

Cranenburgh Oda. V. *The Widening Gyre: The Tanzanian One Party State and Policy Towards Rural Cooperatives.* Eburon Publishers, 1990.

Dill, Brian. "Community-Based Organizations (CBOs) and Norms of Participation in Tanzania: Working against the Grain." *African Studies Review,* vol. 53, no. 2, 2010, pp. 23-48.

Eisenstein, Hester. *Feminism Seduced: How Global Elites Use Women's Labor and Ideas to Exploit the World.* Paradigm Publishers, 2010.

Farrington, John, and John Nelson. *Information Exchange Networking for Agricultural Development: A Review of Concepts and Practices*. Sayce Publishing, 1994.

Geiger, Susan. "Tanganyikan Nationalism as 'Women's Work': Life Histories, Collective Biography and Changing Historiography." *Journal of African History*, vol. 37, no. 3, 1996, 47-67.

Geiger, Susan, *TANU Women: Gender and Culture in the Making of Tanganyikan Nationalism, 1955–1965*. Heinemann, 1997.

Harvey, David, *The Enigma of Capital and the Crises of Capitalism*. Oxford University Press, 2011.

Haverkort Bertus, Kamp Johan, and Water-Bayer, Ann, eds. *Joining Farmers' Experiments: Experiences in Participatory Technology Development*. Intermediate Technology Publications, 1991.

Jackson, Matthew, *Social and Economic Network*. Princeton University Press, 2008.

Joekes, Susan P. *Women in the World Economy*. Oxford University Press, 1990.

Sender, John and Smith, Sheila, *Poverty, Class, and Gender in Rural Africa: A Tanzanian Case Study*. New York: Routledge, 1990.

Jellicoe, Marguerite, *The Long Path: A Case Study of Social Change in Wahi, Singida, Tanzania*. East African Publishing House, 1978.

Kabeer, Naila. "Marriage, Motherhood and Masculinity in the Global Economy: Reconfigurations of Personal and Economic Life." Working Paper No. 290. Sussex: Institute of Development Studies, 2007.

Kasper, Claudia, and Monique B. Mulder. "Who Helps and Why? Cooperative Networks in Mpimbwe." *Current Anthropology*, vol. 56, no. 5, 2015, pp. 701-32

Kendall, Diana. *Sociology in Our Times: The Essentials*. Thomson Wadsworth, 2007.

Lee, Minjin. "Building Regional Networks between Labor Unions and Communities." vol. 44, no. 2, 2015, pp. 275-93.

LeCompte, Margaret D., and Jean J. Schensul. *Designing and Conducting Ethnographic Research*. Walnut Creek, CA, AltaMira, 1999.

Madaha, Rasel. "Organized and Gendered Media Advocacy at the Centre of the Feminist Movement in a Patriarchal Tanzania." *Africa Review*, vol. 6, no. 1, 2014, pp. 18-29.

Madaha, Rasel. *Networking by the Rural Poor as a Mechanism for Community Development Within the Neoliberal Context: the Case of Women's Networks in Mkalama District, Singida Region, Tanzania.* 2017. University of Dar es Salaam, Unpublished PhD Thesis.

Mannon, Susan. E, "Love in the Time of Neo-Liberalism: Gender, Work, and Power in a Costa Rican Marriage." *Gender and Society*, vol. 20, no. 4, 2006, pp. 511-30.

Mannon, Susan. E. "Pampered Sons, (Wo)manly Men, or Do-nothing Machos? Costa Rican Men Coming of Age under Neoliberalism." *Bulletin of Latin American Research*, vol. 29, no. 4, 2010, pp. 477-91.

Mbilinyi, Marjorie. "The State of Women in Tanzania." *Canadian Journal of African Studies*, vol. 6, no. 2, 1972, pp. 371-77.

Mbilinyi, Marjorie. "The 'New Woman' and Traditional Norms in Tanzania." *The Journal of Modern African Studies*, vol. 10, no. 1, 1972, pp. 57-72.

McMahon, Martha. *Engendering Motherhood: Identity and Self-Transformation in Women's Lives.* The Guilford Press, 1995.

Meena, Ruth. *Gender in Southern Africa: Conceptual and Theoretical Issues.* Sapes Books, 1991.

Meena, Ruth. "The Impact of Structural Adjustment Programs on Rural Women in Tanzania." *Structural Adjustment and African Women Farmers.* Edited by C. Gladwin, University of Florida Press, 1991, pp. 169-90.

Mitter, Swasti. *Common Fate, Common Bond: Women in the Global Economy.* Pluto Press, 1986.

Mohanty, Chandra. T. "Women Workers and Capitalist Scripts: Ideologies of Domination, Common Interests and the Politics of Solidarity." *The Socialist Feminist Project: A Contemporary Reader in Theory and Politics.* Edited by Nancy Holmstrom, Monthly Review Press, 2002. pp. 160-80.

Möller-Leimkuhler, Anne Maria. "The Gender Gap in Suicide and Premature Death or: Why Are Men So Vulnerable?" *European Archives of Psychiatry and Clinical Neuroscience*, vol. 253, no. 1, 2003, pp. 1-8.

Msonganzila, Margareth R. "Women and Co-operatives in Tanzania: Separatism or Integration?" *Economic and Political Weekly*, vol. 29, no. 44, 1994, pp. WS86-WS96.

Narayan, Deepa. "Bonds and Bridges: Social Capital and Poverty, Policy Research." Working Paper No. 2167, Poverty Reduction and Economic Management Network, World Bank, 1999.

Nelson, Fiona. *In the Other Room: Entering the Culture of Motherhood.* Fernwood Publishing, 2009.

Nkealah, Naomi. "(West) African Feminisms and their Challenges." *Journal of Literary Studies*, vol. 32, no. 2, 2016, pp. 61-74.

O'Neill, Brenda, and Elisabeth Gidengill, eds. *Gender and Social Capital.* Routledge, 2004.

Oracion, Enrique. "Kinship Networks and Resiliency to Flooding of Pagatban Riverside Communities in Negros Oriental, Philippine." *Sociological Review*, vol. 63, 2015, pp 27-51.

Park, Kyung A. "Women and Development: The Case of South Korea." *Comparative Politics,* vol. 25, no. 2, 1993, pp. 127-145.

Parpart J. L., M. P. Connelly, and V. E. Barriteau. *Theoretical Perspectives on Gender and Development.* International Development Research Centre, 2000.

Pluknell, D. L., N. J. Smith, and Z. S. Ozgediz. *Networking in International Agricultural research in Food Systems and Agrigarian Change.* Cornell University, 1990.

Rainie, Lee, and Barry Wellman. *Networked: The New Social Operating System.* The MIT Press, 2012.

Rice, Eric, and Amanda Yoshioka-Maxwell. "Social Network Analysis as a Toolkit for the Science of Social Work." *Journal of the Society for Social Work and Research*, vol. 6, no. 3, 2015, pp. 369-83.

Sen, Gita, and Piroska Östlin. *Unequal, Unfair, Ineffective and Inefficient Gender Inequity in Health: Why It Exists and How We Can Change It.* WHO, 2007.

Staudt, Kathleen. "Book Review of G. Hyden: Beyond Ujamaa in Tanzania: Underdevelopment and an Uncaptured Peasantry (Heinemann, Nairobi, 1980)." *The African Review*, vol.11, no. 1, 1984, pp. 87-89.

Tripp, Aili Mari. "Gender, Political Participation and the Transformation of Associational Life in Uganda and Tanzania." *African Studies Review*, vol. 37, no. 1, 1994, pp. 107-31.

Tripp, Aili Mari. *Changing the Rules: The Politics of Liberalization and the Urban Informal Economy in Tanzania.* University of California Press, 1997.

Tripp, Aili Mari, et al. *African Women's Movements: Changing Political Landscapes.* Cambridge University Press, 2009.

UNESCO. *Gender Mainstreaming Implementation Framework.* UNESCO, 2003.

URT. *Cooperative Development Policy.* Tanzanian Government Printers, 1997.

Wallace, Adryan. "Holistic Development: Muslim Women's Civil Society Groups in Nigeria, Ghana and Tanzania." *African Sociological Review*, vol. 19, no. 2, 2015, 53-74

Wellman, B, "Structural Analysis: From Method and Metaphor to Theory and Substance." *Contemporary Studies in Sociology*, vol. 15, 1997, 19-61.

West, Candace, and Don H. Zimmerman. "Doing Gender." *Gender & Society*, vol. 1, no. 2, 1987, 125-52.

Woolcock, Michael, and Deepa Narayan. "Social Capital: Implications for Development Theory, Research, and Policy." *The World Bank Research Observer*, vol. 15, no. 2, 2000, pp. 225-49.

World Bank. *World Development Report: Gender Equality and Development.* The World Bank, 2012.

Chapter 12

"More Than a Woman": Exploring Motherhood and Masculinities in Food and Nutrition Security in Northern Vietnam

Andréa Moraes

Introduction

"Child malnutrition is the most serious consequence of food insecurity and has a multitude of health and economic implications" (Chinnakali et al. 227). Despite advances in the last decades, child malnutrition is still a worldwide challenge: one in five children under five years old is at risk of being undernourished (UNICEF), and this risk increased after the COVID-19 pandemic started (Fore et al.). A common and accepted approach to understand and address child malnutrition is through mothers, as the nutritional status of a child is often linked to the nutritional status of the mother (Oniang'o and Mukudi). Thus, research and interventions on child malnutrition are often associated with the mother's education and nutritional knowledge, (Fádáre et al.; IFPRI), mental health (Rahman et al.), social networks (Moestue et al.), and empowerment (Alaofè; Chipili et al.; Cunningham; Debnath and Bhattacharjee). Fewer studies, though, investigate the impact of gender relations in the household and the roles of fathers and extended families in children's nutrition.

Gender relations in general are especially complex in societies that have gone through the upheavals of colonization or political changes, and Vietnam is a good example of such complexities. Over the last decades, the country has undergone important transformations that interact with both Buddhist and Confucianism traditions and gender roles. Today, market socialism fosters some economic independence for women, with mixed results. Whereas Confucianism emphasizes patriarchy and the subordination of women, socialism encourages a more egalitarian society. In rural areas of Northern Vietnam, for instance, men are still more likely to receive agricultural training, and women are often constrained to the economy of subsistence (Zuo). However, new job opportunities for women associated with tourism are emerging in some provinces, but they are still expected to build "happy families" and become sacrificing mothers. The interaction between all these changes impacts gender relations as well as food and nutrition security. Hence, this chapter draws attention to the complexities of rural gender relations and how they could shed light on factors affecting child nutrition beyond targeting only women.

Mother, Child, and Nutrition

Despite the physical separation that occurs with birth, the close interdependence between baby and mother is likely to continue whether the mother is breastfeeding or not. Even if the mother is away most of the day and grandmothers, fathers, sisters, aunts, or other caretakers are responsible for feeding the baby, the nutritional status of a child continues to be linked to the nutritional status of the mother (Oniang'o and Mukudi). Child feeding is part of a mother's reproductive responsibilities in a household and is therefore a common and expected role for mothers worldwide. Although there is no biological dependence between the life of the mother and the baby after birth (as the baby could survive without the mother), the mother is still considered the default person responsible for the development and growth of the baby.

One of the accepted approaches to address and improve child nutrition is to invest in women's education: formal or informal. Olusegun Fádáre et al. argue that "Mothers' limited knowledge about food choices, feeding, and health care seeking practices contributes significantly to negative nutrition outcomes for children in most developing countries" (1). In their research in rural Nigeria, the authors conclude that mothers' educational levels and child nutrition scores correlate. They encourage the promotion of mothers' informal education (literacy and numeracy) as a path to increase their knowledge of nutrition and health and therefore their child's nutrition. They are not alone, as many other studies associate maternal nutritional knowledge with child nutrition (Debela; Oh; Saaka).

In Australia, Karen Campbell et al. found that home food availability mediates the association between maternal nutritional knowledge and children's diets. Highlighting the importance of mothers' nutritional knowledge for food buying and preparation, the authors concluded that their research "supports a focus on nutrition education that expands mothers' understanding of what foods to buy, prepare and serve" (1). The emphasis on nutrition education of mothers is clear, but it is not only education that matters; women's mental and social health as well as their empowerment could also impact child nutrition. In another study, Helen Moestue et al. underline the importance of social networks supporting women and children's nutrition and health, concluding that there is "a positive association between child's height-for-age Z-score and mother's network size and network literacy rate" (1274).

In addition, Atif Rahman et al., argue that treating the mother's mental health is important for addressing not only child malnutrition but also the mother's overall health issues. The concern is with child undernutrition but also with the consumption of cheap ultraprocessed foods by children: "Food insecurity is complex and ... not only can it lead to undernutrition and recurring hunger, but also to overnutrition, which can lead to overweight and obesity" (Tanumihardjo et al. 1966). Obesity is already a significant cause of death in low-income countries.

Moreover, a mother's lack of time to cook has been also related to children's malnourishment. In a study about working mothers and child nutrition in urban Bangalore, India, Sanghita Das argues that children are increasingly consuming more packed ultraprocessed foods and fewer homemade nutritious meals due to mothers' lack of time. Furthermore, she found that eating food from outside the home had a negative impact on the health of children. To address this issue, the author advocates for longer maternity leave for women as well as for policies supporting working moms.

Other studies or interventions concerned with the status of mothers and child nutrition focus on understanding and promoting women's empowerment (Jamal; Chipili; Malapit). The argument that child feeding is part of women's responsibility and experience clearly implies that the less power a woman has in a household or community, the lower will be her ability to feed herself and her children. Therefore, it is not surprising that improving women's abilities to produce food should have an effect on the child's health. Empowering women could have many different meanings (Moraes, *Gendered Waters*) and therefore could lead to many different directions, including nutrition sensitive agriculture (Kumart et al.; Olney et al.; Heckert et al.), increased land rights (Allendorf), or even responding to intrahousehold empowerment gaps. What is very common in most studies about child malnutrition is the focus on mothers.

Without denying the importance of mothers, this chapter proposes a look at gender relations in the household and at the role of fathers and extended families in child nutrition. Using as a starting point partial results from focus groups discussions with men and women participants in the ECOSUN project in Northern Vietnam, this chapter aims to reflect on the complexities of motherhood and masculinities in this context. Motherhood and masculinities, especially regarding the caring role of fathers and their impact on children's health and nutrition, are examined at the crossroads of ethnic minorities, rural poverty, Confucianism, and market changes, as they pose challenges and are negotiated in different ways.

Although there are a few studies on fathers and nutrition (Watterworth), this chapter aims to go a bit further and discuss the changing expectations of motherhood (Rich; O'Reilly) and how they relate to masculinities (Connell) in the context of a food and nutrition security project in Northern Vietnam. This research is inspired by a gender transformative approach (Njuki et al.) that "goes beyond improving women's access to resources: it enables communities to understand and challenge the social norms that create inequalities between men and women and can either help or hinder an individual's capacity to take advantage of available opportunities" (6). Recognizing the importance of women in food and nutrition security, the chapter reflects upon women's roles as mothers being constructed, reinforced, and reconstructed in relation to men, relatives, and communities. The little story below illustrates the importance of understanding gender norms if one aims to support women's empowerment.

> Mercy is a smallholder bean farmer from Chinseu Village who often intercropped her beans with maize on her small plot of land. Using little fertilizer or other farm inputs, Mercy produced between 50 and 100 kilograms of beans in a good year. Her family consumed half her bean crop at home and she sold the remainder on the roadside near her village. She used the money she earned from the sale of the beans to buy food and clothes for her family. When a new farming project was started in Chinseu, Mercy got access to improved bean varieties and markets. Because the new bean variety could not be intercropped, she had to grow the beans on a different plot of land from her maize. The investment paid off, however, and in the first year she produced nearly one ton of beans. To sell the increased produce, she needed to find new markets, and these were far from her village. Her husband thus started to transport the surplus beans to the city for bulking and sale there. He began spending less and less time at home, and sometimes he spent the income from the beans before he reached home. Meanwhile, Mercy remained at home, often with less bean income than she had before she began to adopt the "improvements." (Njuki qtd. in Karaimu)

Jeminah Njuki argues that gender is still the missing link in agriculture, and that projects that aim to empower women regarding food security must also work with men and with the communities where women are situated, yet this is easier said than done (House). Nevertheless, a gender transformative approach to food and nutrition security will be used to examine the focus group discussions of the ECOSUN Project in Northern Vietnam.

The ECOSUN Project in Northern Vietnam

Over the last twenty years, Vietnam has experienced fast economic growth and a significant reduction in malnutrition and food insecurity. Still, twelve million out of ninety-three million people are under-nourished, and most of them are women and children in rural areas, where poverty and food insecurity are still common (ECOSUN): "Malnutrition affects an estimated 780,000 children in Vietnam, with 27.5 percent of them showing stunting and 16 percent being underweight" (Centre for Studies in Food Security).

The ECOSUN project was born from this concern. The National Institute of Nutrition (NIN) had previously produced and distributed fortified complementary foods for young children in Hanoi and aimed at scaling up this model to the northern part of the country, along the border with China, where high rates of child malnutrition have persisted. In addition to poverty, these areas contain a concentration of diverse Indigenous peoples that in Vietnam are classified as ethnic minorities (a term that will be used from now on). Most of the population in the country are from the Kihn ethnic group; however, there are fifty-three ethnic minorities, which make up half of the poor, although they account for only 15 per cent of the population (Moraes, *Negotiating Gender in Food Security*).

The ECOSUN project was implemented between 2016 and 2018 by the National Institute of Nutrition in Vietnam, with support from the School of Nutrition at Ryerson University in Canada, and financial and technical support from Global Affairs Canada and the International Development Research Center (IDRC). The project's main goal was to scale-up the food production of fortified complementary foods for small children in three rural provinces with high levels of child malnutrition: Lao Cai, Lai Chau, and Ha Giang (ECOSUN). These provinces, located in Northern Vietnam alongside the border with China, were chosen because they have some of the highest rates of child malnutrition in the country.

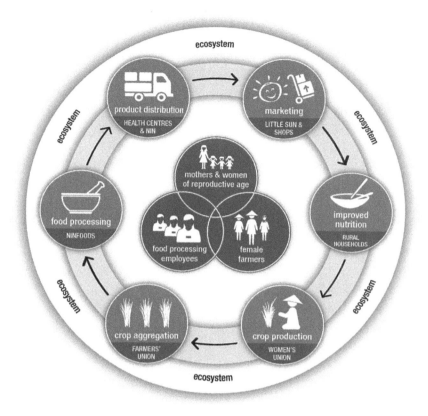

Figure 1. ECOSUN Project: Representation of System's Approach.

Using a food systems approach to address food insecurity (see Figure 1), and with a focus on women, the ECOSUN project aimed to train and support local women farmers to produce vegetables, creating a new market for their produce and therefore economic empowerment. The vegetables produced were then processed in local small-scale food processing facilities (SSFP) to create fortified complementary foods for young children while providing new training and new jobs for local workers. The fortified complementary food produced was then sold in local markets and distributed in health centres to mothers of young children along with nutrition education.

Although the project lasted only two and a half years, its outcomes were remarkable and included the following:

- Ten-year public private partnership formalized between NIN (National Institute of Nutrition) and local businesswomen in Lao Cai for ECOSUN production.
- ISO 22000 compliant SSFP established and operating to produce one hundred tonnes of fortified instant porridge and two million vegetable packets annually.
- Eight local workers trained in food safety and quality assurance at the SSFP, of which five are women.
- 450 farmers trained in good agricultural practices (GAPs).
- Local co-op of seventeen women farmers that use GAPs to supply carrots, pumpkin, and sweet leaf to the SSFP.
- Fifteen easy to access Little SUN nutrition counselling centres set up at community health centers.
- Thirty-six health workers at these Little SUN centers have been trained in preparing ECOSUN products to teach during counselling sessions.
- Market launch and nine mini promotion events held in project communes.
- Twenty-one preschools in Lao Cai use the instant porridge in the school meal programs.
- 14,438 children under the age of two have been reached through 10,561 family nutrition counselling sessions (particularly to mothers) (ECOSUN).

The focus on women was also undeniable, as women participated as project coordinators, researchers, nutritionists, farmers, trainers, workers, health agents, and mothers. As a matter of fact, the focus on women's empowerment was part of the conditions for funding by IDRC. It was, however, after the project had already started that the two gender coordinators in Canada and Vietnam were invited to participate in a workshop in Nairobi organized by IDRC on integrating gender into projects and programs. Beyond women's empowerment, this workshop challenged projects to include actions that could lead in the direction of a gender transformative agenda, understood as "fostering a critical examination of gender norms and dynamics; strengthening or creating systems that support gender equality; strengthening or creating equitable gender norms and dynamics; and changing inequitable gender norms and dynamics" (IDRC 8). One critical approach to integrate gender into the project's agenda was the inclusion of men's perspectives, and for this reason, men were included in the design of the focus groups' discussions. Due to the short period of the project and the design that focused mostly on women, there were limited opportunities to incorporate actions that challenged gender norms or dynamics. Nevertheless, results from two research tools— the English translation of the transcription of the focus groups' discussions in Vietnam and notes from interviews with key informants— will be explored in this chapter as starting points for a reflection on gender roles, masculinities and femininities, mothering and fathering in the context of food insecurity, as well as child malnutrition. It is important to acknowledge that this is not a gender analysis of the ECOSUN project per se but a thematic analysis (Attride-Stirling) of some of the main issues that could shed light on gendered social norms associated with food and nutrition security and the role of mothers and fathers.

Although this chapter uses data from the project to reflect on the roles of mothers and fathers, femininities, and masculinities in the context of Vietnam, its main goal is to reflect on the lessons learned on motherhood and masculinities associated with food insecurity and child malnutrition. One relevant lesson learned in this project was the importance of cross-cultural translation. From the general project meetings, to data collection (from ethnic minority languages to Vietnamese), and to the production of reports (from Vietnamese to English), translation involved not only words but also a diversity of cultural and political perspectives. This was at the same time an enriching factor and a limitation of this project.

Description of the Focus Group Discussions (FGDs) and Interviews

Six focus FGDs were organized in the summer of 2017 with the goal of exploring the existing gender dynamics and decisions about child feeding with men and women in the selected provinces. Each of the three provinces had two groups, one with men and the other with women, with the following composition: Dao Duck Commune, Vi Xeon District, Ha Giang (five men, eleven women); Ban Giang Commune, Tam Duong District, Lai Chau (eleven men, seventeen women); and Trinh Tutu Commune, Boa Dent District, Lao Chai (six men, twelve women).

The FGDs took place at local medical stations and were led by female and male staff from the NIN. Participants were selected with the support of local medical staff; they had to have children under the age of five and had to speak Vietnamese. However, not everybody was fluent in Vietnamese, and translators or interpreters also mediated the conversations. According to the field researchers, this shortened the depth of discussions. In addition, some of the respondents were shy. The age of participants varied from eighteen to sixty and included from young parents to grandparents. Members of different minority ethnic groups participated in the FGDs, such as the Hmong, Dao, Day, and Thai, to name a few.

Overall, participants were asked about a) the role of family members in different activities; b) family decisions, including expenses and caring for children; c) supporting networks; and d) challenges and hopes for their children. In addition, five key informant interviews were conducted with agricultural extension trainers and other partners in the area by a Canadian researcher in Vietnam. The highlights below are based on the report written by the Canadian female researcher (You) as well as notes and translation of transcripts from the FGDs prepared by the male and female staff from the NIN (Ngothiha and Le Van Chi). For the purpose of this chapter, only a few highlights will be shared, including household composition, gender roles in agriculture, parent-ing, support systems, challenges, and wishes.

Household Composition

Several FGD participants lived in multigenerational households (grandparents, parents, and children): nine out of eleven households in the Dao Duc Commune and eight out of twelve households in Trinh Tuu Commune. However, only five out of nineteen households in Ban Giang Commune lived in multigenerational households. The diversity of living arrangements exemplifies the diversity of cultures in the region, as some ethnic groups are patrilocal (wife moves to the husband's family) and a few others are matrilocal (husband moves to wife's family residence). According to one interviewee: "With Nùng people, the women will lead and usually the men will follow ... whereas for the Hmong group, the women don't want to engage with outsiders, so if you want to engage with the women, you need to involve the men" (You).

Gender Roles in Agriculture

Food production plays a large role in the lives of all FGDs participants, either as a source of food for consumption or for income, including paid labour or food sold in market sales. Decisions such as which crops to grow or what foods to consume are generally made as a family. However, men and women have different roles. For women, agriculture is considered part of their domestic work, such as childcare and cooking. Therefore, women are responsible for planting, weeding, pest control, and harvesting. Men, in contrast, do most of the heavy-lifting duties, such as ploughing or transporting harvests. "We are only in charge of the hard works that require strength," said a man from Lao Cai. Men are also expected to work outside the home to bring in income, although women also work for income to a lesser extent. Several women reported that if they were busy or incapacitated, their roles could be interchanged. As one woman in Lao Cai put it: "Generally in ethnic groups, women do a lot. But, if [the women] don't have time, our husband will help." Women do a lot but with fewer resources, as they have less access to technology and training. According to the agricultural trainer interviewed, government and NGO projects in the area did bring equipment and provide training in the past, but both mostly went to men. The production of food for consumption continues to be mostly labour intensive and women's work, which means that any additional agricultural work to increase productivity could be an additional burden to the women. Women lag behind men in agricultural training due to lack of time and inadequate language skills, as most training is done in Vietnamese and not all women speak the language. Thus, most knowledge about farming is shared orally "while working in the fields," said a female participant. Furthermore, grandparents and older generations are often important for passing down traditional knowledge about farming (You). Rice is a staple crop in all three regions, although some families also grow cassava, corn, and bananas; women tend chickens and pigs. Women also go to the forest to find vegetables and other wild foods. One important decision made by men is buying seeds or fertilizers for production. "He [her husband] buys important things like seeds," said a woman from Lao Cai. Decisions about seeds are increasingly important, as government programs and other initiatives are encouraging the purchase of hybrid seeds (such as hybrid rice), which need to be bought every year, unlike their traditional counterparts that can be saved (Bonnin and Turner).

Parenting

As mentioned before, in most of the households, the husband's main role was earning money. In Lao Cai for instance, because men are often hired to work, they do not have much time to stay at home. There were also reports of women having health issues, small babies or being too tired to work. But even when women were working in the field or for income, they had to carry their children on their back until they are three years old. Unfortunately, no discussions on breastfeeding were cited in the FGDs. There was one report in which the mother mentions that the children preferred the father. In her own words: "I don't pamper my children too much. My children are more afraid of me than their father. I am crueller. I control them more strictly. Their dad pampers them more".

Additionally, in Ha Giang, men stated that they do take care of children, although most of the caring work is done by the mothers. Men can help, feed, play, and change diapers for instance. However, "teaching is mostly done by women." It looks like teaching in this context meant education and discipline. According to the researchers, mothers do not feel assured to trust their husband to do this. In their perspective, they are the main ones teaching the children because they are patient. "The fathers are often hot-tempered" one mother argued. When the children are sick, husbands take them to the clinics because they can drive; motorbikes are common in these mountainous areas as well as all over Vietnam. It is not uncommon that husbands and wives do many things together.

Grandmothers also help to care for the children; however, "The grandmothers often have old knowledge; the mothers are younger," a participant from Ha Giang reported. It was interesting to note that a grandmother in the group agreed that mothers are gentler. In Lai Chau, some mothers reported sending their children to the grandparents so they could go to the field in order to plough and get wood, from the morning to the evening. In this case, the grandparents feed the children with porridge or milk in the morning and in the evening. In some families both parents go to the field. "Anyone who is free will take care of the children," one mother stated.

All family members, including grandparents, take part in most family work, such as housework and taking care of children. However, it was reported that mothers rarely trust grandparents to teach the children, as normally grandparents do not speak the Kihn language well. At the same time, mothers acknowledged that "grandmothers love their grandsons and granddaughters, so they are willing to take care of them," but the mothers are still the main caretakers.

Support Systems

When asked about their support systems, most men and women in Ha Giang mentioned their families, relatives, neighbours, and friends. In Lai Chau, women mentioned talking with close people in the family, mostly husbands, sisters, or their family on the mother's side. When asked about participation in groups or associations, such as the Women's Union in Lao Cai, wives declared that they do not take part in women's meetings either because their children are small, they are tired or sick, or the distance is too far.

Challenges

Lack of money was a challenge faced by many families. For the fathers, the difficulty was being poor, especially for the children. They lacked money to take care of children and to raise them until they go to work (at sixteen years old) and can help the parents. For the women in Lai Chau, the pressure to manage money was a challenge. Although they work hard, they often fear not having money if the children get sick. Both men and women mentioned the need to save money for that purpose, although there were different degrees of fathers' engagement and support.

Another challenge revealed by women in Lao Cai was the fear in relation to the future of their kids: "I worry that when he grows up, he will gamble, or he may not get married. I worry when she grows up, she will get married with someone addicted to drugs or gambling. I worry she will be enticed for selling [trafficked] to China." In fact, according to Viet Tuan, 75 per cent of all trafficking victims in Vietnam are women and children from ethnic minority groups living in the northern mountainous regions of the country. It is no surprise that this mother also mentioned her wish to move away from there.

Another concern that appeared in the FGDs was domestic violence, either verbal or physical. In one locality, a woman mentioned conflicts about property with the husband's family. Another woman said that "Some people are scolded by the husband's parents; others are scolded by their husbands, and some scold them back." She also linked the conflicts with the consumption of alcohol: "He often scolds me when he is drunk." Other women also reported conflicts when husbands drink wine or smoke cigarettes. Although the amount of money for buying wine and cigarette is fully decided upon by the husband, the wives will complain. Mothers are the ones who keep the money to spend in the family.

Wishes

Most FGDs ended with a discussion about wishes for the future. Some participants from Ha Giang declared they wished that the economy would get better so that they could make more money. Others wished health for the families, particularly that their sons and daughters would be "good, study well, be healthy, obedient and successful." Participants from Lao Cai also hoped that their kids would have a better life than they have, and one woman wished to move out of the commune. But it was in Lau Chai that other interesting comments emerged. Although this was not discussed in all meetings, one participant stated her family's preference for a baby boy: "I know they still want me to have a boy, so I will continue to give birth. My family has four daughters, and we still try to have another son. We hope he will be good and that we can earn enough money for him to study well." This is not uncommon in Vietnam, where "preference for sons, combined with a decline in fertility, and the availability of sex selection" (UNFPA 7) help explain the unbalanced sex ratio at birth of 112 boys to every one hundred girls in 2017.

Interestingly, it was also in Lau Chai that a couple of participants had a different set of hopes, including access to public services, family support raising children, and to be heard. As one participant said: "I hope the other members of my family can support me more. I hope the government will support us both physically and mentally. I hope the government will support us about disease prevention, vaccination, support us to raise our children because this is still our main job." Moreover, their concern with the health of their children was evident.

One parent from Lai Chau mentioned: "We want to be consulted about which medicines our children should use to improve their resistance."

Motherhood, Child Nutrition, and Masculinities

A first observation that can be made about the FGDs and gender roles is that there is variation. Some families were matrilocal and others patrilocal; sometimes women controlled the money and sometimes men; sometimes the division of labour was strict and sometimes flexible. Insights from the anthropologist Hy Van Luong have helped us to make sense of this diversity. In a study about kinship in Northern Vietnam, he argues that despite the transition to socialism, two fundamental kinship traditions persist in the region: a male-oriented (patrilineal) model and a non-male-oriented (bilateral) model of kinship. Both are important in understanding gender relations.

According to Luong, the male-oriented model emphasizes the "male-centered continuity of the kinship unit" (745), and therefore it privileges the allocation of resources and authority to sons. In fact, it is centred on "the male-female hierarchy and its isomorphic relation to other conceptual dichotomies such as center/periphery and spatially bound/spatially unbound, the male oriented model emphasizing the rule of patrilocal residence, the domestic-centered role of women in patrilineal extended families, and the public-domain orientation of male household members" (745). This model is strongly linked to the Confucian belief system, "in which ancestor worship is ideally of linear continuity" (749). This helps to explain the preference for sons mentioned in the FGDs.

In contrast, the non-male-oriented model incorporates the bilateral principle, which according to Luong, enables a woman to keep her father's name after marriage, to keep in close contact with her relatives, and to participate in ritual obligations towards her natal patrilineage (Luong 747). This model also recognizes both patrilineal and matrilineal kin and nuclear family relations. Moreover, Luong argues that the non-male-oriented model "stresses greater equality in gender relations and a resource allocating pattern in which the distinction between sons and daughters as well as between patrilineal and matrilineal relatives is not emphasized" (749). Accordingly, this model is linked to Buddhism and the notion of cyclical reincarnation, which helps to explain some of the more egalitarian practices described in the FGDs.

Luong acknowledges that the two models coexisted for a long time due to the high degree of village endogamy, but there were also fissions. Furthermore, he recognizes that the "state-sanctioned Confucian doctrine most effectively reinforced the male-oriented kinship model" (748). This has persisted despite changes in legislation on land owner-ship (that used to be exclusive to males), prohibition of polygyny, and the many other recent advances towards greater gender equality.

Motherhood and Confucianism

Despite many advances in female education, legislation, labour market participation, women at the grassroots level in Vietnam "continue to face a range of health, economic and social problems" (Schuler et al. 384-85). For instance, even before having children, women are the ones bearing the "costs and risks associated with fertility regulation" (Schuler et al. 385). Sidney Ruth Schuler and colleagues argue that two overlapping constructions of gender exist in the country: A Confucian and a socialist model (385). The Confucian moral code focuses on the three obediences a woman must follow: "to father before marriage, to husband when married, and to eldest son when widowed" (386). According to the authors, in socialist Vietnam, women also became responsible for the nation, therefore accumulating the responsibility of the "family and the nation" (386). These social norms are often reinforced by national campaigns organized by the Vietnam Women's Union (VWU), a central top-down organization created in the 1930s to promote women's issues within the government (Kaime-Atterhog and Anh). VWU has a vast outreach, with more than fifteen million members across the country, including rural areas populated by ethnic minorities.

One example of the high expectations for women in Vietnam, especially for mothers, is the campaign organized by the Vietnam Women's Union in 1997, which encouraged women to "study actively, work creatively, raise children well and build happy families" (Schuler et al. 386). This campaign was based on three criteria. The first criterion encouraged women to follow government mandates that would improve their family's economic position, such as techniques on animal husbandry. The second criterion conformed with Confucian gender norms (the three obediences). It included "preserving family harmony, which in this society often requires giving in, keeping quiet and making sacrifices to the family" (Schuler et al. 386) and "maintaining a harmonious home," including "doing most or all the housework" (Schuler et al. 386). Finally, the third criterion suggests that as mothers, women are not only responsible for themselves but for their children's education, behaviour, and success in life. This explains why teaching children was mentioned so many times in the FGDs as part of the mother's job. It is interesting that, in this patriarchal configuration, masculinity is honoured through the worship of fathers and ancestors, but the actual work of raising healthy and successful children is considered the responsibility of mothers.

Moreover, Gabi Waibel and Sarah Glück argue that besides the Confucian three obediences, embedded in the Vietnam Women's Union campaigns are the four virtues that women are expected to aspire to: "being hard working, being neat and having a humble physical appearance, possessing self-control and being kind-hearted" (346). The authors argue that since 1986, the "economic system changed to market socialism" and with it, "the co-operative system was abolished, and the family [has] re-emerged as the basic production unit" (Waibel and Glück 346). From then on, the economic development of the country was associated with the idea of promoting the "happy family" and social norms securing women's feminine roles in caring for their family's wellbeing. But this has come at a price: the self-sacrifice of mothers.

Rice and Masculinity

In their research on household livelihoods and gender roles with members of the Hmong and Yao ethnic minority groups in Sa Pa, Lao Cai Province in Northern Vietnam, Christine Bonnin and Sarah Turner explore the "impact of agrarian policies in gender roles, relations and identities through transformations of individual and household livelihoods" (1302). More specifically, they look at the gendered implications of the new agrarian intensification happening in the region with the transition to hybrid rice. Besides small gardens and forest gathering, rice is the staple in Vietnam cuisine, and in the Northern region ethnic minorities are known for cultivating different types of traditional rice for different purposes, from medicinal to ceremonial. Diversity, according to Bonnin and Turner, is key to sustainable livelihoods and food security. The authors also insist that both men and women cultivate rice.

In the 1990s, the government started to donate or sell subsidized hybrid rice to small farmers with the goal of improving "agricultural production yields and local food security" (1304). The area had been lagging in terms of economic growth, and the government also had "an interest in the national integration of minority peoples" (Bonnin and Turner 1308). The traditional mixtures of rice (up to eight different types) were considered by the state "neither marketable nor valuable" (1309). Traditionally, and as mentioned in the FGDs, rice is cultivated by all members of the family, including husband and wife and even grandparents (doing different types of work). Most decisions about crop production are also shared. However, according to Bonnin and Turner, decision making about production has been increasingly challenged with the introduction of hybrid rice. Access to training is gendered, and as described in the FGDs, women are underrepresented in agricultural training for many reasons, from lack of time to language skills. So, it is not surprising that men were the ones being trained and therefore the ones transitioning to hybrid rice. However, not all families adopted it, for different reasons. Some were cautious to become dependent on government subsidies; others were concerned with the cash payments for seeds and fertilizers. Finally, there were the ones who were worried about losing their traditional seed varieties (Bonnin and Turner 1310). It is important to note that the knowledge about medicinal and ceremonial uses of the mixed rice is kept by women.

For those who adopted the hybrid rice, productivity increased, but with it also the farmers' vulnerability. Seeds for the hybrid variety need to be bought every year and require the purchase of fertilizers and irrigation, so there are more costs for inputs. In addition, because seed purchase depended on the government distribution schedule, farmers no longer had control of when to plant, as conditions could change with the weather. Third, because of less control of timing, farmers reported having a short period to plant, therefore needing to hire farm workers. Bonnin and Turner argue that families needed more cash to pay for seeds, fertilizers, and labour, and that in four years, the costs for seeds and inputs doubled (1310). Meanwhile, tourism reopened in Sa Pa starting in 1993 and with it an increased interest in ethnic handicrafts and textiles from tourists. Because women were already involved in traditional textile production and there was a need for cash for the family, they increasingly entered this new trade opportunity. In parallel, there was also a growing number of women working as trekking guides for cash, for tourists based in Sa Pa town.

According to Bonnin and Turner, the impact of such changes on gender roles was not fixed. They found that with some younger couples, after some jealousy and negotiations, the husbands started to appreciate their wives' new economic autonomy (1312). Moreover, some couples even shifted customary gender divisions of labour, as husbands began taking care of the house and the children when women were away or even giving them a ride to Sa Pa on their motorbike for their work.

The authors note that there were more conflicts at the inter-generational level, with fathers feeling threatened by the autonomy of their daughters and in-laws resisting changes to the autonomy of wives (1312). Many of the mothers continued bringing their babies and children to work with them. Bonnin and Turner observe that women often did not feel appreciated or respected for bringing home cash and that this change in gender norms and livelihood created a crisis of masculinity in the region, after all "a good wife stays at home" (Bonnin and Turner, 1302).

Based on the FGDs, it does not seem to be just a coincidence that more conflicts were cited in the discourses of women from Lao Cai, considering all these changes occurring in the region. One might argue that the reported cases of drunkenness and domestic abuse were associated with this masculinity crisis and changes in livelihood.

Conclusion

This chapter aimed at raising questions and exposing complexities. It started by highlighting the link between mother and child nutrition and how mothers are often the target of studies and interventions addressing this problem. Without denying the importance of mothers, the chapter embraced the challenge of looking at child malnutrition and food insecurity from a gender transformative agenda by considering mothers and the construction of motherhood in relation not only to men and masculinities but also to their relatives, communities, and the state.

As a starting point, it used a thematic analysis of the FGDs about gender roles from the ECOSUN project (2016–2018) in three provinces of Northern Vietnam. It also acknowledged the challenges of creating a cross-cultural perspective on gender roles and social norms of diverse Indigenous groups through the selective eyes of Vietnamese researchers. More than anything, it highlighted the "critical need of gender awareness in debates over food security and nutrition" (Bonnin, and Turner, 1302), as it takes more than a woman to address the structural causes of child malnutrition and food insecurity. Women do not live or make decisions about their health and the nutrition of their children in isolation. Policies and programs aiming at reducing food insecurity and child malnutrition need to include more complexity.

Works Cited

Alaofè, Halimatou, et al. "Association Between Women's Empowerment and Maternal and Child Nutrition in Kalalé District of Northern Benin." *Food and Nutrition Bulletin*, vol. 38, no. 3, 2017, pp. 302-18.

Allendorf, Keera. "Do Women's Land Rights Promote Empowerment and Child Health in Nepal?" *World Development*, vol. 35, no. 11, 2007, pp. 1975-88.

Attride-Stirling, Jennifer. "Thematic Networks: An Analytic Tool for Qualitative Research." *Qualitative Research*, vol. 1., no. 3., pp. 385-405.

Bonnin, Christine, and Sarah Turner. "'A Good Wife Stays Home': Gendered Negotiations over State Agricultural Programmes, Upland Vietnam." *Gender, Place & Culture*, vol. 21, no. 10, 2013, pp. 1302-20.

Campbell, Karen J., et al. "Home Food Availability Mediates Associations between Mothers' Nutrition Knowledge and Child Diet." *Appetite*, vol. 71, 2013, pp. 1-6.

Centre for Studies in Food Security. *ECOSUN: Healthy Farm, Healthy Food, Healthy Kids— Scaling up Small-Scale Food Processing of Therapeutic and Complementary Foods for Children in Vietnam.* Ryerson, www.ryerson.ca/foodsecurity/activities/activity_ecosun/. Accessed 22 Apr. 2021.

Chinnakali, Palanivel, et al. "Prevalence of Household-Level Food Insecurity and Its Determinants in an Urban Resettlement Colony in North India." *Journal of Health, Population and Nutrition*, vol. 32, no. 2, 2014, pp. 227-36.

Chipili, G., et al. "Women Empowerment and the Nutrition Status of Children Aged Between 6-59 Months." *Journal of Nutrition and Health Sciences*, vol. 5, no. 2, 2018.

Connell, Raewyn. "The Study of Masculinities." *Qualitative Research Journal*, vol. 14, no. 1, 2014, pp. 5-15.

Cunningham, Kenda, et al. "Women's Empowerment and Child Nutritional Status in South Asia: a Synthesis of the Literature." *Maternal & Child Nutrition*, vol. 11, no. 1, 2014, pp. 1-19.

Das, Sanghita. "A Study on Working Mothers and Child Nutrition in Bangalore Urban." *The Indian Economic Journal*, vol. 62, no. 4, 2015, pp. 1204-14.

Debela, Bethelhem Legesse, et al. "Maternal Nutrition Knowledge and Child Nutritional Outcomes in Urban Kenya." *Appetite*, vol. 116, 2017, pp. 518-526.

Debnath, Avijit, and Nairita Bhattacharjee. "Understanding Malnutrition of Tribal Children in India: The Role of Women's Empowerment." *Ecology of Food and Nutrition*, vol. 55, no. 6, 2016, pp. 508-27.

ECOSUN. *Scaling Up Small-Scale Food Processing, A Strategy to Promote Food Security Among Women Subsistence Farmers in Rural Vietnam. Final Technical Report.* Ryerson University, November 1, 2015–June 30, 2018, Ryerson University.

Fádáre, Olusegun, et al. "Mother's Nutrition-Related Knowledge and Child Nutrition Outcomes: Empirical Evidence from Nigeria." *Plos One*, vol. 14, no. 2, 2019, https://doi.org/10.1371/journal.pone.0212775. Accessed 22 Apr. 2021.

Heckert, Jessica, et al. "Is Women's Empowerment a Pathway to Improving Child Nutrition Outcomes in a Nutrition-Sensitive Agriculture Program?: Evidence from a Randomized Controlled Trial in Burkina Faso." *Social Science & Medicine*, vol. 233, 2019, pp. 93-102.

House, Sarah. "Easier to Say, Harder to Do: Gender Equity and Water." *Gender, Water and Development*. Edited by Anne Coles and Tina Wallace, Berg Publishers, 2005, pp. 209-226.

IDRC—International Development Research Centre. "Integrating Gender into Projects & Programs: A Guide for Research Teams." IDRC Gender Integration Workshop in Nairobi, Kenya, April 2017, Microsoft PowerPoint presentation.

IFPRI—International Food Policy Research Institute. "Women's Empowerment and Nutrition, An Evidence Review." *IFPRI Discussion Paper* 01294, http://www.fsnnetwork.org/sites/default/files/ifpridp01294.pdf. Accessed 18 Jan. 2018.

Jamal, Haroon. "Exploring the Relationship Between Mother's Empowerment and Child Nutritional Status: An Evidence from Pakistan." *Pakistan Journal of Applied Economics*, vol. 28, no. 2, 2018, pp. 189-211.

Kaime-Atterhog, Waniku, and Thi Van, Than Anh. "Vietnam Women's Union: Promoting Gender Equality." *Sida Evaluation*, Asia Department, www.sida.se/contentassets/1591a6324de44a8988a5455d6b0f3c41/vietnam-womens-union---promoting-gender-equality_2312.pdf. Accessed 22 Apr. 2021.

Karaimu, Paul. "'It Takes an Orchestra to Play a Symphony': Jemimah Njuki on Making Market-Oriented Agriculture Work for Women." *ILRI News*, 31. Jan. 2011. https://abinani.wordpress.com/category/countries/malawi/. Accessed 1 May 2019.

Kumar, Neha, et al. "What It Takes: Evidence from a Nutrition-and Gender-Sensitive Agriculture Intervention in Rural Zambia." *Journal of Development Effectiveness*, vol. 10, no. 3, 2018, pp. 341-372.

Luong, Hy Van. "Vietnamese Kinship: Structural Principles and the Socialist Transformation in Northern Vietnam." *The Journal of Asian Studies*, vol. 48, no. 4, 1989, pp. 741-56.

Malapit, Hazel Jean L., et al. "Women's Empowerment Mitigates the Negative Effects of Low Production Diversity on Maternal and Child Nutrition in Nepal." *The Journal of Development Studies*, vol. 51, no. 8, 2015, pp. 1097-1123.

Moestue, Helen, et al. "'The Bigger the Better'—Mothers' Social Networks and Child Nutrition in Andhra Pradesh." *Public Health Nutrition,* vol. 10, no. 11, 2007, pp. 1274-1282.

Moraes, Andréa. *Gendered Waters: The Participation of Women on the Program 'One Million Cisterns' in the Brazilian Semi-Arid Region.* 2011. University of Columbia, Missouri. PhD dissertation.

Moraes, Andréa. *Negotiating Gender in Food Security: The case of women's participation in small-scale food processing in Vietnam.* IRSA XIV World Congress of Rural Sociology: Sustainable and Just Rural Transitions: Connections and Complexities, Toronto, Canada, 10–14 August 2016. Microsoft PowerPoint presentation.

Njuki, Jemimah, et al. *Transforming Gender and Food Security in the Global South.* Routledge Studies in Food, Society, and the Environment. Earthscan from Routledge, International Development Research Centre, 2016, idl-bnc-idrc.dspacedirect.org/bitstream/handle/10625/55820/IDL-55820.pdf?sequence=1&isAllowed=y. Accessed 22 Apr. 2021.

Ngothiha, Phuong, and Le Van Chi. "English Translations of Transcriptions and Notes from the Focus Group Discussions on *Ha Giang, Lai Chau & Lao Chai.*" ECOSUN Project, Ryerson University, November 2017.

Oh, Hye-Kyung, et al. "Factors Influencing Nutritional Practices among Mothers in Dakar, Senegal." *Plos One,* vol. 14, no. 2, 2019, doi:10.1371/journal.pone.0211787.

Olney, Deanna K, et al. "A 2-Year Integrated Agriculture and Nutrition Program Targeted to Mothers of Young Children in Burkina Faso Reduces Underweight among Mothers and Increases Their Empowerment: A Cluster-Randomized Controlled Trial." vol. 146, no. 5, 2016, pp. 1109-17.

Oniang'o, Ruth, and Edith Mukudi. "Nutrition and Gender." *Nutrition: A Foundation for Development,* ACC/SCN, 2002, www.bvsde.paho.org/texcom/nutricion/intnut7.pdf. Accessed 11 Jan. 2018.

O'Reilly, Andrea. *From Motherhood to Mothering: The Legacy of Adrianne Rich's Of Woman Born.* State University of New York Press, 2004.

Rahman, Atif, et al. "The Neglected 'm' in MCH Programmes—Why Mental Health of Mothers Is Important for Child Nutrition."

Tropical Medicine & International Health, vol. 13, no. 4, 2008, pp. 579-83.

Rich, Adrienne. *Of Woman Born: Motherhood as Experience and Institution.* Norton, 1976.

Saaka, Mahana. "Relationship between Mothers' Nutritional Knowledge in Childcare Practices and the Growth of Children Living in Impoverished Rural Communities." *Journal of Health, Population, and Nutrition*, vol. 32, no. 2, June 2014, pp. 237-48.

Schuler, Sidney Ruth, et al. "Constructions of Gender in Vietnam: In Pursuit of the 'Three Criteria.'" *Culture, Health & Sexuality*, vol. 8, no. 5, 2006, pp. 383-94.

Tanumihardjo S.A., et al. "Poverty, Obesity, and Malnutrition: An International Perspective Recognizing the Paradox." *Journal of the American Dietetics Association,* 2007, vol. 107, no. 11, pp. 1966-72.

Tuan, Viet. "China is Main Destination for Vietnamese Trafficking Victims: Official." *VNE Express International Edition*, 24 Aug. 2018, e.vnexpress.net/news/news/china-is-main-destination-for-viet namese-trafficking-victims-official-3797546.html. Accessed 22 Apr. 2021.

UNFPA. *Viet Nam Country Profile: Global Programme to Prevent Son Preference and the Undervaluing of Girls.* UNFPA Viet Nam, 2019, www.un.org.vn/en/publications/doc_details/579-viet-nam-country-profile-global-programme-to-prevent-son-preference-and-the-undervaluing-of-girls.html. Accessed 22 Apr. 2021.

UNICEF. *Child Nutrition and Covid 19. UNICEF Data*, July 2020, data.unicef.org/topic/nutrition/child-nutrition-and-covid-19/. Accessed 22 Apr. 2021.

Waibel, Gabi, and Sarah Glück. "More than 13 Million: Mass Mobilization and Gender Politics in the Vietnam Women's Union." *Gender & Development*, vol. 21, no. 2, 2013, pp. 343-61.

Watterworth, Jessica C., et al. "Food Parenting Practices and Their Association with Child Nutrition Risk Status: Comparing Mothers and Fathers." *Applied Physiology, Nutrition, and Metabolism,* vol. 42, no. 6, 2017, pp. 667-71.

You, Catherine. "A Gender Analysis of the Food System in Northern Vietnam." *TS. ECOSUN Project*, Ryerson University, February 2018.

Zuo, J. "Feminization of Agriculture, Relational Exchange, and Perceived Fairness in China: A Case in Guangxi Province." *Rural Sociology*, vol. 69, no. 4, 2004, pp. 510-31.

Notes on Contributors

Miriam Araya is committed to achieving social justice and Black liberation. Miriam received her master's degree in justice studies from San Jose State University in 2017 and is currently a second year PhD student in justice and social inquiry at Arizona State University. Miriam is also a dedicated BLM organiser.

Renée E. Mazinegiizhigoo-kwe Bédard is of Anishinaabeg, Kanien'kehá:ka, and French-Canadian ancestry. She is a member of Okikendawdt (Dokis First Nation). She holds a Ph.D. from Trent University in Indigenous Studies. Currently, she is an Assistant Professor at Western University in the Faculty of Education. Her areas of publication include practices of Anishinaabeg motherhood, maternal philosophy and spirituality, along with environmental issues, women's rights, Indigenous Elders, Anishinaabeg artistic expressions, and Indigenous education.

Sevan Beukian is an immigrant woman of colour in Canada, born and raised in Lebanon in an Armenian family, currently settled on Amiskwacîwâskahikan on Treaty 6 territory. She is a mother raising two children with her partner. Sevan completed a PhD in political science from the University of Alberta. Her experience has spanned over a decade in teaching, research, and policy work in EDI, trauma/memory, intersectional feminism, and antiracism.

Meghna Bhat earned her PhD in criminology, law, and justice from the University of Illinois at Chicago with a specialization in gender and women's studies. Her research explores portrayals of gender violence in cinema. Dr. Bhat is also a trained storyteller, preventionist, and a first-generation immigrant in the US.

Stuti Das holds a degree in sociology from the University of Hyderabad, India. Her interests include sociological engagements with alternative sexualities, gender and sexuality activism, and issues at the interface of sexuality and disability. She is presently a PhD student in the Department of Sociology, Boston University, USA.

Cheryl Lynch Lawler, PhD, LCS, is a board-certified training and supervising psychoanalyst on the Faculty of the Saint Louis Psycho-analytic Institute where she previously has served as president, clinical director, and academic dean. Her interests are transdisciplinary, involving psychoanalytic theory, feminist love studies, ancient Sufi hermeneutics, and pre-Socratic philosophy. She has published widely on the topics of feminist psychoanalysis and feminist theology, always with an emphasis on a (r)evolution in Western consciousness.

Rasel Madaha holds a PhD from the University of Dar es Salaam. He is a lecturer/assistant professor at Sokoine University of Agriculture in Tanzania. Rasel is also the president of AGEN, a national NGO that empowers Tanzanian marginalized people. Rasel specializes in local government, community development, gender, economics, and not-for-profits. He has won several international awards. Rasel has membership in international associations and has over fifteen inter-nationally recognized publications.

Andréa Ferreira Jacques de Moraes holds a PhD in rural sociology from the University of Columbia, Missouri. She is a research associate at the Centre for Studies in Food Security and a contract lecturer at the School of Nutrition and the Chang School of Continuing Studies at Ryerson University in Toronto, Canada. Her research interests are centred on gender, food and water security, food studies and Brazilian democracy. Recently, she served as the Canadian gender coordinator for the project Scaling-up Small-scale Food Processing: a Strategy to Promote Food Security among Women Subsistence Farmers in Rural Vietnam (ECOSUN), funded by the Canadian International Develop-ment Research Centre.

Kierra J. Otis is a gender studies PhD student at Arizona State University and birth doula serving in the Phoenix area. Her scholarship focuses on pregnancy, labour, and childbirth for women of colour, particularly queer Black diasporic women. Otis's favourite place to read is a coffee shop close to campus or cuddled up with her pup, Basil.

Tólá Olú Pearce is a sociologist (PhD, Brown University, RI) and professor emerita, Departments of Sociology and Women's and Gender Studies, University of Missouri, Columbia. Previously, she taught at the Obafemi Awolowo University, Nigeria. Her scholarship interests are maternal/child health in Africa, globalization, social inequalities, and human rights. Recent publications include *Reconstructing Sexuality in the Shadow of Neoliberal Globalization: Investigating the Approach of Charismatic Churches in South Western Nigeria; Dispelling the Myth of Pre-colonial Gender Equality in Yoruba Culture; These People Have No Clue about Us, the Land, or How We Live: Human Rights along the Texas/ Mexico Border* (with Jennifer Correa).

Katharine I. Ransom has a PhD in transformative studies, with a focus in feminist economics, from the California Institute of Integral Studies. Her research interests include the viability of matristic or matrilineal forms of social organization and their attendant characteristics as an alternative form of socio-economic organization to modern capitalism.

Victoria Team, MD, MPH, DrPH, is a senior research fellow in the School of Nursing and Midwifery at Monash University and health services research fellow at Monash Partners Academic Health Science Centre, Australia. Victoria trained as a medical doctor in Europe and practiced in Africa for almost ten years. Her current research is in the field of wound management.

Zairunisha has a PhD in motherhood, rhetorics of choice and coercion, reproductive technology and feminist bioethics from Jawaharlal Nehru University, India. Her research interests include feminist bioethics, Indian philosophy, philosophy of technology, and sociopolitical philosophy. Presently, she is working as an assistant professor of philosophy in Ramanujan College, University of Delhi, Delhi, India.

Deepest appreciation to
Demeter's monthly Donors

DEMETER

Daughters
Paul Chu
Rebecca Bromwich
Summer Cunningham
Tatjana Takseva
Debbie Byrd
Fiona Green
Tanya Cassidy
Vicki Noble
Bridget Boland
Naomi McPherson
Myrel Chernick

Sisters
Kirsten Goa
Amber Kinser
Nicole Willey
Christine Peets